HEAD and HEART

HEAD and HEART

Affection, Cognition, Volition
as Triune Consciousness

by
ANDREW TALLON

Fordham University Press
New York
1997

Copyright © 1997 by Fordham University Press
All rights reserved.
LC 97–12417
ISBN 0–8232–1771–X (hardcover)
ISBN 0–8232–1772–8 (paperback)

Library of Congress Cataloguing-in Publication Data

Tallon, Andrew.
    Head and heart : affection, cognition, volition as triune
consciousness / by Andrew Tallon.
        p.   cm.
    Includes bibliographical references and index.
    ISBN 0–8232–1771–X (hardcover : alk. paper). —
    ISBN 0–8232–1772–8 (pbk. : alk. paper)
    1. Emotions (Philosophy)   2. Intentionality (Philosophy)
3. Consciousness.   I. Title.
B815.T35   1997
128'.37—dc21   97–12417
                                                    CIP

Printed in the United States of America

for

Mary Beth,
Andrew, & Clare

Contents

Preface: Restoring Feeling to Consciousness

> Our hearts are uncircumcised; little will they believe.
> Koran, ii, 82 (c. 622).

> A faithless heart betrays the head unsound.
> John Armstrong, *The Art of Preserving Health*, bk. 4, l. 284 (1744).

> The heart has its reasons, which reason doesn't know.
> Blaise Pascal (1625–1661), *Pensées*, pt. 2, art. 17, no. 5 (1660).

> Heart speaks to heart. (*Cor ad cor loquitur.*) (1879)
> John Henry Newman (1801–1890),
> Motto of his cardinal coat of arms.

HEAD AND HEART HAVE BATTLED LONG ENOUGH.[1] It's time they got their acts together, literally. If heart means feeling, and head means knowing, with both of these subject, directly or indirectly, to willing, then triune consciousness would mean the union of affection, cognition, and volition as an operational synthesis. This thesis seems simple enough to state, and is even self-evident to whoever places practice before theory, but philosophy questions everything: a theory must be articulated clearly, argued successfully, and defended against all comers. The dominant rationalist tradition currently still holding the turf, even as we find new challenges to it emerging, has methodically excluded one kind of consciousness from this trilogy: affection. This book defends the right of feeling—meaning the whole realm of passion, emotion, mood, and affection in general—to be admitted to equal partnership with reason and will in human consciousness. It does so not only by proving the *existence* of affectivity as a distinct kind of consciousness inseparable from the other two, but also by showing precisely *how* affection works, how it operates in synthesis with those two, and by offering a new concept of triune consciousness as a paradigm for the human spirit.

The problem is, of course, that no theory of triadic or triune consciousness (I use these terms interchangeably), as the higher operational synthesis of head and heart through will, can be argued successfully while the entire realm of affectivity is accorded secondary status, in fact considered a mark of inferiority in some speculative comparison of humans with supposedly higher intelligences—like Mr. Spock, Commander Data, or Lt. Tuvok of *Star Trek*—as though feelings reveal our evolution from animals and the sooner we get over that the better. So entrenched is the prejudice against accepting affectivity as part of consciousness that books like Goleman's *Emotional Intelligence* (1995), Damasio's *Descartes' Error* (1994), Turski's *Toward a Rationality of Emotions* (1994), Smith's *The Felt Meanings of the World* (1986), Restak's *The Modular Brain* (1994), and MacLean's *The Triune Brain* (1990),[2] to mention only a few recent works, continue to fight uphill to gain recognition for affectivity as necessary for sound reasoning and responsible decision making. The thesis that *no* feeling is just as bad as—and probably worse than—*too much* feeling, is long overdue.

What has been lacking up to now is a single philosophical argument that takes seriously the challenge of integrating head and heart from start to finish on the basis of one consistent principle. That principle is *intentionality*, the central thesis of any contemporary phenomenology of consciousness. The question then becomes: Are some (not all) feelings *intentional* (in the technical sense to be explained)? And the thesis would be that insofar as an affection is intentional, it merits being included in human consciousness as a full and equal partner along with cognition and volition. Once affective intentionality (irreducible to either cognitional or volitional intentionality) has been established as the best contemporary explanation of feeling (the heart)—and I need seven chapters to do so, constituting the phenomenological "half" of this book—then comes the task of taking this phenomenology and interpreting it (the hermeneutical "half"), that is, of proposing a theory to "cover the phenomena" described in the first seven chapters. The theory of triune consciousness becomes possible only when affectivity has been shown to participate in intentionality, which is the price of admission.

Admission is not enough, however: *how* affective intentionality itself actually *works*—something not explained by the sources I consult in the first seven chapters (although Ricoeur provides the crucial clues with the concepts of *connaturality* and *habit* [as virtue])—is a necessary step in arguing the thesis of triune consciousness. In other words, in order to integrate heart and head, I must show how human consciousness without affection operates at a lower level of performance, or, put another way, how affective intentionality raises human consciousness closer to the paradigm that is both theoretically conceivable as the natural goal of the human spirit in its vertical finality, and also fully within the experience of persons who progress along a developmental continuum in the value domains of truth, goodness, and beauty. The clues, then, to showing that feeling is best understood in terms of affective intentionality are (1) the ancient concept of connaturality, sometimes called "affective connaturality," retrieved by Ricoeur, Rousselot, Maritain, Lonergan, and others, and (2) to help understand and update that somewhat esoteric idea, the concept of habit qua virtue, also suggested by Ricoeur and developed by others like von Hildebrand, Strasser, and Rousselot and Lonergan again.

Our agenda, then, is clear: to show how feeling is best described phenomenologically as affective intentionality, and then to show how affective intentionality is itself best understood through connaturality, with help from the concept of virtue. The result is a unified theory of human consciousness as a triad, as never adequately understood until and unless the full range of intentional affectivity is included. Now, in order to make the prima facie case that this agenda is indeed both plausible and necessary, so that attempting less would be worthless, let me offer a brief review of a few sources to confirm the above suggestions. The idea in what follows is merely to get in the ballpark, as it were, and to situate the discussion both in philosophical and in nonphilosophical literature. I hope the next few pages will serve to legitimate my approach for anyone unfamiliar with it, and to persuade the skeptical to give it a try. Then, following this preface, there is a brief introduction further to situate the discussion within the general structure of consciousness, so that affective intentionality as a distinct and irreducible mode of consciousness in its own right can be shown to fit into a clear schema.

One of the best and clearest presentations of triadic consciousness is Calvin Schrag's *Experience and Being* (1969), chapter 3, "The Intentional Structure of Experience." His differentiation of consciousness into three modes based on three irreducibly distinct intentionalities is in exact agreement with mine. For Schrag, "intentionality . . . is a structural component of affective and volitional as well as noetic acts" (Schrag 1969, 82). "Intentional or meaning-bearing connections pervade the whole of experience and underlie its varied affective, volitional, and conceptual permutations" (82).

Schrag understands intentionality as a "vectorial connection" (83) with a clearly identifiable structure such that the three modes of intending—affection, cognition, and volition—establish three worlds of being, three domains of experience, three ways of being, of being humanly in the world.

I wonder how seriously we take this fact, or whether we believe it at all. Three vectors of experience constitute three meanings: felt meanings (see Smith, *The Felt Meanings of the World* 1986; Tallon 1995b), cognitive meanings, and willed meanings. "They provide the basis for affective styles, volitional tendencies, and noetic forms. By virtue of them, felt, willed, and noetic meanings surge up in the world" (Schrag 1969, 84). Schrag then divides his chapter into sections entitled "Felt Meaning" (89–99), "Willed Meaning" (99–108), and "Noetic Meaning" (108–21). The section on noetic meaning is noteworthy for distinguishing, after Heidegger (as I also do in chapter 2), two kinds of thinking, representational and nonrepresentational (his terms are "representational" and "hermeneutical"), saying that "when phenomenology becomes existential phenomenology, it becomes hermeneutical phenomenology . . ." (117). His section on willed meaning depends chiefly on Ricoeur's study of the voluntary and involuntary. Both of these sections were on the leading edge of this discussion when they appeared, and they are still important today.

The chief value of the section on felt meaning is to distinguish unequivocally Schrag's understanding of consciousness as one and yet triune—based on its three distinct but not separate intentionalities—from anything like a "psychic tripartism" (90) or a "tripartite self, endowed with separate faculties containing distinct powers . . ." (90). His position is rather that felt, willed, and noetic meanings emanate from a common center of experience and partake of the common intentional structure that is embedded in the vectorial bonds that connect experiencer-experiencing-figure-with-background. Feelings, volitions, and concepts intend figures against a background. They are differentiated not with respect to a separation of faculties but by the particular focus of attention which each assumes (90). As George Turski says, in complete agreement with Schrag:

The traditional dichotomies between thought, emotion, and volition simply break down in favor of a more fluid transition between these phenomenologically *different modes of intentionality*. The multipartite self of the old faculty psychology . . . is definitively put to rest [1994, 34; my ital.].

One of Schrag's insights in this section can be misunderstood, and has been misunderstood by a tradition (for example, Plato, Scholasticism in general, Descartes) that removed affection from consciousness and located it exclusively in the body considered separate from the soul. Schrag says:

> The intentionality of feeling is in one of its expressions an intentionality of self-reference, functioning as a *lumen naturale* with respect to the experiencer. The intentional vectors of anxiety and hope reveal the sense of anxious and hopeful situations in such a manner that the experiencer becomes an issue and possible thematic topic. The intentionality of feeling discloses the sentient experiencer . . . with the situation and within the horizon-forms of time and space. . . . The intentional vectors of feeling radiate into a world and concomitantly reveal an embodied, speaking, and communal experiencer who lives in an oriented time and space [98–99].

This does not mean that feeling is entirely subjective, disclosing not the world but only one's own embodied experience of it, taken as some abstract state. That would deny the whole meaning of the intentionality of feelings and moods, and the very concept of affective *intentionality* would become self-contradictory. It does mean, as his expression *lumen naturale* shows, that affective intentionality, equal to and in some cases better than cognition at grounding action, is simply embodied in a way *different* from the other two intentionalities, a way that attunes us connaturally to our world differently from the way cognition does (Tallon 1979; 1993). Make no mistake: cognition and volition are also very much embodied, as the whole epistemological tradition—from Aristotle through Kant into today—of reason's dependence on sense perception and imagination clearly attests. The modest but necessary conclusion is that without this third intentionality, this third way of meaning, our world would be radically less, drastically poorer, a paper-thin flatland devoid of value; both phenomenologically and hermeneutically our meanings and worlds would be false because untrue to human experience in its triadic unity. Schrag's consciousness is threefold.

The fine line between, on the one hand, relegating feeling only to embodiment—excluding it from "spiritual" consciousness as an equal partner with cognition and volition—and, on the other, recognizing the different and special way affection connects with embodiment, was Merleau-Ponty's lifelong obsession, and we devote part of a chapter to his work. Merleau-Ponty fought Cartesianism all his life and promoted a "good ambiguity" to describe embodied intentionality. Sue Cataldi's *Emotion, Depth, and Flesh: A Study of Sensitive Space* (1993) bears the subtitle "Reflections on Merleau-Ponty's Philosophy of Embodiment." What is different about her approach is its focus on the experience of depth (see her ch. 1, "Flat Affects vs. Deep Emotional Experience"). What is emotional depth, and why is it important? When we use the expression "flat affect" to describe persons whose responses to value, positive or negative, are disproportional and inadequate to the stimulus, we imply that something is missing from them. They are out of tune with being, with their world, with *our* world—with *the* world, we would even say—which we take to be richly textured and sometimes highly charged, so that someone whose affective responses are grossly deficient seems humanly defective.

Cataldi's fine analyses are independently confirmed by neuroscience (Damasio 1994). As Damasio shows, patients who suffered brain injury, for example, the famous Phineas Gage, who had a steel rod blasted through his head, or, in cases when tumors destroyed certain parts of the brain, were found not only to have their *affective* responses damaged, but also to have become incapable of *rational thinking* and *responsible decisions. Reduced affection meant defective thinking and deciding—especially in personal and moral matters.* Their reasoning and volition led to actions destructive of themselves and others insofar as they were impaired by affective disorder— and not by too *much* emotion but by too *little!*

This is not the place to present the details of these sources; the conclusions, however, will help show why the thesis of this study, centered on the necessity of triune consciousness for full humanity, and especially as approached through connaturality, has a prima facie plausibility. For example, Cataldi makes the point that depth implies motion (e-motion, disposition), citing forgotten meanings and evoking Quentin Smith's (1986) careful analyses of "feeling flows." As feeling or emotion deepens, it moves toward the center of the person, no matter how physical or corporeal its origin. Cataldi gives many examples from ordinary language to show how one no longer *has* an emotion but *becomes* and *is* the emotion. This insight connects well with explaining connaturality through habit (meaning a "having," from the Latin *habitus,* that mediates between a being [that is, its nature] and its doing or action). Connaturality, as habit (virtue or vice), is the midpoint between being and doing, which in turn argues strongly for locating affectivity at the *center* of consciousness, right there with cognition and volition, not out somewhere in a mechanical *res extensa.* On the other hand, it does not mean, again, a purely subjective state, as though without reference to an objective world. Feeling (emotion) is always an ambiguous mix of affection (as being moved or touched—a being-affected) and intention (as reference to otherness).

Damasio's concept of "somatic markers" addresses this issue. The point is as easily misunderstood as the affirmation of affectivity as only a special experience of embodiment (rather than as intentional as cognition and volition) because it looks as though one is affirming both sides of an irreconcilable dichotomy: are feelings "in the body" or "in the mind"? The answer has to be "in both," but that answer has to be explained (and I devote many chapters to doing so). As Damasio puts it, "The body provides a ground reference for the mind" (1994, 223), which is not such a bad way to paraphrase connaturality, the way finite consciousness uses embodiment as its felt resonance to being and world as value, the "gut reaction," "vibes," and "woman's intuition"—the heart of interpersonal life. The "connaturality thesis" is to (at least) affection what the "sense intuition thesis" is to cognition. As Damasio says, "[F]eelings are the sensors for the match or lack thereof between nature and circumstance" (xv). That our nature is a law or standard for what befits or suits us is not a new idea, of course, nor is the corollary that "second nature"—our habits—are further attunements of our (first) nature to our world as we develop skills in dealing with that world in better ways. Damasio recognizes this:

> And by nature I mean both the nature we inherited as a pack of genetically engineered adaptations, and the nature we have acquired in individual development, through interactions with our social environment, mindfully and willfully as well as not. Feelings, along with emotions they come from, are not a luxury. They serve as internal guides, and they help us communicate to others signals that can also guide them. . . . Contrary to traditional scientific opinion, feelings are just as cognitive as other percepts. They are the result of a most curious physiological arrangement that has turned the brain into the body's captive audience. . . . [T]he body, as represented in the brain, may constitute the indispensable frame of reference for the neural processes that we experience as the mind; . . . our most refined thoughts and best actions, our greatest joys and deepest sorrows, use the body as a yardstick [xv].

This, again, is another way to express connaturality. Feeling is necessary not merely for the correct operations of reason-

ing and willing but is also the necessary condition for the
higher operational synthesis of cognition and volition with
affection, a synthesis that constitutes so much better a performance of reasoning and will as virtually to replace them—
at higher skill levels, when one becomes more competent,
proficient, expert—with more intuitive knowing and spontaneous action. As Damasio says:

> First, there is a region of the human brain, the ventrome-
> dial prefrontal cortices, whose damage consistently com-
> promises, in as pure a fashion as one is likely to find, both
> reasoning/decision making, and emotion/feeling, espe-
> cially in the personal and social domain. . . . [M]etaphori-
> cally . . . reason and emotion "intersect" in the ventrome-
> dial prefrontal cortices. . . . Second, there is a region of the
> human brain, the complex of somatosensory cortices in
> the right hemisphere, whose damage also compromises rea-
> soning/decision making and emotion/feeling, and, in ad-
> dition, disrupts the process of basic body signaling. . . . In
> short, there appears to be a collection of systems in the
> human brain consistently dedicated to the goal-oriented
> thinking process we call reasoning, and to the response
> selection we call decision making, with a special emphasis
> on the personal and social domain. This *same collection of
> systems is also involved in emotion and feeling, and is partly dedi-
> cated to processing body signals* [70; my ital.].

This text links the three modes of consciousness together
in a functional interdependency that Damasio and many others in neuroscience increasingly recognize. To emphasize the
plausibility of using connaturality (and habit as its "engine")
to explain how affectivity works and integrates with cognition and volition at the interior of a triad of consciousness,
let us listen to Damasio once more. He contrasts what he calls
a "traditional 'high-reason' view of decision making" with his
"somatic-marker hypothesis":

The "high-reason" view, which is none other than the common-sense view, assumes that when we are our decision-making best, we are the pride and joy of Plato, Descartes, and Kant. Formal logic will, by itself, get us the best available solution for any problem. An important aspect of the rationalist conception is that to obtain the best results, emotions must be kept out. Rational processing must be unencumbered by passion [171].

If we think of the high-reason view as performing a perfect cost/benefit analysis, he says,

[I]magine that before you apply any kind of cost/benefit analysis to the premises, and before you reason toward the solution of the problem, something quite important happens: When the bad outcome connected with a given response option comes into mind, however fleetingly, you experience an unpleasant gut feeling. Because the feeling is about the body, I gave the phenomenon the technical term *somatic* state ("soma" is Greek for body); and because it "marks" an image, I called it a *marker.* . . . What does the *somatic marker* achieve? It forces attention on the negative outcome to which a given action may lead, and functions as an automated alarm signal which says: Beware of danger ahead if you choose the option which leads to this outcome. The signal may lead you to reject, *immediately,* the negative course of action and thus make you choose among other alternatives. . . . Somatic markers probably increase the accuracy and efficiency of the decision process. Their absence reduces them [173; his parentheses].

This is connaturality reduced to about as simple and familiar a description of "gut reaction" or "woman's intuition" as could be desired. When it comes to explaining this description, Damasio states:

In short, *somatic markers are a special instance of feelings generated from secondary emotions* ["secondary emotions" come from "second nature," that is, habits]. Those emotions and feelings *have been connected, by learning, to predicted future outcomes of certain scenarios.* When a negative somatic marker is juxtaposed to a particular future outcome the combination functions as an alarm bell. When a positive somatic marker is juxtaposed instead, it becomes a beacon of incentive [174; his ital.; my brackets].

Connaturality is the old name for this experience, like the concept of "discernment of spirits," familiar in another context, whereby someone in the throes of making an important career decision listens to the contrasting movements of immanent motives, tries to detect a resonance or dissonance between the proposed action and one's whole nature—the *first* nature of one's basic essence, and the *second* nature of acquired virtues and vices (good and bad habits), those habits or second nature which Damasio sees as the ground of what he calls secondary emotions (because based on second nature).

It is important to note that connaturality and somatic markers are not reducible to cognition, they are affections, they are felt. As Damasio says:

Somatic markers do not deliberate for us. They assist the deliberation by highlighting some options (either dangerous or favorable), and eliminating them rapidly from subsequent consideration. You may think of it as a system for automated qualification of predictions, which acts, whether you want it or not, to evaluate the extremely diverse scenarios of the anticipated future before you. Think of it as a basic biasing device [174].[3]

So affective intentionalities are essential to optimal operation of both cognitional and volitional consciousness, it would be fair to say, according to recent neuroscience theory. Not that scientific explanations should be accorded more persuasive power than those based on personal experience, phenomenological description, and hermeneutical interpretation, which all science eventually requires anyway; but they do *add* rather than subtract from the accumulation of evidence in favor of a triadic conception of human consciousness.

Finally, according to a growing consensus in enneagram psychology, which is attracting considerable attention and more critical study today, human personality types derive from the interaction of three triads or centers[4] of consciousness which correlate with affection, cognition, and volition. Most important is the universal goal of overcoming the dominance of one center to achieve an integrated balance of all three.

With this very broad sketch of philosophy, psychology, and neuroscience we have set a context for asking whether and how affective consciousness fits into consciousness in general, a necessary preface to this study. To make these preparatory steps more useful we still have to move from the general to the specific. So we need now briefly to outline a more detailed sketch of consciousness into which to integrate affection. To do so I turn, in the following introduction, to Lonergan's *Insight* (1957) and his *Method . . .* (1972) for the best overall approach to a schema of the structure of consciousness.

Notes

1. Thomas Jefferson spoke of head and heart; see Jefferson (1954), Bullock (1945), and Brodie (1974).

2. See MacLean (1980; 1990) and De Sousa (1987, 59–61) for the phrase "the triune brain."

3. There is an analogy with electronics that may help. In a diode, the cathode radiates electrons which the plate collects as they flow across the vacuum. But without a bias screen, with its own charge, between the cathode and plate, there is no way for the operator to control (to amplify or attenuate) the current flowing from cathode to plate. By making the diode a triode, the operator takes control of the process by varying the bias voltage. Something similar happens when consciousness is a triad of affection, cognition, and volition. Thus affection also influences volition, for example, as willpower: ". . . how would one explain willpower? Willpower draws on the evaluation of a prospect, and that evaluation may not take place if attention is not properly driven to both the immediate trouble and the future payoff, to both the suffering *now* and the *future* gratification. Remove the latter and you remove the lift from under your willpower's wings" (Damasio 1994, 175; his ital.). Again, it takes all three to explain normal human functioning. Restak speaks of the three streams of thought, movement, and feeling: "In 1937 Papez proposed as the brain's mechanism of emotion a circuit centered around the hypothalamus. The Papez circuit, as it came to be called, is composed of a collection of interrelated structures that include the hippocampus, the fornix leading to the hypothalamus, the mammilthalamic tract leading to the anterior thalamic nuclei, and the cingulum bundle leading to the cingulate gyrus. Papez's purpose was to explain how sensory information that passes through the thalamus en route to the cerebral cortex takes on emotional significance. He suggested three exit pathways from the thalamus: to the cortex, responsible for the 'stream of thought'; to the basal ganglia below the cortex, responsible for the 'stream of movement'; and to the hypothalamus, responsible for the 'stream of feeling'" (1994, 141).

4. Riso (1987, 24–35) speaks of the "relating," "feeling," and "doing" triads. He prefers the terminology of "triads" to that of "centers" (1990, 20, 27–34; 1992, 12–15). Beesing et al. (1984, 145–55) speak of gut, head, and heart centers, as do Rohr and Ebert (1993, 25–28), Baron and Wagele (1994, 6–7), and Hurley and Dobson, who first call them the affective, theoretical, and effective centers (1991, 67–78) and, later, the intellectual, relational, and creative centers (1993, 4–6, and, with reference to the three layers of the brain, reptilian, mammalian, and neocortex, 84–87, 184–203). Palmer (1988, 46–65) and Riordan (1975, 297–301), add variants for the names of the centers.

Ricoeur (1965/1986, 161–91) refers to Kant's "trilogy of passions formed by possession (*Habsucht*), domination (*Herrsucht*), and honor (*Ehrsucht*) . . . a trilogy of human passions" (ibid., 169), which Ricoeur translates into French as *avoir, pouvoir, valoir*—to have, to be able (power), to value. This "triple *Sucht*" (ibid.) is a *Suchen*, a seeking to overcome human finitude through the three modes of consciousness, since it is through knowing that we possess being, through will that we dominate, and through feeling that we apprehend and appreciate values.

Introduction: The Structure of Consciousness

That really which is called Brahman,
that indeed is the space external;
and that indeed which is the space external,
that really is the space internal;
and that space which is internal
is verily this space within the heart.
That is the Full.
Chandogya Upanishad, 3.12.7-9 (c. 800–400 B.C.).

The heart is everything, the rest is useless.
La Fontaine (1621–1695), *Belphégor* (1678)

Said the Sun to the Moon—"When you are but a lonely white crone,
And I, a dead King in my golden armor somewhere in a dark wood,
Remember only this of our hopeless love
That never till Time is done
Will the fire of the heart and the fire of the mind be one."
Dame Edith Sitwell (1887–1964)

OUR FIRST TASK IS TO IDENTIFY THE GENERAL STRUCTURE of consciousness by describing its four levels and twelve operations (se Figure 1, p. 18). Following the terminology of Lonergan's *Insight* (1957), and beginning with sense perception (seeing, hearing, and so forth), imagination, and memory, let us call this first group of cognitive operations "experience," or "empirical consciousness." Although feelings are most definitely part of experience, and in fact part of con-

```
┌─────────────────────────────────────────────────────────────┐
│            Cognitional and Volitional Consciousness           │
│                                                               │
│   4. Responsible Consciousness (Level of Decision: Volition)  │
│      Acting                                                   │
│  ↑   Deciding                                                 │
│      Deliberating                                             │
│      ──────────────────────────────────────────►             │
│                                            Evaluating         │
│                                                      ↑        │
│   3. Rational Consciousness (Level of Judgment)               │
│      Judging                                                  │
│      Grasping the Virtually Unconditioned                     │
│      Marshalling and Weighing the Evidence                    │
│                                                               │
│   2. Intelligent Consciousness (Level of Understanding)       │
│      Formulating Concepts and Hypotheses                      │
│      Insights                                                 │
│      Inquiring—Asking Questions                               │
│                                                               │
│   1. Empirical Consciousness (Level of Experience)            │
│      Imagining                                                │
│      ──────────────────────────────────────────►  Feeling    │
│      Perceiving                                               │
│      Sensing                                                  │
└─────────────────────────────────────────────────────────────┘
```

Figure 1

sciousness at every level, I purposely prescind from attending to them at this time because they will occupy the next seven chapters: feeling as affective intentionality is the "q.e.d." If the term "feeling" is *analogous*, then feeling at the first level of consciousness, that of experience, is analogous (but not identical) to feeling at the second (understanding), and analogous (but not identical) to feeling at the third (judgment), and finally analogous (but not identical) to feeling at the fourth (choice, decision, action). The common but false idea of feelings as solely and merely "accompaniments" to cognition and volition, riding "piggyback," as it were, upon the intentionalities of knowing and willing but deprived of true intentionality in their own right, is part of the problem to be addressed.

If we wanted to present an abstraction by the name of "head–consciousness," we could exclude feelings altogether from the schema, not even mentioning "heart–consciousness" at all.[1] But clearly we have to acknowledge the existence of feelings in consciousness, no matter how they may subsequently be explained, or even explained "away" from "spiritual" consciousness. Our Figure 1 represents a compromise: while head-consciousness is highly differentiated (as analyzed into at least four levels and twelve operations, when volition is included), heart-consciousness will remain *for now* completely undifferentiated, appearing only as a line running vertically along the right side of the diagram of head-consciousness from Feeling to Evaluation.

To explain Figure 1: Experience, conceived within the context of a consciousness streaming toward being as "to-be-known" (without claiming that knowing is the only way to approach being, of course), raises questions: we want to *understand* what we experience. Naturally this statement is not meant to be a reduction of being to meaning, nor to exclude the possibility that some experiences, like basking in the sunshine on the beach, are simply enjoyed. But in the present context of an analysis of cognitive consciousness, we conceive experience as arousing curiosity. As Aristotle said, we find within ourselves the pure desire to know. That desire is like a motor propelling us from the first level of consciousness to the second level, that of understanding, urging us from empirical to intelligent consciousness. If the imperative of the first level, that of experience, is "Be attentive" ("Pay attention!") that of the second is "Be intelligent" ("Use your head," "Try to understand," "Think!"). The goal and intention of the first level of consciousness is to see, hear, imagine, remember, perceive (and, let us merely mention it again for now: to experience feelings, emotions, moods, passions—immediate presentations of being as intentional as those of sensation, perception, and the like).

At the second level of consciousness, then, the first operation is questioning, inquiry, asking for the meaning of what we experience. The main question asked is "*What* is this? *What* is the *meaning* of my experience?" "*What* am I experiencing, seeing, hearing, perceiving?" It is a search for the essence, nature, whatness, quiddity of experience. (The hunger or desire to know, of course—and again we merely mention what will be fully treated later—is itself a passion, a felt appetite: the mind is not empty like a wastebasket, but like a stomach, and fulfillment brings joy, peace, which are *emotions*, and, at least for now, worthy of being granted the status of feelings that at least accompany in consciousness the cognitive intentionality experienced in the search for truth.)

The second operation of intelligent consciousness is insight, the apprehension of intelligibility found in the immediate presentations of empirical consciousness. Insight is the "eureka" experience, an act frequent in the intelligent, scarce in the stupid. Insight is the act of understanding, occurring as a response to questioning, as a satisfaction of a dynamic intending toward meaning. Insight is not an image, not a picture, not a sound, but an act that is unimaginable, intangible; it is entirely an act of intelligence, irreducible to any other operation of consciousness, often coming unbidden, suddenly surprising us in moments when we least expect it, although usually after a time of imagining, thinking, ruminating, comparing immediate experience with remembered experience, and so on. Let us simply give the collective name "thinking" to the many mental processes that go on between the (first) operation of questioning and the (second) operation of insight, with insight as our "clicking" together enough intelligible elements of an experience to find some form (*eidos*) or idea in that complex of empirical consciousness. Each insight is expressed in some manner that constitutes the *third* operation of intelligent consciousness: prescinding from the possibility of the *artist* expressing insight by, for example, throwing a pot, dancing, or painting a canvas, the most classical expression of insight in a *cognitive* context is the formation of a *concept*.

Conceptualization is the third operation of intelligent consciousness, the (simple) "mental word" spoken by reason or intellect. This "verbum" *represents*, in the sense of "presents again" at the level of intelligence, the experience of some being that was presented first at the level of empirical consciousness (sense perception). Here it has a new life, that of the mind (intelligent experience). Intelligence gives birth to idea as its own self-expression; it is as consciousness experienced as thinking that it has answers to the questions raised by sense experience. It is both interesting and important to note that ideas and concepts are the *result* of insight. We do not have ideas and then get insights into the ideas, but the other way around: concepts, ideas, hypotheses, theories, guesses, hunches, surmises—the whole gamut of answers to questions (all provisional at this second level of cognition, as we shall see in a moment)—are the *products* of acts of insight, of our attempts to "make sense" of our experience, of our creative efforts to tell ourselves, in the mental words of thought, what a being given in our experience is and means.

But, as Lonergan was fond of saying, "Insights are a dime a dozen." When you are trying to figure out why your car won't start, insight after insight flashes through your mind as the myriad possibilities unfold from past memories, present context, and future possible experiments. We are therefore propelled beyond intelligent consciousness to a third level of cognition, that most important proving ground of our ideas, hypotheses, and theories, where we test our insights to *verify* which are true and which false. Lonergan calls this the level of judgment—"rational consciousness," or "critical consciousness"—and its imperative is "Be reasonable" or "Be critical." Its essence is to question a *second* time, to seek a *second* insight—this time into the possibility of verifying one's insights through evidence—to put to the proof one's answers to the questions for intelligence by asking "But *is it so?* Is it really *true?*" Truth or falsity enter first at this *third* level of cognitive consciousness.

We can again identify three operations. If we think of the classical model of what is somewhat simplistically called "scientific method"—where the scientist sets up, in the field or in the lab, an experiment devised precisely to test a hypothesis—we can recognize in the phrase "gathering and weighing the evidence" a summary of the controlled arrangement of the conditions necessary to facilitate a new, second insight, now at a higher level of cognition. The purpose of bringing together the necessary and sufficient conditions for judgment parallels the patterning of data (everything relevant that is "given" to consciousness in its search for truth) presented by the senses in immediate perception and offered to intelligence by imagination. The pattern is similar, but the question is different, like the imperative. At the second level the question was "*What* is it?," while at the third the questions is "Is it *so?*" The first question aims at *essence*; the second aims at *existence;* from *forma* to *esse.* A possible truth, at the second level, becomes an actual truth at the third, and does so only if another insight occurs and the conditions of verifying the insight of intelligence are fulfilled.

Lonergan speaks of grasping the "virtually unconditioned" when naming the second operation of the third level: certain conditions had to be fulfilled in order for an intelligent insight to be confirmed as true in rational, critical consciousness. If those conditions are in fact fulfilled, we may proceed to *judgment,* to speak another (complex) mental word, as it were, and claim that our insight is true.

This brief sketch shows that the first three levels of consciousness constitute the unit called "cognitive consciousness" only when all three are taken together. They are the preparation and necessary condition for ascent to the fourth level, that of decision, where the purpose of cognition is fulfilled when knowledge leads to action. The arrow running up the left side of Figure 1 represents the vertical finality of consciousness: cognition is for decision and action. The imperative at the fourth level is "Be responsible," and volitional, voluntary, or responsible consciousness is the name and nature of this level. We may again identify three operations in our experience, although, as before, these operations are more like groupings of complex multiples of activities, themselves further able to be differentiated by further analysis. We could call them deliberation, decision, and action; evidently, such terms encompass whole series of individual "mental" activities. Let us call the first three levels taken together the head, that is, cognition, ultimately most intelligible when grasped as fully integrated with volition as having a vertical finality toward action—the left side of Figure 1—excluding (for now) affection, the heart, which is the still undifferentiated right side of Figure 1, represented by the vertical arrow from Feeling to Evaluation.

A remarkable virtue of this schema is its self-verifiability: anyone can test its validity by trying to disprove or revise it. Here it helps to quote Lonergan:

> Moreover, for it to be possible for a revision to take place certain conditions must be fulfilled. For, in the first place, any possible revision will appeal to data which the opinion under review either overlooked or misapprehended, and so any possible revision must presuppose at least an empirical level of operations. Secondly, any possible revision will offer a better explanation of the data, and so any possible revision must presuppose an intellectual level of operations. Thirdly, any possible revision will claim that the better explanation is more probable, and so any possible revision must presuppose a rational level of operations. Fourthly, a revision is not a mere possibility but an accomplished fact only as the result of a judgment of value and a decision. One undertakes the labor with all its risks of fail-

ure and frustration only because one holds, not only in theory but also in practice, that it is worth while to get things straight, to know with exactitude, to contribute to the advancement of science. So at the root of all method there has to be presupposed a level of operations on which we evaluate and choose responsibly at least the method of our operations.

It follows that there is a sense in which the objectification of the normative pattern of our conscious and intentional operations does not admit revision. The sense in question is that the activity of revising consists in such operations in accord with such a pattern, so that a revision rejecting the pattern would be rejecting itself.

There is then a rock on which one can build. But let me repeat the precise character of the rock. Any theory, description, account of our conscious and intentional operations is bound to be incomplete and to admit further clarifications and extensions. But all such clarifications and extensions are to be derived from the conscious and intentional operations themselves. They as given in consciousness are the rock; they confirm every exact account; they refute every inexact or incomplete account. The rock, then, is the subject in his or her consciousness, unobjectified attentiveness, intelligence, reasonableness, responsibility. The point to the labor of objectifying the subject and his or her conscious operations is that thereby one begins to learn what these are and that they are [Lonergan 1972, 19–20].

Heart consciousness is indicated, in a purely heuristic way, by the arrow joining Feeling with Evaluation and running along the right side from the first level to the fourth. As stated above, the reason for this particular sketch of the general structure of consciousness is to facilitate the introduction of the notion of the heart as affective *consciousness*, based on interpreting feeling, mood, and temperament as affective *intentionality*. To present a phenomenology of feeling as affective consciousness is to justify conceiving *some* feelings (specifically the æsthetic, ethical, and mystical, not, for example, mere physiological feelings such as thirst or fatigue) as intentional, and to define the relations among the three intentionalities as triune consciousness.

The path has now been prepared by our preface and introduction for the seven chapters aimed at arguing in such a way as to leave no doubt that the best way to understand the heart, the domain of feelings and moods in general, is through the contemporary phenomenology of affective intentionality. Then the task will be to offer a hermeneutics of triune consciousness as the higher operational synthesis of all three intentionalities.

Note

1. While Lonergan's *Insight* leaves affective consciousness undifferentiated, his later work, *Method in Theology*, has a philosophical preamble that goes a long way toward clarifying that differentiation. Robert Doran's *Subject and Psyche* (1994), as well as his other excellent works (1981b; 1990; 1996) may be seen in part as an attempt to continue that differentiation, while my own work may be seen as its completion and integration with cognition and volition.

Chapter 1

Phenomenology, Intentionality, Embodiment

Exalt not thy heart, that it be not brought low.
Ptah-Hotep, *Instruction*, no. 25 (c. 3550 B.C.).

The human heart is more dangerous than mountains and rivers,
more difficult to understand than Heaven itself.
Chuang-Tze, *Philosophy*, ch. 11. (400 B.C.).

The heart perceives that which the eye cannot see.
Algazali (1059-1111), *Ethics*, Bk. 2, ch. 21, maxim 38 (c. 1100).

Summary

First, we note the general idea of phenomenology as descriptive philosophy and distinguish two kinds of phenomenology according to the central idea of the phenomenological method: intentionality. Second, we begin to move from the physical and psychical space between persons toward the center of consciousness. Third, we show how embodiment, especially in motion, manifests its own affective intentionality. The *possibility* of affective intentionality is established in this chapter, as is the sense of the embodied, felt intentionality of the space between persons, setting the *general* context for triune consciousness.

Phenomenology: Transcendental & Dialogal

B Y "TRANSCENDENTAL PHENOMENOLOGY" I mean the phenomenology of Husserl himself, and by "existential" and "dialogal phenomenology," that of those who deal with intersubjectivity without his Cartesian starting point, that is, who begin not with the idealistic methodological condition called "constitution of the other," but rather with the already always given real world of the "we" prior to any subsequent "I" or "Thou," to use Buber's terms. Buber represents one strain (the dialogal) of the non-Husserlian approach to personal relations, just as Heidegger can be taken to represent existential phenomenology. Both dialogal and existential phenomenology admit the irreducibility of affectivity to cognitive representations.

Ready access to a first understanding of dialogal phenomenology is given in Strasser's *The Idea of Dialogal Phenomenology* (1969; Tallon 1978). Strasser there presents, without argument, as though it had by then become consensus, the view that Husserl's approach to intersubjectivity was a failure;[1] he then goes on to suggest that issue from failure is to be had in a dialogal approach. His recourse, like Theunissen's (1965), is to Buber, though neither of them is satisfied that Buber actually brought the problem to full resolution. Why did Buber seem to hold out hope for doing what full deployment of the Husserlian heavy artillery could not manage? How could the slim, poetic, provocative, and obscure opusculum *I and Thou* ever be expected to succeed where the monumental massiveness and detail of Husserl's intentional analyses did not?

The Husserlian error, like Descartes's error, one must suspect, had to have been so small as to go unnoticed, and it must have occurred very early, for the derouting was thorough. And indeed the mistake came at the very beginning, consisting in Husserl's repeating Descartes's starting point in the "I *think*, therefore I am" (the *cogito*), rather than going back to a world lived in *before thinking*, to a more primordial starting-point in the prereflective and prevoluntary lived world, the world that forms the field or ground in and on which all reason, feeling, and willing occur. This prereflective world, always already given, does not evade all knowledge, though it does escape a phenomenology convinced that meaning is restricted to those intentions that are reducible to cognitional representations; the lived world cannot be reached by a knowledge that makes everything an object. Sensations, perceptions, and feelings are *present*-ations; images and ideas are *re*-presentations.

The crucial difference between the very scientific method of Husserl and the elusive and evocative style of Buber consists in the event called nonrepresentational intentionality. Now this fact does not clearly emerge by a direct contrast of Husserl with Buber but rather requires that we show, through a much more roundabout way, that this event, completely unnamed in Buber, is actually what underlay his philosophy of dialogue and what was intuited by those who resorted to Buber in despairing of Husserl (even if only to despair later of Buber as well).

Buber's category of "the between" is the keystone of his thought.[2] To explain "the between" requires recourse to the concept of affective intentionality, that is, to an intending by the I of the Thou in an actual, present relation, the I-Thou relation (the *Ich-Du Beziehung*) which is prior, chronologically and ontologically, to the subsequent experience which for Buber is loss of the present Thou in an I-It relationship (the *Ich-Es Verhältnis*). In partial agreement with Buber, Levinas called this modality "affective intentionality," "nonrepresentationality," and, later, "proximity" (Tallon 1976a; 1976b; 1989; 1995b; 1996). More important than the consensus that Husserl's idealistic or transcendental phenomenology failed is the reason *why* it failed. It failed because it rigidly remained in the head, whereas recourse to affective consciousness (the heart) underlies Buber's mystifying and poetic expressions, and cuts the Gordian knot of the whole misconceived "problem" of intersubjectivity. A pseudoproblem arises from ignoring affection as an independent intentionality.

Access to "the between" is given primarily through affective intentionality, but, naturally, everything depends on what affective intentionality turns out to mean. Beginning in the space between persons, let us try to get hold of the idea of affective intentionality as the philosophical explanation of feeling. Is the space or "the between" of affective intentionality different enough from the "objective" space of cognitive intentionality to justify following it as a clue? Strasser answers that ". . . transcendental phenomenology, by introducing the transcendental subject and the constituted object, has carried to extremes the tendency of Western philosophy to constantly increase the distance between subject and object" (1969, 55). Let us take this clue—the bias in favor of one version of objectivity—and use it as a bridge to intentionality.

Encounter & Pre-encounter

Rémy Kwant's brief and cogent critique of objective bias takes the form of a thesis that "our familiarity with the things that surround us comes to us through our familiarity with our fellow human persons."[3] "Objectivity" as a total way of viewing the world and understanding reality is secondary and learned, not merely natural and to be presumed correct and complete, as though Buber's I-It relationship were primary rather than derivative. For Kwant, ". . . interhuman communication [Buber's *das Zwischenmenschliche*] is . . . the most primordial and fundamental form of knowledge. . . . [T]his knowledge is not itself reducible to something else. . . . [A]ll other knowledge depends on it" (1960, 13; my brackets).

How does Kwant establish this thesis? His argumentation, in short, is a mixture of experience and the phenomenology of Merleau-Ponty. Its simplest statement, kept within the confines of knowledge and further narrowed to speak only of knowledge involving thinking, says: "The primordial and most primitive form of thinking is not found in thinking-put-into-words, but in behavior" (18). "As a person I 'think' with my hands, with the movements of my body, in one word, through my behavior" (19). Whether we call this "thinking" or "meaning," that is, whether conceptual operations are involved or a nonconceptual dealing with our world could be included, seems secondary, since Kwant means to include all understanding in his word "thinking," as is clear from the context, where freedom is its complement. It is also clear that encounter presupposes a potentiality broader than verbal discourse, prior to dialogue in words: ". . . [T]he person is an ever-developing possibility to encounter things and people. As a person I am always actualizing myself, but this actualization is always partial and never terminal" (21). "This is knowledge through human activity, which is behavior. . . . This is prereflective knowledge. The world in which we move about has meaning for us, but this meaning is not reflected upon" (25).

In this section, Kwant takes us one small step closer to recognizing the existence of some notion or tradition other than the perhaps naively accepted one usually offered to explain human nature, an explanation too quick in its recourse to reflection, to language in words, to a rationalism or logocentrism, to a primacy of reason over every other kind of consciousness.

Acts, Social & Asocial

The suggestion that meaningful behavior occurs before mind, prereflectively, could also be put in terms of the *quality* of our encounters, and not only in terms of a certain *temporal* development in them. No one would say that *all* encounters can move from pre-encounter (as the potential for meaningful dialogue and communication), through encounter, to full verbal expression, for such is not our experience: some encounters resist reflective appropriation in representational language (that is, in images and ideas). We can and do act, but often we cannot imagine our body movements adequately or verbalize them; for example, we demonstrate with a body motion, rather then say in words, a tennis stroke or a ballet movement. One could invoke recent split-brain research (the bicameral mind, hemisphericity, left lobe dominance, and so on) to highlight this everyday experience, typically exemplified by the way people spontaneously make an upward-spinning-hand movement when describing a spiral staircase rather than defining it in words.

But to continue Kwant's emphasis on the primacy of the embodied over the objective (on knowing persons prior to things) in encounter, we can briefly cite the distinction made by Reinach in his theory of social acts (Spiegelberg 1964, 1: 202–03). Reinach calls spontaneous those acts "characterized by an inner activity that takes place entirely within the agent, like the taking of a decision or giving preference to something" (1: 202). These he distinguishes from "others by being essentially directed toward other persons, like envying, forgiving, or giving commands. Within this second group of 'other-regarding' acts Reinach then subdivides further between those acts that need not be expressed or received by others, like forgiveness, and those that make sense only as expressed and received by others, such as commands, requests, admonitions, questions, answers, and communications" (1: 202–03).

The value of this distinction is to open the way, in a less technical manner than usual, to the notion of intentionality. These other-regarding acts "intend" others (in the sense of "attend to" and "tend toward") quite differently from the way in which mental events or states of consciousness that are entirely self-regarding do not refer to others. Other-regarding acts establish (or presuppose as already established) Buber's "between," that force-field of meaning within which its participants live and move.

The Intentional & the Nonintentional

There is another way to approach this same insight into experience,[4] this time through the work of von Hildebrand: "In order to understand the nature of 'intentionality,' we have to distinguish intentional experiences, not only from mere states lacking any direction toward an object, but also from merely teleological trends in human nature" (1953, 194). Examples of pure states are fatigue, "being in a bad humor, [or] being irritated," all of which "have no conscious relation with an object" (191). In contrast to relatively static states, teleological trends are dynamic. "In undergoing an experience such as thirst or a craving for food, we clearly grasp that these are not mere states, for they possess an immanent direction toward something" (194).

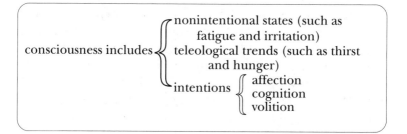

Figure 2

Now the first two categories (that is, states and trends) of consciousness are not intentional in the sense that affection, cognition, and volition are. In other words, to distinguish cognition and volition from affection does not mean claiming to find some deep, hidden meaning in states of fatigue, or in trends, no matter how teleological, as though shot through with a finality perceptible only to hawkeyed phenomenologists. The so-called wisdom of the body does not reside therein. When later we distinguish the intentional into "preintentional," "intentional," and "postintentional" (or "metaintentional"), we will not be falling back to some doctrine of privileged access available only to specialists, but will be referring to the simple, everyday notion of disposition and habit.

To summarize our first few points: there is a phenomenology that could be called existential or dialogal, concerned with a version of intentionality that takes its starting point in embodiment and intersubjectivity. The possibility of affective intentionality within such a phenomenology now sets our agenda.

Intentionality, the Heart, & Triune Consciousness

Under the general notion of intentionality we are testing whether affective intentionality describes feeling. Affective intentionality would be the philosophical explanation of feelings as the "reasons of the heart." The goal is to justify its formal, *technical* usage; its informal usage in everyday language is provocative, suggestive, and even instructive, but cannot be taken as substituting for philosophical argument. The numerous headings that follow contain some parallels and partial redundancies, for emphasis and clarification, but intend to build upon one another. The aim is an accumulative insight, appropriate to a tradition more often implicit than explicit. Each subsequent section, rather than being an exhaustive treatment of any one theme or source, intends only to furnish enough material to add to the one insight, namely, that affective intentionality is the best way to describe feeling and to integrate affection with cognition and volition into a triadic conception of consciousness.

Representational Intentionality & Kinetic Intentionality

Levinas's (1973) critique of Husserl's doctrine on intentionality goes back to his 1930 thesis. To go straight to the point:

> [I]ntentionality is not an act which is always identical, which is present in all forms of consciousness, and which alone exercises the function of relating to an object, while specifically affective or voluntary coefficients, relegated to the rank of purely subjective phenomena, are added to an always identical intention. *Intentionality itself is different in each of these cases.* In each act the *voluntary and affective elements are special ways of being directed toward* an outside object, special ways of transcending oneself [Levinas 1973, 43; my ital.].

It would be hard to find a more unequivocal claim that there are three distinct kinds of consciousness—affection, cognition, volition—each kind based on its *own intentionality*, its *distinct way of intending* otherness.

Now the most fundamental criterion for dividing classes or kinds of intentionality is representationality. Levinas makes this quite clear:

> [C]oncrete life must be taken in all its forms and not merely in the theoretical form [44] [not merely as objectivations or representations;] . . . the real world is a world of objects of practical use and *values*; [thus] . . . *objectivity does not mean* that they are given in a *theoretical representation.* But *"to have a sense" does not mean* the same as *"to represent."* The act of love has a sense, but this *does not mean that it includes a representation* of the object loved together with a purely *subjective feeling which has no sense* and which *accompanies* the representation. The characteristic of the loved object is precisely to be given in a *love intention, an intention which is irreducible to a purely theoretical representation* [44–45]; my ital. and brackets).

Here we find clearly distinguished two radically different senses of intentionality, themselves rooted in attitudes as irreducibly twofold as Buber's two word-pairs, I-Thou and I-It. Levinas eventually finds it necessary to side (temporarily) with

Heidegger against Husserl, accusing Husserl of an ". . . intellectualism . . . seeing the concrete world as a world of objects that are *primarily perceived.* Is our main attitude toward reality that of *theoretical contemplation?* Is not the world presented in its very being as a *center of action,* as a *field of activity* or of care—to speak the language of Martin Heidegger?" (119; my ital.).

Note how this rationalism is described: ". . . [A]cts of valuing, willing, etc., in all their forms are based on a *representation.* This pre-eminence of *theory,* established in the *Logische Untersuchungen,* has never been denounced by Husserl" (132; my ital.). The other (heart) tradition says that ". . . in addition to theoretical truths, there can also be '*practical* and *axiological* truths'" (133; my ital.).

Clearly there is a fundamental difference between the way these two philosophers approach the world. According to Levinas, for Husserl "the real world is the world of knowledge" (62): ". . . the assertion of the dominant role of theory, perception, and judgment in our life, in which the world is constituted, is a thesis that Husserl has never abandoned. For him, representation will always be the foundation of all acts" (62). Husserl's "intellectualism," then, is for Levinas the tradition of the primacy of the mind; "the primacy of theoretical consciousness [means that] the act of intuition, which brings us into contact with being, will be first and foremost a theoretical act, an objectifying act . . ." (63; my brackets).

For Levinas, Husserl's ambiguity in both opening the door to nonrepresentational intentionality and then closing it, goes back to his inability to transcend his intellectualism, to break out of the head tradition into the heart tradition. Thus we find this sentence, the last in his book on Husserl: "But isn't the possibility of overcoming this difficulty or fluctuation in Husserl's thought provided with the affirmation of the *intentional character of practical and axiological life?*" (158; my ital.). Here Levinas has intimated his own preoccupation and project, which is to show as meaningful, independently of representations as theoretical, the ethical (practical, axiological) life given in its *own intentionality*; in his *Totality and Infinity* (1969) this became Levinas's thesis of the primacy of ethics over ontology. Thus Heidegger, too, because of his neglect of the ethical, is ultimately found to be an unreliable guide. And, in his *Otherwise than Being* (1981), it became the primacy of beings over Being.

The term "kinetic" also appears in the title of this section. Kinetic refers to an interpretation (Sheehan 1982) of Heidegger's revision of intentionality in *Being and Time*. In an important study Sheehan demonstrates the Aristotelian basis of Heidegger's rereading of intentionality; Heidegger, too, struggled to overcome Husserl's reductively idealistic concept of intentionality, first rejecting the very term "intentionality," as he does in *Being and Time*, where he prefers to say "transcendence," and then later, when he drops transcendence also (Emad 1981, 145–58).

Whereas for Husserl intentionality is "intentionality as 'constitution' . . . performed by the absolutely self-positing transcendental ego, . . . for Heidegger everyday intentionality already understands being . . ." (Sheehan 1987, 8–9). *This* intentionality—unlike one more at home *with* itself (*bei sich*), as would be a pure spirit, a pure reason or will (or a transcendental ego)—is more naturally *outside* itself (*ausser sich*), and in the world. And affective intentionality is more primitively— as a mark of finitude and dependence on otherness—outwardly oriented, other-directed (*bei dem Andern*), revealing what Sheehan calls its "kinetic structure: . . . Human existence is nothing other than this disclosive movement of transcendence and return: excess to being and access to entities" (16).

Sheehan coins the expression "pres-ab-sentiality" to name "the moving entity's being-structure . . . . Aristotle's word for the pres-ab-sentiality of moving entities is *dynamis*, a word for 'being.' It does not mean 'mere possibility' but rather 'imperfect presence' or 'movement into presence.' As Heidegger interprets it, it means the same as kinesis . . . . *Dynamis* and kinesis, properly retrieved, are the basis of the term *Ereignis*. This word describes a moving entity's disclosive structure, its being" (19).

More will be made of this reading of Heidegger later. For now we need only note the sharp contrast between the exclusively representational interpretation of intentionality, and the kinetic and nonrepresentational interpretation. This second understanding, the substance of Levinas's "proximity," is an opening wedge to an understanding of another tradition than the head tradition (as tied to representations), to one that gradually becomes more understandable when recognized to be describable in terms of movement, kinesis, proximity, space, *dynamis, potentia,* embodiment: this other, alternate tradition, then, speaks of human being felt as bodily movement in space and time before knowing in concepts and ideas, that is, as motion before notion, kinesis before noesis, body movement before conceptual knowledge.

Ethical Space

Having begun to articulate—starting out in the space between persons—a complementary interpretation of how we consciously and unconsciously intend the persons and furniture of our world, let us now continue to explore the manifold of nonrepresentationalities, in order to facilitate a gradual accumulation of a sense or feel of what affectivity means and of what the heart tradition implies in its explicit and implicit usages.

We have begun with embodiment in space. In passing we could refer to the riches to be found in the human and social sciences, such as in anthropologist Edward T. Hall's "proxemics" (1959; 1966; 1976), communication theorist Ray Birdwhistell's "kinesics" (1952; 1970), and psychologist William S. Condon's "synchronics" (1967; 1974; 1979), three more ways that space is said to mean—beneath, below, or beside the mind. In these and other studies we find confirmed the prereflective, prevoluntary meaningfulness of space, especially interpersonal space. In Buber's terms, "the between" (1965), must be described as "encounter," not "experience"; "encounter" is an affective consciousness that keeps the distance that makes relation possible, whereas "experience" is a cognitive consciousness that absorbs the otherness, reducing others to my mental state of mind and making others the same as my ideas or images of them, "totalizing" them, as Levinas would also say. Space makes relation possible as our embodied motion transforms space into place. The territoriality of animals, birds, and fishes is too well known to require documentation. The sense of space that is the "room" (*Raum*), the wherein of one's embodiment in motion, is not the product of a logical reasoning or act of the will. It is in and of our bodies "before we know it."

Roger Poole calls the higher degree of this sense of nearness, as felt intersubjectively, "ethical space" (1972, 40), and he, too, bases it upon embodiment; the sense of space is the first manifestation in consciousness of the meaning of the human body. Space becomes intentional through embodiment, which is already intentional and "makes" space "mean" through motion. Poole's book includes a photograph; we see three Russian soldiers and four Czech citizens sitting on two park benches:

> The time is late summer 1968. The three Russians sit in a row, staring before them. One of them has leant his weapon casually against his knee. Further along the bench, two Czech citizens are bent forward, staring at the ground. At right angles to the Russians, a young man and a girl are sitting. Both of them are looking at the Russians. Both are immobile, reflective. The young man stares directly at the Russians, who all three take care to avoid his glance. The girl looks at the Russians only obliquely, her eyes covering them in swift forays. The Russians stare ahead of them,

creating a kind of neutral space where their looks cannot
be intercepted [3].

What is happening here? By sheer presence in space, these
seven human beings are wordlessly constituting meaning.
They actively, meaningfully, intentionally interact: "Acts in
space are embodied intentions" (6) "The intentions structure the space . . . [E]thical space is set up instantaneously
. . . as an achieved intentional structure . . ." (7). These people
are intuitively aware that speech is secondary to the sheer
fact of embodied meaning, their nonverbal communication
of hostility in the face-to-face situation that they enact by their
sharing space and time even as they avoid further "affront"
by resisting the urge to "confront" the soldiers; but the event
is already ethical. The intersubjective space between them
embodies value and is affectively intentional.

Now this intentionality, establishing meaningful and value-
laden space between persons, is a function of their spatial
and temporal nearness; without rational linguistic discourse
and without any set, voluntary sign-making they are embodied meanings, not users of bodies sending signals or making
signs. There is an immediacy in their intuitive acts.

> The body is established as the locus of all ethical experi-
> ence. Nothing happens to me which does not happen to
> my body. Insult the body and you insult the freedom within
> it . . . . The body is the locus of all ethical experience, and
> all experience is, because spatial, ethical. There can be no
> act which does not take place in ethical space [27].

This meaningful constitution of space is a moment prior
to and enabling of subsequent explicitations, articulations,
verbalizations, and so on, that is, as a knowing in one's heart,
as an intimation or sense of the event before mind and will
arrive on the scene. Thought will come, and eventually some
degree of self-appropriation in rational freedom, but before
that "the destruction of ethical space is itself the destruction

of the very possibility of thought . . . . The terrorist attempt to deprive space of its ethical significance, to deprive the body of its semantic function as sign and symbol, of its meaningful disposition in space, is in fact an attack upon human reason itself. It becomes impossible to think under the new spatial conditions" (27).

Intersubjective space, as a coconstitution by persons, is already filled with meaning in the present, before reflectively appropriated in thought as *re*-presented by speech.[5] There is an intentionality prior to representation; a step before head, the two are linked by a relation so tight that if the "presenting" intentionality were destroyed, so also would be the mind's "re-presenting." In other words, if we cannot first know in that material, embodied, felt subjectivity called heart, we will not know in that formal, rational subjectivity called mind or head.

The general meaning of intentionality, then, has room to include affective intentionality as our primary access to the meaning of feeling as emotion. Poole tries to make its meaning clearer in this way:

> Intentionality . . . refers to our power of conferring meaning . . . . Intentionality . . . is . . . a hypothesis. I operate a sort of spatial supposition, I "intend" what I see, hear, smell, want, fear, and so on, in a certain manner. This "intentionality" is thus open to others in the world to confirm or disconfirm. Once we have realized the connections between subjectivity as intentionality and the role of intentionality in bringing my world into being and canceling it out again in a series of infinitely fast "inspired guesses," we arrive at the point where we have to turn the objective hypothesis around 180 degrees and observe the subjectivity we are studying, not as a body operated upon by forces in a mechanical world, but as a freely emitting center of meanings. We attain a certain vantage from where we find out that we are conferring meaning upon the world instead of letting the world shove its meanings down over us [92].

Poole's consistent use of the pronoun "we" is not editorial, for he means to emphasize that intentionality, like intersubjective space itself, is relational. The world neither is already a meaning without us, imposing itself mechanically upon us, nor am I, as though I were a solipsistic subjectivity, able to impose my meaning upon a neutral, until then, meaningless world: "Subjectivity itself turns out to be, not only an intentionality, a meaning-conferring ability, but a relationship" (95), an intersubjectivity. Meaning is thus neither *in* you nor *in* me but, as Buber insisted, *between* us, in the space he called a metaphysical and metapsychical reality, neither a neutral construct nor merely imaginary—not a representation. It is quite evident that this " between," this ethical space, is not reflectively, voluntarily constituted by so many acts of mind and will; later we shall note how Merleau-Ponty, after Husserl, distinguishes two intentionalities, called "act-intentionality" and "operative-intentionality": the "flesh of the world" is given in affective intentionality. It is embodied sense intuition, where intuition is allowed to mean more than representation, allowed to comprise all embodied, felt meaning. (See Cataldi 1993.)

There is more to Poole's essay than is brought forth here. We consulted him to help show that even "before we know it" (that is, know conceptually in the thinking mind by cognitive intentionality) intersubjectivity is already ethical and valuable as sensed and felt in affectivity, and only "later" (at least logically, and usually also chronologically) objective, when the immediacy of affective intentionality opens the way to cognitive intentionality.

Existence as Intentional (Embodiment, Motility)

If we now again imagine a methodological movement inward, from space, through the concept of motion or motility, to its ground, which is embodiment, we can begin to explore embodiment itself more thoroughly. Intentionality is not single or monolithic in meaning, but manifold; embodiment, in space and movement, gradually brings to consciousness a prereflective and prevoluntary (=not-mind and not-will) meaning of intentionality.

Access to a new shading of the meaning of intentionality is Merleau-Ponty's clear statement that ". . . representative consciousness is only one of the forms of consciousness . . . ."[6] Merleau-Ponty is a primary source for the (implicit) heart tradition as based on the phenomenology of affective intentionality. There are simply too many themes and quotable passages from which to choose; his early emphasis on embodiment as intentional and his later concept of the "flesh" clearly integrate the multiplicity of his themes, however, and so we can organize our brief reference to his *Phenomenology of Perception* (1962), *Signs* (1964), and *The Visible and the Invisible* (1968) around these pivotal points.

Merleau-Ponty places himself squarely in the alternative tradition that admits of a kind of pararational or prerational knowing when he announces his intention: "To return to things themselves is to return to that world which precedes knowledge" (1963, ix). To paraphrase Pascal, for Merleau-Ponty "the heart has its perceptions": ". . . I cannot put perception into the same category as the synthesis represented by judgments, acts, or predications" (x). "*Perceptions* of the heart," we might say, precede "*reasons* of the heart" and also precede the representations of reason, which would not be true ". . . if the reality of my perceptions were based solely on the intrinsic coherence of 'representations'" (xv). "Looking for the world's essence is not looking for what it is as an idea once it has been reduced to a theme of discourse; it is looking for what it is as a fact for us, before any thematization" (xv). "The world is not what I think, but what I live through" (xvi–xvii).

These statements clearly suggest an understanding of our human way of being in the world, of intending it meaningfully, other than one based on the primacy of mind as representational. Merleau-Ponty's nonrepresentational intention-

ality is presented as a contrast between Kant and Husserl:
"What distinguishes intentionality from a Kantian relation to
a possible object is that the unity of the world, before being
posited by knowledge in a specific act of identification, is
'lived' as ready-made or already there . . . without any concept" (xvii). Following Husserl, Merleau-Ponty calls the
Kantian intentionality an "intentionality of act" (xviii), while
he calls the "broadened notion of intentionality operative
intentionality (Husserl's term is *fungierende Intentionalität*) . . .
which produces the natural and ante-predicative unity of the
world and of our life, being apparent in our desires, our evaluations, and in the landscape we see, more clearly than in objective knowledge . . ." (xviii); it is "phenomenological
'comprehension' . . . distinguished from traditional 'intellection' . . ." (xviii).

Merleau-Ponty clearly has a keen sense of proposing another tradition than that of reason or intellect as primary
access to meaning. Knowledge must not be equated solely
with the rational/intellectual tradition but must also include
desiring, valuing, perceiving in nature, without concepts,
which arrive later. Thus, ". . . to 'understand' is to take in the
total intention—not only what these things are for representation . . ." (xviii).

All this is familiar to anyone who knows Merleau-Ponty.
We need only note what is easily missed, namely, that by that
everyday word "heart" an ægis is ready at hand under which
to rank what is otherwise usually only named negatively
(nonrational, nonmental, nonrepresentational, nonobjective,
and so on). Let us keep these three terms joined together:
intentionality, perception, and embodiment, as this chapter's
major organizing ideas, along with three others: motion,
space, and time as corollary ideas. Central to Merleau-Ponty's
thesis of the primacy of perception is the primacy of embodiment.

Here are a few pertinent quotations that will not need my
brief interpretation:

[T]he thinking subject must have its basis in the subject incarnate [193]. Space and perception generally represent, at the core of the subject . . . the perpetual contribution of one's bodily being, a communication with the world more ancient than thought [254]; . . . [M]otility [is] an original mode of intentionality or meaning which amounts to conceiving human nature, no longer in terms of consciousness, but in terms of existence [254, n1]. Husserl's originality lies beyond the notion of intentionality; it is to be found in the elaboration of this notion and in the *discovery, beneath the intentionality of representations, of a deeper intentionality,* which others have called existence [121, n5]. Consciousness is being towards the thing through the intermediary of the body [138–39; my ital.].

Again, trying to name this embodied intentionality, Merleau-Ponty speaks of ". . . this third term between the psychic and the physiological . . . which we call existence" (22), later called "the flesh." Neither the psychic without a body nor the physical without a psyche, but something else, a *tertium quid.* He says "the body is an affective object" (154); on 217 he speaks of our being "connatural with the world" and on 137 of "motility as basic intentionality," and on 144 of "knowledge in the hands," and of "the body which understands." Here again is motion before notion, kinesis before noesis.

These references all precede his even more powerful treatment of sexuality and intersubjectivity, where affective intentionality offers privileged access to others. Little commentary is needed to bring the foregoing statements to focus. In sum, primacy should not go to mind and will but to a way of bodily being in the world, already meaning-ful (*sinnvoll*). Call it "the phenomenal body beside the objective one," or "knowing-body . . . [;] in short, we substitute for [representational] consciousness, as the subject of perception, existence, or being in the world through a body" (309, n1; my brackets).

There are many more ways, in just this one source, to approach our theme (for example, the contrast of grasping

[*Greifen*] and pointing or indicating [*Zeigen*], in the sense of meaning), but we may conclude with only one: "[B]ehind the spoken cogito, the one which is converted into discourse and into essential truth, there lies a tacit cogito . . . presence of oneself to oneself, being no less than existence . . . anterior to any philosophy . . ." (403–04). This self-presence, this subjectivity, this existence, is embodied: ". . . [M]y existence as subjectivity is merely one with my existence as a body . . ." (408), and "at the heart of the subject we discovered, then, the presence of the world, so that the subject was no longer understood as a synthetic activity, but as ek-stase [a standing out from oneself toward otherness] . . . . We found beneath the intentionality of acts, or thetic intentionality, another kind which is the condition of the former's possibility: namely an operative intentionality already at work before any position or any judgment . . ." (429; my brackets). Affection is the "other kind" of intentionality.

In sum, then, Merleau-Ponty has an affective intending prior to reason and will, equated with existence and embodiment, phenomenologically descriptive of what counts in ordinary language as a knowing and loving in the heart. This is the meaning of his central concept of the flesh (Cataldi 1993), and of the body-subject (that is, *le corps sujet*). It is not simply equated with saying "my body knows" or "my body loves," but it is a third something between *psyche* (soul) and *soma* (body), by being ambiguously both. Merleau-Ponty, content to describe, offers only hints of how we may later interpret that third mode of consciousness, affective consciousness.

When Seeing Is More than Seeing

Partly as a bridge to Sartre's rich descriptions of affective intentionality and partly to gain another access to the important category of "the between," let us move a step closer to the center of embodiment as affective. We began with space, considered motion and a certain somewhat preliminary view of embodiment as intentional, and now wish to establish even more solidly the phenomenological priority of this embodiment.

John Heron has written a very insightful essay (1970) on our theme. His phenomenology of encounter sheds light on Buber's between. Heron states that

> in only two cases does simultaneous reciprocal interaction between qualitatively similar processes occur: in the case when two people touch each other, make bodily contact; and in the case when two people look into each other's eyes, make eye contact . . . . In the strict sense of the term, actual encounter occurs only in mutual touching and mutual gazing, for it is only in these instances that each meets the other who is meeting oneself. In mutual touching as in mutual gazing, each person both gives and receives in the same act . . . [243].

Heron concentrates on the gaze, introducing the capital distinction between looking *at* another's eyes and looking *into* them. To say to someone, "Look me in the eye" is to invite an encounter totally different from the clinical inspection by the oculist, ". . . an invitation or a challenge to the other to find something which is not a physical property in and through the eyes of the speaker" (248). One "may directly encounter some personal quality . . . : 'Look into my eyes' is equivalent to 'Meet me in my gaze,' with the corollary 'And let me meet you in yours'" (248).

Heron calls this "quiet gazing . . . a feeding of the heart..." (249) and describes it thus:

> The luminosity of the gaze or the gaze-light of the other is a distinct phenomenal reality which is transphysical, although supervenient upon and mediated by physical phenomena: . . . the phenomenal reality of the gaze-light of the other is such that it is continuous with the other; the other is revealed in it, it discloses the other, s/he is the presence of it . . . . The purely physical properties of the

eyes of the other are not continuous with him or her in the
way the luminosity of the gaze is . . ." [253].

Heron further describes this intersubjective encounter in
terms of a field, a kind of force field generated by the two
interacting persons:

> The interaction of the twofold gazing . . . is a necessary
> condition of the irradiation of each by each being. This
> interpenetration, then, is a transphysical unitive reality or
> field—which is also a unitive field of consciousness . . . : my
> awareness of your awareness of me both reveals me to my-
> self and reveals you to me, and your simultaneous aware-
> ness of my awareness of you both reveals you to yourself
> and reveals me to you. But further, in my awareness of your
> awareness of my awareness, whether of myself or you, I re-
> veal myself to you; and in your awareness of my awareness
> of your awareness, whether of yourself or me, you reveal
> yourself to me. Thus in the unitive field of consciousness
> established through the interfused transphysical stream-
> ing of mutual gazing, each is revealed to oneself, each is
> revealed to the other, and each reveals oneself to the other
> [255–56].

Note two qualities of the encounter, the streaming and
the field, for Heron's thesis is that there is a genuine corre-
spondence of gaze and consciousness. Heron refers to Buber
for this term "streaming," claiming that

> under optimal conditions of interpersonal encounter, the
> gaze of the other may be experienced as streaming into
> my whole being—I am filled out and irradiated by it . . . .
> The transphysical streaming of the gaze of the other
> interfuses my whole being; the transphysical streaming of
> my gaze interfuses the whole being of the other; but in
> each case this only occurs by virtue of the thorough inter-
> penetration of the mutual streaming . . . [255].

This mutual streaming is the lived experience of embodied intentionality. It is the prereflective, prevoluntary, preverbal mutual presence wherein two persons are nourished by being in the "elemental," in Levinas's term, in the field of meaning they constitute together. We experience neither bodies without meaning nor meaning without bodies but rather embodied meaning.

No one will miss the very fundamental nature of such encounter, its immediacy, directness, and irreducibility. Heron insists that none of this meaning is inferential (258–63). There is one field of consciousness and in that field, between its constituting embodied intentionalities, two consciousnesses become mutually aware. (Similar analysis could be made of touch, and Heron offers indications of how it would proceed.) These two features of the encounter—the gazes streaming into one another and the single field of consciousness, so completely different from noting, by looking at the eyes, their physical properties like their color, their bloodshot lines, their shape, and so on, or from reflecting upon one's mental state of consciousness—point to Merleau-Ponty's third something, between the psychical and the physiological, like Buber's "between," in fact the very ground of the latter's possibility in all its ambiguity. The heart's unspoken reasons met in the mutual streaming of the gazes, establishing "the between" wherein consciousnesses arise to and for one another, already having been there before reason sets out to dispel the ambiguity.

Note an important implication of this reciprocal encounter. The so-called problem of how we know other minds, as Heron points out, is based on "a false starting point, that of reflective alienation from intensely lived experience. And in this state of alienation the problem presupposes a false assumption: that it is always and only our own self and its experience that are given us in immediate and direct awareness" (263). Such reflective knowing (like Buber's target of critique, the "mental state," so radically contrasted with "the between"), is by no means the foundation of all truth, any more than Husserl's representations were. Rather than this conceptual knowing, there is a genuine nonrepresentational knowing the other in one's heart, a case of the other being given in immediate and direct nonobjective awareness. Thus proofs for knowing other minds are always easily shown to be circular. As Heron states:

> It may be suggested that the physical properties of the eyes alone are sufficient to account for the emotional reaction that is consequent upon their appraisal. But if so, this re-action should be enhanced when one attends exclusively to the physical properties of the other's eyes; however, it is precisely then, as the crucial test shows, that the special impact of perceiving the other disappears. The emotional reaction is a function of perceiving the gaze . . . [263].

Thus our first descriptive approach to the idea of feeling as affective intentionality, with the heart as its metaphor.

Notes

1. Strasser notes: "Husserl declared . . . that his 'transcendental idealism stands or falls with the possibility of solving the problem of intersubjectivity by means of the method of intentional analysis.' Scheler, Reinach, Schapp, Heidegger, Löwith, Sartre, and Merleau-Ponty (and Ricoeur) are all witness to '. . . the inability of Husserl's transcendental phenomenology to solve the problem of intersubjectivity'" [1969, xi].

For Ricoeur's part in this consensus, see his Husserl (1967), esp. ch. 5.

2. Tallon 1976a; 1976b. The centrality of "the between" is also the view of Robert E. Wood: "The Between actualized in relation is the central notion of Buber's thought" (1969, 41), and ". . . the center of all his thinking" (ibid., 9).

3. Kwant 1960, 10. He cites (7) Marx's dictum: "It is not our way of thinking which determines our being, but our social being which determines our way of thinking" (1951, 13).

4. As Spiegelberg puts it, we are in the realm of experiences usually presumed to be self-evident: "Here again the phenomenologist is faced with the lack of adequate studies of phenomena which thus far have been simply taken for granted. Yet that which is 'self-explanatory' in this sense is often merely something 'which one has passed a thousand times and is just passing for the thousand and first time'" (1964, 1: 202).

5. Poole 1972, 71: "Meaning is, of course, wider than verbal. Meaning is just as easily living meaning, the meaning of intersubjective space, art, the lived body, signs of all kinds, the activities of war and peace."

6. Merleau-Ponty 1963, 172, my ital.; see also 171–73. *Représentationnel* does not exist as an "official" French word; to say representational one must say *représentative*, which Fisher translates as representative. Representational and nonrepresentational are perfectly acceptable English words, of course, for example in the realm of art. Some French writers have begun to use the word *représentationnel.*

Chapter 2

Intentionality of Affection & Emotion

> The heart of the wise, like a mirror,
> should reflect all objects, without being sullied by any.
> Confucius (551–479 B.C.), *Analects* (c. 500 B.C.).

> There is nothing more unfathomable than the human heart.
> Unknown, *Homer's Epigrams*. no. 5 (c. 400 B.C.).

> But still the heart doth need a language.
> Samuel Taylor Coleridge (1771–1834), *Piccolomini* 2. 4.

> Then nature rul'd, and love, devoid of art
> Spoke the consenting language of the heart.
> John Gay (1685–1732), *Dione*, prologue

Summary

This chapter is devoted to the philosophy of Jean-Paul Sartre, two of whose central ideas, affective intentionality, from *Being and Nothingness*, and dialectical reason, from the *Critique of Dialectical Reason*, are interpreted as evidence of a solid alternative to the representational intentionality of Cartesian analytic reason. The existence of affective intentionality as an independent and irreducible mode of consciousness is confirmed and its nature begins to emerge more clearly.

W E TURN NOW TO SARTRE, to continue our phenomenology of affective intentionality. Partly by undermin-
ing anything like a transcendental ego—which
would mean a soul somehow able to be or to do without radical dependence on embodiment—and by disproving any
meaningless bodily action, any deed that would escape responsibility, Sartre implicitly affirms the heart tradition. Neither Cartesian analytic reason, on the one hand, nor "mere"
body, on the other, but rather "psychic body" (1953a, 443), is
his way of approximating our theme. Once again, as with
Merleau-Ponty, since we face a prolific author whose interests ranged widely, we must be as parsimonious as possible.

Early Texts

Let us divide our treatment of Sartre according to the two
negations mentioned above, first his eliminating "soul without body," then his emphasizing "body with soul." Perhaps
here, for some skeptics, the metaphor of the heart will lose
its Valentine's Day, tender-minded, "sweetness and light" aura,
and enter soberly into philosophical language, for no one
will accuse Sartre of softness or concession to popular
(*vulgaire*) usage in his view of human existence. In his analyses, only a thoroughgoing human humanity survives, with no
patience for either a disembodied meaning or meaningless
materiality.

First, then, as to the problem of a detachable ego—a cryp-
tic spirit going by another name—Sartre's attack (dating from
1936) on Husserl's transcendental ego is well known (1957).
Sartre's essay is a negative moment of his own anthropology,
removing an obstacle to an existential and humanistic understanding of humanity. His essays on imagination (in 1936)
and emotion (1939; 1940)—as well as *Being and Nothingness*
(1953, dating from 1943), particularly on body, space, time,
and especially the interhuman—are all mixtures of positive
and negative elements of the positive moment of his anthropology, which is the reinstatement of affectively intentional

embodiment. Put simply, first he gets rid of pure spirit (as transcendental ego), then he gets rid of pure body (as mechanistic materialism).

One can easily perceive parallels with Merleau-Ponty's antispiritualist and antiphysicalist position. If we bring to Sartre's negative moment, in *The Transcendence of the Ego*, the heuristic hint that he is in the (implicit) heart tradition, we can make sense of his otherwise seemingly too strongly put expressions like the "transcendental field" being "impersonal" or "pre-personal, *without an I*" (1957, 36); all the many apparently overstated reductions of ego to its content or to reflection, and the emphasis on an almost adamantly altruistic (that is, outwardly turned, not naturally inward) intentionality finally make sense when Sartre says: ". . . [A]s long as the I remains a structure of absolute consciousness, one will still be able to reproach phenomenology for being an escapist doctrine, for again pulling a part of human existence out of the world . . ." (1936, 106) which would again result in a pure mind or spirit—Platonic, Cartesian, or Husserlian, using a body—but would not give us a human being.

On the more positive side, however, once the substantiality of a kind of separable and separately posited spirit, soul, or ego has been challenged, the other side of the coin, the retrieved and reconstituted status of embodiment and its feeling (affectivity), as well as its realities (space, time, and motion), predictably must attract Sartre's attention, and they do. Again, not just for their own sake, as would interest a pure physicalist or a mere materialist, but for the sake of intentionality, they interest an existentialist.

Radical Conversion as Change of Heart

How shall we approach the mass of words in Sartre's works appropriate to the second half of his anthropology? What access promises to yield the most insight? If traditional heart talk is inseparable from the concept of *change* of heart (conversion), we may take a clue from the idea of change in Sartre's "radical conversion" as a change of heart. If we take for an axiom that the *person* acts, not (on the one hand) the soul or consciousness (or intellect or will) nor (on the other) the body or *any* part of the whole—then we can cautiously ask about the effect of, for example., emotion or imagination— or even the material conditions of workers—upon the whole person's actions. This would be like asking: What mediates me to myself as agent? How shall freedom recover itself, as Sartre says on the last page of *Being and Nothingness?* Or pursue being? Or how shall the for-itself be(come) in-itself? Is this an idle, vain passion, a desire to be God—or an ethical idealism? Socially is it overcoming unfreedom by detotalizing the political totalities that terrorize us? Sartre says that "we humans are 'mediated' by things to the same extent as things are 'mediated' by us" (1976, 79). This dialectical circularity, as he calls it, is the very opposite of any rationally analytic power to dominate matter, or any blind, mindless materiality or materialist power to pretend to be history without dialectic interaction with human freedom. Neither mind nor matter, but both in dialectical circularity, in dialectical reason, constitute the third, embodied meaning.

Dialectical Reason as Heart

To make the claim, then, perhaps surprising at first, but by no means outrageous, that by *dialectical* reason Sartre means what another tradition calls heart, requires only the recognition that his entire corpus aims at reinstating embodiment and materiality to full ontological status against *analytic* reason, that is, against a Cartesian or any other rationalization of human existence, especially in its religious form. He aims at nothing less than regaining a true anthropology, a whole not to be lost reductively to either of its mistakenly substantialized parts. "Thus the dialectic is a totalizing activity" (47). And "the intelligibility of dialectical reason . . . is the very movement of its totalization" (46).[1] This is his way of overcoming the nemesis of every French philosopher: Cartesian

dualism. What he adds that is new is how affective intentionality is our mode of experiencing embodied meaning, and
how reason becomes dialectical in embodiment.

To our clue (which is also a question) about change, then,
Sartre would respond by calling attention to all those diverse
ways in which one unifies oneself in act by the diverse ways
one mediates things, by embodying action that mediates one
to oneself. No direct "spiritual" self-transformation is possible,
nor any interior freedom oblivious of exterior conditions.
Imagination and emotion are but the same doctrine writ small;
in other words, in those early studies, more anthropological
and psychological than the later social and political ones,
Sartre sets down his unitary concept of human being. Thus
emotion is a way one "transforms one's body as synthetic totality in such a way that one can live and grasp this new world
through it. In other words, consciousness changes the body,
or, if you like, the body . . . puts itself on the level of behavior"
(1948a, 76), acting thus as a single whole, whether seen from
the side of consciousness (soul, ego) or of body; thus "emotion is not an accident [not something that 'happens' to me].
It is a mode of existence of consciousness, one of the ways in
which it *understands* (in the Heideggerian sense of *Verstehen*)
its 'being-in-the-world'" (1948a, 91; my brackets). For Sartre
there is no evading the intentionality of emotions; ultimately
I am responsible for them and how they bring about changes
in my whole person.

Imagination, too, is intentional. As I form images I intend an object in that precise way, organizing my consciousness in that way, imaginatively (1962, ch. 9; 1948b, 4–21). But
the most interesting phenomenological observations Sartre
makes in *The Psychology of Imagination* have to do with affectivity, and brief consideration of affective intentionality there
bridges to his treatment in *Being and Nothingness*. If we bring
our clue-question to Sartre again, asking how we might
change, for example, how we might cease being selfish and
become compassionate, he would answer:

As the love becomes impoverished and schematized (for-
mulized) it also becomes very weak. In every person we
love, and for the very reason of his or her inexhaustible
wealth, there is something that surpasses us, an independence, an imperviousness which exacts ever renewed efforts of approximation: The unreal object has nothing of
this imperviousness. It is never more than what we know of
it [1948b, 208].

To understand what Sartre means here let us take up the re-
verse situation, that is, hating someone: What renewed efforts go into working up hatred? Sartre says:

Try to bring about in yourself the subjective phenomena
of hatred, of indignation, without having those phenomena oriented *on* some hated person, on an unjust act, and
you can tremble, pound your fists, blush, but your internal
condition will be devoid of indignation, of hatred. To hate
Paul is to intention [*sic*] Paul as a transcendent object of a
consciousness. But neither must we commit the intellectu-
alistic error by believing that Paul is present as the object
of an intellectual representation. The feeling envisions an
object but it does so in its own way, which is affective [1948b,
98].

Intentionally Affective Body

Here we are full circle again: ". . . [I]n a word, feelings have
special intentionalities, they represent one way—among others—of self-*transcendence*. Hatred is hatred *of* someone, love is
love *of* someone" (1948b, 98). No amount of "pure spirit," as
though merely willing could make love or hatred arise, nor
"pure bodily" motion, such as incessant genuflecting or gri-
macing (or pounding one's fists), could make one holy or
angry. Neither of these extremes respects the unitary condition of human existence as embodied consciousness. Instead
of keeping consciousness and body separate we need to get

them together. Sartre's approach is to say that in order to understand fully the nature of this type of synthesis we must renounce all comparisons drawn from physical intermixtures: ". . . [A] consciousness of knowledge which is at the same time a consciousness of feeling is not *part* knowledge and *part* feeling . . . [but] entirely knowledge and entirely affectivity" (1948b, 103). The context of this remark is the nature of an image and the value of images in the change or self-transformation in becoming someone who loves or hates. So let us rejoin the context: ". . . [M]ost affective states are supposed to be accompanied by images, which represent for desire that which is desired. This theory is guilty of the error of confusing the image with its object, the illusion of immanence, negation of *affective intentionality,* and complete misunderstanding of the nature of consciousness" (1948b, 102; my ital.). What does this mean if not that an image is *not* an accompaniment to affectivity but, as he says, "a synthesis of affectivity and knowledge," where "the image presents itself as the lower limit towards which knowledge tends when it becomes debased [and] as the upper limit toward which affectivity tends when it seeks to know itself" (1948b, 103). Thus, though an image is less than perception when it comes to knowing, it offers *some* knowledge, for "desire is also a knowledge" (103), a kind of knowledge. But *what* kind? Is this knowledge (the reasons) of the heart? A strange hypothesis to test on a philosopher of Sartre's reputation, one may protest, but only if one persists in reducing heart to its sentimental version, and refuses to acknowledge the heart that hates, that brings forth good and evil, that, after all, and above all, needs conversion and change. We have now set up the conditions proper to an examination of *Being and Nothingness* wherein Sartre's contribution to the thesis of triadic consciousness, in terms of affectivity, emotion, and embodiment are most accessible and developed.

Being and Nothingness

Let us first restate the question, and restate also, very briefly, a summary of what Sartre has answered to this point. It would be a mistake to make too much of a single word in a single footnote, but no mistake at all to make something of it (especially in light of Sartre's interviews shortly before his death). I refer to the famous footnote 13 relevant to "the possibility of an ethics of deliverance and salvation" that Sartre says "can be achieved only after a radical conversion" (1953a, 534, n13). The value of this note is to continue the theme of change (as conversion, change of heart), and to ask what must "existence" (that is, human being or nature) be in order that such change and its ethics be possible. If it is true that to understand Sartre's rejection of the transcendental ego is to see it as a rejection of an existence or anthropology wherein the human person is reduced to *analytic* (that is, Cartesian) reason, then to understand his views on emotion, imagination, and even his Marxism is to recognize his rejection of any mechanistic physicalism or materialism. *His* materialism is that of a psychic body, a materialism pregnant with intentionality.

Now intentionality, if not to mean some disguised self-subsisting soul or spirit—Platonic, Cartesian, or Husserlian—and yet also to be compatible with a strongly professed materialism, must resist facile comprehension into clear and distinct, unambiguous concepts; rather it must first and foremost participate in an immediacy and directness, perhaps the truest case where "there is only intuitive knowledge" (240), that of lived intersubjective existence (*le vécu*). Conversion is precisely this regaining of the present after the bad faith of a refusal of consciousness, a refusal that takes the form of an introspection that tries to evade freedom and responsibility: "In introspection I try to determine exactly what I am, to make up my mind to be my true self without delay—even though it means consequently to set about searching for ways to *change* myself" (106; my ital.). This introspection is the act of the

Cartesian *cogito,* a disintegrating act that Sartre calls "an inner disintegration in the heart of being" (116), which happens to the unconverted because "the first act of bad faith is to flee what it cannot flee, to flee what it is" (115). Conversion would be what Sartre calls a "self-recovery of being which was previously corrupted," for he clearly asserts that being in the bad faith of self-deception "does not mean that we cannot radically escape bad faith." In fact, "this self-recovery we shall call authenticity" (116, n10), a regaining of self that is *integrated* rather than corrupted, rather than decomposed into a soul (separate as a pure "I think," *cogito, ich denke*) and a body of irresponsible emotion or passion, like that of the self-deluded woman who divorces herself from her body, "not noticing" that she leaves her hand "between the warm hands of her companion," because, Sartre says, "she is at this moment all intellect" by "not being her body" (97–98): she is in bad faith. Sartre is not advocating, as some moralists suggest, an identification with oneself wallowing, as it were, in one's "true" self no matter what, as pederast, as flirt, and so on. He is attacking any *decomposing* of the person into "what one is not," namely, one's "parts," whereas one is a whole. This requires some explanation.

Take, for example, the whole business of the vain desire to be, like God, both in and for oneself. Human reality, as split, is *for*-itself but not *in*-itself: consciousness is not its embodiment. But, as Sartre says,

> [I]t is necessary that one be for oneself only what one is. But is this not precisely the definition of the in-itself, or, if you prefer, the principle of identity? To posit as an ideal the being of things, is this not to assert by the same stroke that this being does not belong to human reality and that the principle of identity, far from being a universal axiom universally applied, is only a synthetic principle enjoying a merely regional universality? . . . [I]n order that the candor of "pure hearts" can have any validity for human real-

ity as an ideal, the principle of identity must not represent
a constitutive principle of human reality, and human reality must not be necessarily what it is but must be able to be
what it is not. What does this mean? If one is what one is,
bad faith is impossible and candor ceases to be one's ideal
and becomes one's being. But is one what one is? And more
generally, how can one be what one is when one exists as
consciousness of being? [101].

Sartre is here recommending neither the unconscious
self-identity of things, nor, of course, the conscious self-object-
ification of some introspected "pure" consciousness, but the
humanly impossible coincidence of conscious embodiment
with itself. Identity is a desired but never-to-be-achieved ideal,
and thus a vain ideal—*unless*, he says, conversion enables a
self-recovery and authenticity, again, *not* by becoming unconscious (so that the disintegrating negating that consciousness
is and introduces into human reality be stilled) *nor* by denying embodiment. Somehow both the for-itself of consciousness and the in-itself of its (thinglike) embodiment (facticity)
must be recovered. Do we find anywhere in *Being and Nothingness* an instance of such an integration? We do, and affective intentionality is its essence.

Affective Intentionality Is Not Analytic Reason
Note what is at issue. Sartre is keenly aware of the alienating
split that consciousness introduces into human being, resulting in its substantialization, as in Descartes's first principle,
the spiritual "thinking thing" (the *res cogitans)*, with embodiment reduced to Descartes's second principle, the material,
spatial and temporal, "extended thing" (the *res extensa)*. Once
put asunder these two selves (the "for" and the "in") ensure
an equally disintegrated psychology and ethics. So we seek
an instance either prior to the advent of this consciousness,
or, if after consciousness's splitting of being, a recovery of
integrated identity: "I am the project of the recovery of my

being," Sartre says (475). "Human reality is a perpetual surpassing toward a coincidence with itself which is never given"
(139).

Here we rejoin the main line of previous considerations,
where affective intentionality was shown to be a consciousness of a different sort, where one is not all intellect. "Not all
consciousness is knowledge (there are states of affective consciousness . . .)" (11). "Pleasure . . . is not a representation . . ."
(15). For Sartre it is clear that "we must abandon the primacy
of knowledge . . . : consciousness . . . is in itself something
other than knowledge turned back upon itself" (10–11). Affective intentions are neither conceptual nor representational:
"I do not 'conceive' them or 'represent' them to myself; expressions like these would refer us again to 'knowing,' which
on principle is removed from consideration" (363). What do
we avoid by recourse to affective intentionality, and what do
we accomplish? We avoid this disintegrating split, escape rationalism, and get to the prereflective *cogito*: ". . . [T]he reduction of consciousness to knowledge in fact involves our
introducing into consciousness the subject-object dualism
which is typical of knowledge" (12) and so we avoid that. And,
second: ". . . [T]here is a pre-reflective *cogito* which is the condition of the Cartesian *cogito*," and we attain that (13).

Now the place where we can most profitably look for
events of affective intentionality, as we have seen in previous
sections, is intersubjectivity, encounter with others, "the between." This is also Sartre's preferred locus, as is evident from
his dominant and extensive treatment of embodiment, especially in concrete relations with others. Again we must be clear
about what we seek. If the heart tradition is to appear anywhere and be a relevant factor in Sartre's anthropology, it
must overcome the several dualisms we have already noted
(the *en soi* [being in itself] and *pour soi* [being for itself], being and (analytic) cognitive consciousness, object and subject, and *res extensa* and *res cogitans*, soul as substance and psychology without a psyche, and so on). Now Sartre spends many

pages overcoming solipsism, which he sees as the logical outcome of any intersubjectivity based on the classical dualisms.
But since these dualisms derive from confusing consciousness with knowledge, to regain an affective, nonrepresentational consciousness that is irreducible to knowledge is to recover the integrated person and a different world of human
relations altogether, one based on another consciousness, another (dialectical) "knowing," a "knowing in the heart," which
is not an unambiguous knowledge like that of clear and distinct ideas, but rather a being-with that is a genuine intending that is not knowledge, that is, not head-knowledge, but
heart-knowledge. It is Sartre's *inclusive* knowledge, which he
calls *compréhension,* parallel to Heidegger's "existential understanding," *Verstehen,* arising from affective intentionality.

Now this is what Sartre says, without, of course, explicitly
calling it heart-knowledge (Pascal perhaps not being one of
his primary inspirations). He says "if we are to refute solip-
sism, then my relation to the other is first and fundamentally
a relation of being to being, not of knowledge to knowledge"
(329). (Later we use the term "connaturality" for this knowing by resonance with one's *being* rather than by reference to
one's *knowing.*) This original being-with precedes any representational intentionality. "Heidegger's being-with . . . is not
knowledge" (332). It is not head-knowledge, yet something *is*
conscious, nonrepresentationally, not in image or word, but,
beyond Hegel, Husserl, and Heidegger, "in the look," that is,
in no previously assured structure in me or in others, but
strictly and solely in actual *mutual encounter.*

Radical Conversion from
Analytical to Dialectical Reason

And here we find ourselves once more in the realm of "the
between," of a reciprocity that, because grounded in embodiment, tries to transcend objectivity and be an intersubjectivity, tries, I say, because there is a condition to be met: ". . . [A]
radical conversion . . . is necessary if one is to escape objec-

tivity" (345). How are we to understand this radical conversion, the same expression that appears in the famous footnote 13 mentioned above? The answer lies nowhere else than in Sartre's understanding of embodiment, experienced and expressed in affective intentionality as distinct from cognitive intentionality:

> The body . . . is the in-itself . . . surpassed by the nihilating for-itself . . . . [T]he body is a *necessary characteristic* of the for-itself . . . . *The very nature of the for-itself demands that it be body*; . . . its nihilating escape from being should be made in the form of an engagement in the world [409]. The body is the contingent form which is taken up by the necessity of my contingency [432]. The body is nothing other than the for-itself; it is not an in-itself in the for-itself [408]. Consequently the body-for-itself is never a given which I can know [409]. In order to add cognitive structures to the body as it has been given in reflection, we will have to resort to the other [443].

This chain of quotations is meant to lead us to recognize that we must think of embodiment much more integrally than would Plato, Descartes, or Husserl or, on the opposite pole, than would a mechanistic materialist. Being embodied is the mediation of affective intentionality because ". . . consciousness *exists* its body . . . . Therefore my body is a conscious structure of my consciousness" (434).[2]

Later Texts

Sartre experienced an important development in his view of intersubjectivity, at least if we can judge from an interview published a month before his death. Whereas other persons, whether met in the look or otherwise, were originally "conflict" for the Sartre of *Being and Nothingness,* for the Sartre of forty years later "fraternity, not violence, was the fundamental bond among human beings" (Anderson 1981, 447). Prior to conflict there existed a positive ground, eventually (inevitably?) lost, through a natural degradation in the real world (of need [and scarcity], à la Marx?), later able to be recovered through the famous radical conversion. Let us explore this point.

If dehumanization has resulted from one's being reduced either to a disembodied soul (to an ego, to a *cogito*), or to a mechanistic body (without the psychic, without intentionality or meaning), or both, whether by religion, by rationalist analytic philosophy, by capitalism, or by all of the above, then for as long as one remains in this dehumanized bad faith one is inauthentic, a failure. Now, "when Sartre states that all human actions are in vain he refers only to our bad-faith attempts, on the level of impure reflection, to be God" (445). "But it is because a human being is a unity of two dimensions, facticity and freedom [embodiment and consciousness] that bad faith is possible" (443; my brackets). This is the split noted often above.

But further, "for Sartre bad faith is not an inevitable condition of being human. An authentic self-recovery, a proper synthesis of facticity and transcendence, is possible" (443). Such a proper synthesis would be a converted being, one whose heart is changed, turned from fragmentary spirit or body, from analytical to dialectical reason, and integrated into a new humanism, which Jeanson calls a "morally authentic 'humanism'" (446), which, in fact, is precisely the new human project, namely, "the humanization of humanity," in Sartre's words, which can come only from a radically converted, integrated, whole person, not from an ego (transcendental or otherwise) or from a mechanism (materialist or otherwise) but from the heart, from embodied consciousness and freedom. Now overcoming this bad faith, this failure in authenticity, through conversion, though always expressed as freedom, results from a reflection, a turning or converting in consciousness: ". . . [T]his failure can be overcome if one extricates oneself by a purifying reflection from one's 'natural attitude.' That is, if one undergoes a pure reflection and sees

the vanity of one's natural desire, one can give up this unat-
tainable goal" (444). As Anderson explains, following Jeanson,
in ". . . impure reflection . . . one refuses to question one's
chosen fundamental project and simply goes along with one's
natural desire to attain the fullness of being. In pure reflection . . . reduction of the natural attitude, one confronts one's
spontaneous desire and ultimate choice and recognizes its
lack of objective justification. Thus a fundamental project
other than God can be chosen . . ." (444).

Pure reflection, therefore, has the virtue of calling into
question the false ambition of being God:

> With purifying reflection one can see the absurdity of this
> spontaneous belief and freely choose some other goal. If
> one does so, and accepts one's human existence as a con-
> tingent being in the world, conflict loses its meaning. The
> other is no threat to me if I am not attempting to be the
> total foundation of myself. In place of this vain goal, Jeanson
> suggests that philosophy on the level of pure reflection will
> introduce to us an authentic value, "the free invention of
> our humanity." . . . [P]urifying reflection enables us to
> choose a different project, human existence as freedom,
> that is, the "humanization of humanity" [445].

Lest we be distracted from our primarily anthropological
and intersubjective (social) question by considerations seemingly ontological, recall that ultimately the real context of
Sartre's entire phenomenology, whether expressed in terms
of being, nonbeing, freedom, ethics, consciousness, the
look—whatever its verbalization—is always the concrete (ultimately ethical) world of one human being facing another.
No one would lose sight of this were Sartre's entire corpus
kept in view. Thus to introduce God (as a limit-concept) into
the discussion is not to leave the anthropological. Anderson
has seen this and clearly relates transcendence of bad faith,
elimination of conflict, and a corrected attitude toward God
to one basically intersubjective truth; in Sartre's own words:

". . . [O]ntologically 'consciousnesses are not isolated; there are planes in which they enter into one another'" (447). Thus anthropology and ontology unite where persons realize themselves through others, not alone, that is, in "the between" of intersubjectivity. Forsaking the vain desire to be God, one desires instead to be human, or, better, to become human, in a new, "unnatural" (and difficult) attitude, the result of turning away from the two "natural" (and easy) errors of egoism and mechanism, of person as soul alone or as body alone, to undergo a radical conversion to person as embodied, affective intentionality.

Neither a Monism nor a Dualism of Monisms

Sartre's analysis tries to save human nature from the monisms of spirit and matter as well as from the dualisms that resulted from the "colloidal suspension" that rationalism made of human nature. Note that although one can negate "ready–made,"[3] natural-attitude freedom ("God" as natural goal), in principle one can also freely choose God as the new, now freely appropriated and valued goal, as a partner in the humanization of humanity; the negation is a moment of freeing oneself from the natural attitude, making free choice possible. Thus one's freely choosing (that is, accepting and valuing) God also constitutes a radical conversion, as radical and as much a conversion as would be choosing freedom against God, and thus also a reintegrating of consciousness and facticity, of the whole person.[4]

Sartre's philosophy, then, is a powerful expression of a humanism based on the primacy of affective intentionality over cognitive intentionality. An integral understanding of human nature has always been the most fragile, has always had the most attackers, and has consistently been the most difficult both to describe and especially to live. Monisms usually are clearer and seem to attract energetic proponents; "all is spirit" is so clear, "all is matter" is so simple. The dualisms that put together these two monisms with a Band-Aid end up with the usual parallelisms that no one can experience: they are clear concepts, easily known, never lived. Sartre, fighting Descartes as every up-and-coming French philosopher had to, and also encountering Marx, as was also de rigueur for a philosopher of his era, attempted a humanism that avoided both of their reductions, and worked out, partially, a hard-headed heart tradition, not a simpleminded one, by offering us a "critique of the dialectical reasons of the heart." No one can struggle through his sometimes careless and self-indulgent prose without being a witness to something more important than style or clear and distinct conclusions, namely, his sense, never lost, of human dignity, even glory, in being fully and freely responsible for oneself, shown most dramatically in the perpetual possibility for the radical conversion for the sake of the humanization of humankind.[5]

Conclusion

Sartre's contribution to the unfolding in the modern expression of what we are calling the heart tradition needs a brief final word so that one clearly grasps why and how affective intentionality, already emerging from prior expositions, continues to suggest itself as an apt access to that tradition. The point that Sartre makes is the one Heron also made clear (after Sartre, to be sure, and no doubt thanks, in part, at least indirectly, to Sartre's analysis of embodiment), namely, that though the body, whether my own or the other's, mediates knowledge, love, hatred, and all intersubjectivity, it is never the "body" that is known, loved, or hated, unless before or after relation to the whole person. Heron's "transphysical" and Sartre's "psychic body," like Merleau-Ponty's "body-subject," both indicate an overcoming of dualism and a strong attempt to recover the integral event, the concrete whole before (or after) reason or mind dissolve the unity into abstract body or disembodied soul. "The appearance of the Other's body is not therefore the primary encounter; on the contrary, it is only one episode in my relations with the Other

. . . making an object of the Other. Or, if you prefer, the Other exists for me *first* and I apprehend someone in his or her body *subsequently*" (Sartre 1953a, 446; my ital.). One is first conscious, in affective intentions, of the person as a concrete whole, later reduced by abstraction into mind and body; hence the problem of other minds is a false problem because, as Heron said, it is considered primary, whereas it is really secondary, that is, coming after experience of the whole person; the transphysical presence of the person, as an integral human, is primary: ". . . [T]he Other's body is therefore the Other herself or himself as a transcendence instrument" (447). Affective intentionality attains the person nonrepresentationally, nonthematically, yet meaningfully: ". . . [T]hus the Other's body is meaningful. Meaning is a temporally and temporarily fixed moment of transcendence."[6] "The body is the totality of meaningful relations to the world" (447).

Now obviously Sartre cannot possibly mean a body considered merely or only as a body—he has rejected that as mechanistic materialism—but as besouled, as transcendence, as passing limits (*dépassement:* transcendence, surpassing, bypassing) that no mechanistic body could; thus he never deals with body and soul seen separately in any dualism ("meanings do not refer to a mysterious psychism; they *are* this psychism insofar as it is a transcendence transcended" [454]), but rather ". . . the Other's body . . . is given to us immediately as what the Other is . . ." (456). "There is therefore an enormous error in believing that the Other's body . . . is the body of anatomical-physiology" (457). If one still doubted that underlying Sartre's humanism persists this consistent battle against Cartesian ego and mechanistic (empty of intentions) materialism, a review of his treatment of matter as totalized totality, instead of the detotalized totality that is humanized intersubjectivity, would be enough to remove the last doubts (1976, ch. 3). There Sartre says, as clearly as could be desired, that we humans are wholly meaning and wholly matter, and no better antidualistic, antimonistic formula could be coined. As Sartre says, ". . . [I]f a group of human beings can act as a quasi-mechanical system and a thing can produce its own idea, what becomes of matter, that is to say, Being totally without meaning? The answer is simple: it does not appear anywhere in human experience" (180).

Unfortunately we do not, in the present context, have the leisure of a long meditation on the rich theme of materiality in Sartre, for it would repay such an extended study, with revisions of monistic and dualistic interpretations. During his long career as "Mr. Existentialism," Sartre spent himself in an effort to save the subject from all objectifying systems, an anti-Hegelian motif honed in the style of Kierkegaard. But then, true to his awareness of human being's integrity, he saw the need to save embodiment from being lost to subjectivity, transformed into an unreal epiphenomenon, as he saw transcendental phenomenology doing by overemphasizing the primacy of the transcendental ego. He preferred Marx for showing matter's power to touch and move consciousness and for entering fully into dialectical rather than analytical reason (Sartre 1953b, 9–10, n6, and 32–33, n9). In basing his argument on affective intentionality Sartre established beyond cavil not only the undeniable existence of the reality and concept of affective intentionality, but also its nature as the *dialectical* idea of integrated human being.

It is time to leave Sartre. I will not dwell on his visual bias and its need for correction by dialogal phenomenology (Tallon 1978), nor on other changes Sartre made as he became more "socialized" himself (Poster 1975), nor on his many contradictions. We have recently seen a Sartre revival in France, based on the relatively recently published posthumous *Morale* and other materials that bring to light such a "social" Sartre. Beneath all of Sartre's work lay a desire to redeem human reality from every attack upon its oneness. Sartre's share in the heart tradition consists not only in his explicit recourse to affective intentionality as a distinct kind of consciousness, a *dialectical* reason of the heart radically different from the Cartesian *analytic* reason of the head. He also opened up the ethical and interpersonal possibility of conversion as regaining an *integrated* humanity, of embodiment as being and knowing in a way not reducible to representations. Embodiment is the first and most basic way human finite intentionality tries to overcome its finitude, and habitude, as we shall see later, is the further transformation of the *acts* of self-transcendent knowledge and love into their *habits* or virtues, which accounts for the higher, converted, interpersonal levels of affective intentionality that Sartre envisioned in his openness to radical conversion.

Notes

1. This totalization must not be confused with the "totality" that Levinas accuses of destroying the infinities that individuals are. Sartre wishes his word "totalize" to name "the relation among the parts" of the whole, as "a mediation between the parts," so that the individuals remain dynamically related, not statically opposed, which would "result in totality: . . . [A] 'whole' is not a totality, but the unity of the totalizing act in so far as it diversifies itself and embodies itself in totalized diversities" (1976, 47–48, n22).

2. Dinan agrees that for Sartre ". . . representational intention-alities . . . do not enable us to get outside our own consciousness (1971, 93), and that ". . . Sartre's doctrine of intentionality is every-where an attempt to escape from all such representational theories of knowledge" (93). He also finds it important that Sartre explic-itly singles out affective consciousness, as a nonrepresentational consciousness, an affective intentionality that does overcome solip-sism and gives us the other in a real intersubjectivity (96).

3. Ibid., 444–45: "Thus a fundamental project other than God can be chosen, and Jeanson suggests freedom as that new goal. To critics who claim that such a project is nonsense if a human being is already absolutely free by nature, Jeanson replies that we must distinguish freedom as fact and freedom as a chosen value. All hu-man beings are by nature free and do in fact act freely, but not all choose to accept and value this freedom. Indeed, to move from 'ready-made' freedom to its valuation requires a difficult 'radical conversion.'"

4. Dinan concurs that Sartre's philosophy is best understood as a recovery of what might be called a "surpassed dualism" or a "detotalized dualism," which is a recovered humanism. As he says (referring to Sartre 1953a, 305), "Being-for-itself is not composed of body and consciousness; it is wholly body and wholly conscious-ness" (1979, 281). And he repeats often that this consciousness is not cognitive but lived (281–84), especially in the experience of the body-for-others (but not solely—see 290, n5).

Another way of expressing transcendence of dualism (repre-sented in another tradition by heart talk) is in terms of the mind-body problem. As Dinan puts it: "Regardless of the validity of his theory of the body, Sartre's approach to the 'body-mind' problem has the salutary effect of forcing us to question the adequacy of the concepts, 'body' and 'mind' in terms of which the problem has been expressed. This hallowed philosophical problem will never be solved as long as its terms essentially exclude one another, rendering interaction between body and mind incomprehensible. Clearly, alternative conceptions of subjectivity must be considered which permit the integration of the physical and the psychic without reducing one to the other . . . . Yet the presupposition of the unity of man's being seems to impose itself on us necessarily as soon as we try to make sense out of our self-experience. It can even be called a secondary phenomenological datum insofar as it forms an essential part of the meaning of our self-experience once we have discovered it" [286–87].

5. Dinan shows how Sartre succeeds in overcoming Descartes's dualism, and how he does not (1979, 288-89). As long as Sartre is read as using the term "consciousness" in an undifferentiated sense, that is, without distinguishing affective from representational cognitive consciousness, he will always end up contradicting himself. But if we continually recall that the body's intentionality (whether for-itself or for-others) is affective and nonrepresentational, then the non-identity within consciousness that Sartre calls a "nihilating," is possible as a reflecting of cognitive consciousness on affective consciousness rather than an (impossible) reflecting (cognitive) consciousness trying in vain to escape from a reflected (cognitive) consciousness. Thus I would disagree with Dinan on this point, allowing an alternative conception of subjectivity, as he calls it, that derives, with Levinas, from affectivity, that is, from an affective intentionality, from a consciousness that intends the other in terms not of cognition but of affection, touching and being touched and moved, prereflectively, nonrepresentationally.

6. Ibid., 452. In other words, meaning, intending, sense; the French *sens* means direction and meaning, as the German *deuten* means pointing; to get "the point" is to get the meaning, as in the German *Bedeutung* (meaning); meaning does not come solely from a *Sinngebung* (a "bestowal of meaning," or, more simply, "making sense") supposedly from a transcendental ego alone, but from embodied being and its movement in some direction.

Chapter 3

Mood & Affective Tonality

The heart in my breast is not of iron, but hath compassion.
Homer, *Odyssey*, 5. 190 (c. 850 B.C.).

. . . Here the heart
May give a useful lesson to the head,
And Learning wiser grow without his books.
William Cowper (1731–1800), *The Task*, 6. 85. (1784).

A good heart is better than all the heads in the world.
Edward Bulwer-Lytton (1803–1873), *The Disowned*, ch. 33 (1828).

Summary
Ricoeur is our main source in building upon the existence of
affective intentionality by beginning the detailed description
of its nature and characteristics. Heidegger's fundamental
statement on affectivity, in general, and especially on affective tonality and mood, in particular, as revelation of Being
and of finite human existence, sets the stage for differentiating affective consciousness. Langer provides an independent
confirmation (from outside continental phenomenology) of
feeling as affective intentionality. Ricoeur's philosophy of feeling returns us to the French and German sources and also
differentiates the two elements of feeling: affectivity and intentionality.

Affective Intentionality of Mood

OUR TREATMENT OF HEIDEGGER will be transitional, for he mediated an interpretation of and reaction to Husserl that initiated a different understanding of the central phenomenological category, intentionality, without developing it to the extent of those we have yet to treat. There is no question that Sartre, Levinas, Merleau-Ponty, and even Gabriel Marcel could not have thought and written as and what they did without Heidegger. Yet despite the clear fact that he is also a major figure in the recovery of an integral humanism that we call triune consciousness, his writings resist, by his own design, a strongly humanistic emphasis. In fact, one of Levinas's most anguished disappointments in Heidegger is his (according to Levinas) reduction of beings to Being, the many to one, and thus his fall into the classical Greek embarrassment with multiplicity and exteriority— ultimately a totalizing and totalitarian fall. This is to oversimplify Levinas's accusation, of course; what he means is that Heidegger failed to emphasize the idea that individual human beings exist as resistant (Levinas would say "allergic") to any homogenizing (Levinas would say "totalizing") principle or force—including Being—that would focus on what they are or have in *common* (even that they *are*, that they all have "being") rather than on how they *differ*. Levinas focused on the *difference*, the otherness, not on the sameness. Levinas's *Totality and Infinity* gets its title from his focus on each of us as irreducible and inaccessible to a conceptual knowledge that would claim to capture or grasp us in representations (images, ideas, concepts, ontology, science, system); our "infinity" is our excess of meaning and reality beyond cognitive intentionality, yet accessible to affective intentionality, which keeps its distance and respects otherness (Tallon 1995b; 1996).

Thus to consider Heidegger as tangential and introductory to any humanism is to take him at his word. Heidegger's enterprise is thinking Being. Yet for Heidegger it is precisely representational thinking that is at the core of dualisms that dissolve a human being into *res cogitans*—a rational soul, with the focus on *rational* knowledge—and *res extensa,* the mechanistic "soulless" body that Sartre rejected. Any metaphysics, as he uses the term, that is quick to substantialize or reify soul and body, because it is hobbled by an epistemology of representations, must, according to Heidegger, be transcended: ". . . [M]etaphysics thinks beings . . . in the manner of representational thinking . . ." (1972, 56). Now if human being is *res cogitans,* for Heidegger, in order for this *res cogitans* to be the founder of the modern world of science, *cogito* will be interpreted by him to mean *co-agitare,* a gathering or driving together of many into one:

> Representing is making-stand-over-against, an objectifying that goes forward and masters. In this way representing drives everything together into the unit of that which is thus given the character of object. Representing is *coagitatio* [1977a, 150]. In the *co-agitatio,* representing gathers all that is objective into the "all together" of representedness. The *ego* of the *cogitare* now finds in the self-securing "together" of representedness, in *con-scientia,* its essence [152].

Difference and otherness are absorbed, overcome, ignored.

Heidegger considers this primacy of representational thought a fundamental error with widespread repercussions: as one sees oneself, so one conceives one's world, one's place in it, and the institutions mediating self and world. As Heidegger says, "For representational thinking everything comes to be a being" (1975, 87). If to be human is "to be a representer," then the world is the "to be represented," and theory and speculation take precedence over action:

> A human being has become *subjectum.* Therefore as human I can determine and realize the essence of subjectivity, always in keeping with the way in which I conceive and will myself. As a rational being of the age of the Enlightenment I am no less subject than those who grasp themselves

as a nation, will themselves as a people, foster themselves
as a race, and, finally, empower themselves as lords of the
earth. Still, in all of these fundamental positions of subjectivity, a different kind of I-ness and egoism is also possible;
for as human we constantly remain determined as I and
thou, we and you. Subjective egoism . . . can be canceled
out through the insertion of the I into the we [87].

Meditative Thinking as Taking to Heart

How is this insertion accomplished? By retrieval of an intentionality that precedes abstraction. Insertion has to happen
later only because it was lost, whereas actually the we is prior
to the I and you. The being-with (*Mitsein*) that is prior to
knowledge is rooted in an intentionality more primitive than
that of representations. The world is much more than my
thought, exceeding my representations. This is true, first and
foremost, about persons: persons so transcend every representation that to try to equate cognitive intentionality with
others as persons is to do them violence. The most fundamental intentionality is, according to Heidegger, the affective, nonrepresentational intentionality called mood (*Befindlichkeit, Stimmung*; for *Befindlichkeit* the new translation of *Sein
und Zeit* has "attunement" [Heidegger 1996, 126]), to which
we must now turn, because here is the source of a new kind
of thinking, one Heidegger calls sometimes "meditative thinking,"[1] sometimes "taking to heart" (1968). The point is the
same.

To pursue this point let us turn to a work where Heidegger,
instead of speaking of "insertion into the we" speaks now of
"entering the domain of belonging together":

We do not as yet enter the domain of the belonging together. How can such an entry come about? By our *moving
away from the attitude of representational thinking*. This move
is a leap in the sense of a spring. The spring leaps away,
away from our habitual idea of ourselves as the rational

animals who in modern times have become subjects for our objects [1969, 32; my ital.].

To reduce a human being by definition to "rational animal" risks the same intellectualizing that Levinas found in Husserl: only cognitive intentionality was credited with truth and value, not affective intentionality. "Springing away," as Heidegger puts it, from representational intentionality toward nonrepresentationality means transcending these fixations toward a different idea of what "rational animal" means, namely, one including the so-called irrational. As Heidegger says:

> Perhaps however what we call feeling or mood . . . is more reasonable—that is, more intelligently perceptive—because more open to being than all that reason which, having meanwhile become *ratio*, was misinterpreted as being rational. The hankering after the irrational, as abortive offspring of the unthought rational, therewith performed a curious service" [1971, 25].

This means that the term "irrational" at least opens up the possibility of another intentionality, which, while not against reason (not contrarational), is irreducibly distinct (albeit inseparable) from cognitive intentionality, namely, affective intentionality.

Thus Heidegger's well-known attribution of intentionality to a human way of being-in-the-world nonrepresentationally, namely, to moods, underlies the affective intentionality of particular feelings. Heidegger's *Stimmung* is, of course, in a class of terms some of which are rendered as state of mind, attitude, attunement, affects, feelings, moods.[2] It would be pedantic to repeat this familiar discussion (1962b, esp. §29). What needs noting, however, is how important affective intentionality is to human self-understanding. So we ask: What might Heidegger have had in mind, underlying and

uniting his vast productivity, to call for the complete and radical rethinking he felt absolutely necessary for human being
to retrieve *true* relation to Being? Why the need to "destroy"
the old metaphysics in order to recover *true* philosophy?[3] In
both cases, as we have seen, equating knowing with representing[4] was the problem, because it means equating human
being with reason, where reason (read: consciousness) is too
narrowly conceived.[5]

In his Kant book, Heidegger set down as clearly as could
be desired the two sources of human knowledge and their
necessary complementarity, namely, sense as finite intuition,
which he identifies as essentially affective, and thought, which
is essentially representational (1962a, 27–41), with the former
having a natural priority. The primacy of a kinetic, temporal
being-in-the-world, logically prior to thought (that is, earlier
than cognitive intentionality), an intentionality that is experienced as affectivity, received the status of serious philosophy thanks to Heidegger, though Kierkegaard's reflections
on anxiety certainly paved the way. Few have claimed so much
for affectivity.[6]

It would be hard to find a more significant quotation than
the following to bridge to those writers yet to make their contribution to a retrieval of affectivity:

> The continuation of the interpretation of the affects in the
> Stoics as well as their tradition in patristic and scholastic
> theology down to modern times are well known. What has
> not been noted is the fact that the fundamental ontologi-
> cal interpretation of the affects has hardly been able to
> take one step worthy of mention since Aristotle. On the
> contrary, the affects and feelings fall thematically under
> the *psychic* phenomena, functioning as a *third class* of these,
> mostly along with *representational thinking and willing. They
> sink to the level of accompanying phenomena.* It is the merit of
> *phenomenological investigation that it has again created the freer
> view of these phenomena.* Not only that: Scheler, adopting the
> suggestions of Augustine and Pascal, steered the problem-

atic toward the foundational context between "representing" and "interested" acts [1996, 130–31; my ital.].

Here Heidegger mentions all three, affection, cognition, and
volition, and we can agree with him that affective intentionality, as the "third" intentionality, along with representational
intentionality and volitional intentionality, needs something
like "affirmative action." He is also correct in saying that phenomenology has done the most toward achieving this goal of
remedying a mistake and filling a need for a more integral
understanding of human consciousness as triune by including this "third class," the affective. The knowing in one's heart
that is not thinking is not far from Heidegger's understanding as dialectically related to what he calls *Befindlichkeit*, which
is how one "finds" oneself (*comment je me trouve*), one's affective tone,[7] that affect or mood, the feel of one's embodied
being—how one feels [*Mut* as mood], how it is with one's
heart (*Gemüt*). Heidegger's characterization of representational thinking as not the "real" thinking that is *taking to heart,*
but as a ("violent") driving together of the many into one
(*cogitare* as *co-agitare*), ultimately a totalizing and dehumanizing totalitarian thinking, must have influenced Levinas. Cognitive intentionality without affective intentionality, head without heart, is not the best definition of human nature. "Rational animal" neither says it all, nor says it well, because it does
not say enough. Only the triad of affection, cognition, and
volition adequately constitutes human consciousness.

Intentionality of Feeling

From the (back)ground we turn to the foreground of feeling, from states to acts of consciousness. Not that mood
(*Befindlichkeit*: attunement), temperament, or tonality (*tonalité
affective,* as the French renders *Stimmen* [Bollnow 1943; French
tr. 1953]) are inadequate, but because certain authors used
different terms for sometimes interesting reasons. Feeling has
the virtue of being a broader term than nearly any term but

affectivity itself; unlike emotion, affection, and passion, feeling has a verbal form (see Macquarrie 1972, ch. 8, "Feeling," and ch. 1 & 13).

Langer has written some very sane pages on feelings and has introduced useful distinctions and definitions. Would that her health had permitted the anxiously anticipated third volume of her *Mind: An Essay on Human Feeling,* for which the first two volumes in 1967 and 1972 raised such hopes, to have fulfilled expectations; as published, volume 3 was too incomplete to add substantially to the first two. In other writings, however, she had guardedly tried to recover for philosophy a new key that was not so much new as lost and forsaken and now very much in need of being found again (1942). Her resistance to the same equation of thinking with representing that Heidegger and others have voiced is evident when she says: ". . . [S]o long as we admit only *discursive* symbolism as a bearer of ideas, 'thought' in this restricted sense must be regarded as our only intellectual activity. It begins and ends with language" (1942, 71; my ital.).

Now what is the alternative to the discursive, to thought? The chapter from which the quotation is taken is entitled "Discursive and Presentational Forms." *Presentation,* quite the contrary of *re*-presentation, means direct contact: ". . . [T]he nondiscursive mode that speaks directly to sense . . . is first and foremost a direct *presentation* of an individual object" (78). Langer has recourse to Bergson and Creighton to explore the nature of this sort of knowledge.

> Is it possible that the sort of "intuitive" knowledge which Bergson extols above all rational knowledge because it is supposedly not mediated by any formulating (and hence deforming) symbol is itself perfectly rational, but not to be conceived through language—a product of that presentational symbolism which the mind reads in a flash, and preserves in a disposition or an attitude? This hypothesis, though unfamiliar and therefore somewhat difficult, seems to me well worth exploring [80].

Notice what is at issue. Unlike attributing to human being a sort of irrational power, completely distinct from mind, not altogether unlike certain "moral sense" or "æsthetic sense" theories, what is to be explored is a rational yet nonrepresentational mode of consciousness, that is, a presentational way of understanding: ". . . the very idea of a nonrational source of any knowledge vitiates the concept of mind as an organ of understanding" (80). As one mystical author (Aelred of Rivaulx) has put it: "the mind must be in the heart." Langer next turns to Creighton's essay "Reason and Feeling."

> Rationality is the essence of mind . . . if there is something in our mental life besides "reason," by which he [Creighton] means, of course, discursive thinking, then it cannot be an alogical factor, but must be in essence cognitive, too; and since the only alternative to this reason is feeling . . . *feeling itself must somehow participate in knowledge and understanding.* . . . "In the development of mind," he says, "*feeling does not remain a static element, constant in form and content at all levels, but . . . is transformed and disciplined through its interplay with other aspects of experience* . . . [the meaning of feeling is analogous to the level of consciousness on which it occurs]. Indeed, the *character of the feeling in any experience may be taken as an index of the mind's grasp of its object* . . ." [80–81; my ital. and brackets].

This helpful observation recalls Kant's and Heidegger's agreement that there is a common root of sense and understanding; it also recalls von Hildebrand's conviction (to be addressed later) that one has a certain responsibility for how one is affected by values, so that failing to be compassionate in the presence of someone in need is blameworthy and not to be written off as a neutral response that one then overrides by will; even the acquired ability to respond is ethical. Similarly, as we shall note later, Lonergan, influenced by Scheler, also affirms this idea of a *development* of feeling, a maturation of affect. Langer's favorite phrase in this context is "symbolic transformation." For her, "the significant observation voiced in this passage is that feelings have definite forms, which become progressively articulated" (81).

How does this development, maturation, progressive articulation—this education of the heart—take place? Langer's own personal answer, as is well known, is art, especially music, the art the least discursive and least representational, the art most unlike language (173). Music is not a language, she says, nor is any art, but a feeling with a form of its own: "Music articulates forms which language cannot set forth" (19). But beyond the particular instance of music, there is a legitimate generalization not only for art but for other forms of feeling as well.

Langer has much to say about these forms of feeling, and her book is itself a classic treatment. Without being "antiscientific" she recognizes two distinct traditions; as she says:

> Discursive thought gives rise to science and a theory of knowledge restricted to its products culminates in the critique of science; but the recognition of nondiscursive thought makes it just as possible to construct a theory of understanding that naturally culminates in a critique of art. The parent stock of both conceptual types, of verbal and nonverbal formulation, is the basic human act of symbolic transformation. The root is the same, only the flower is different [116].

Langer advances our understanding of the nonrepresentational, affective mode of consciousness especially in her essay "The Process of Feeling" (1962, ch. 1). There she tries to dispel the idea of feeling as a separate power or faculty of the soul. "The misconception leading us into sterile theories of mind is the notion of feeling as a separate sort of entity, ontologically distinct from physical entities and therefore belonging to a different order or constituting a different 'realm'" (1962, 8). To avoid this mistake she begins by taking feeling "in its widest possible sense, that is, to designate *anything that may be felt* . . . both sensation and emotion—the felt responses of our sense organs to the environment, of our proprioceptive mechanism to internal changes, and of the organism as a whole to its situation as a whole, the so-called 'emotive feelings'" (8).

Now this stipulation of feeling as the genus, as it were, of which sensation and emotion are species, can be useful, because *some* way to keep these notoriously overlapping terms apart is required, and Langer does more than simply declare them different; she offers a plausible argument for doing so.

> Feeling . . . is divided almost from the outset into two general categories . . . sensibility and emotivity. Some very interesting work has been done on the problem of this division, especially by psychologists who postulate an original undifferentiated *Gemeingefühl* [common, basic, fundamental, or "ground" feeling or experience] in which sensation and emotive response are not yet distinguishable. Perhaps the differentiation of these two orders goes farther back than any other, as the difference between the neural actions at the periphery of the organism and in its spinocerebral structures very generally does . . . . Briefly, one may say that peripherally started nervous excitations are normally though not always felt as impact, centrally started ones felt as action [11–12; my brackets].

As one can readily see, "feeling" and "experience" are practically indistinguishable in her usage from consciousness, allowing Langer to say "we experience as *objective* whatever is felt as impact, and as *subjective* what is felt as action" (13). This pair of definitions then enables her to define consciousness as "the general mode or degree of feeling which marks a creature's mental activities as a whole at a given time . . ." (13), so that the category of "'the unconscious' . . . is simply not needed once we treat feeling as a phase of processes which in most of their stages are not felt . . . . According to the view here proposed, a great deal of cerebration goes on below the limen of feeling . . ." (14–15).

Now no one will miss the already noted Kantian idea of the common root of sense and reason as it recurs here as affectability, the capacity for "ground experience," the *Gemeingefühl,* which we could think of as *basic consciousness, beneath triadic differentiation.* Langer goes so far as to include under the ægis of emotivity all those "articulations," as she calls them, traditionally classified with reason, or, better put (in light of the above discussion, based on Creighton, of reason and feeling), rationality. Thus she says:

> The specializations of sensibility, as so many senses, have been fairly widely studied; less so, the articulations of what may, by way of distinction, be called "emotivity" into specialized processes, such as image formation (under the influence of sensory impressions), subjectification and the whole gamut of emotions, objectification, and symbolic projection, and with the advent (apparently not below the human level) of symbol-making and symbol-using functions, the highly articulated process of discursive thought [15].

If she has not gone too far, we have here a consistent way to interpret consciousness as having a common affective root, the *Gemeingefühl,* plausible as a translation of the even broader biblical "heart," still undifferentiated, in all its primitive power, and encompassing emotion, cognition, and conation, as did that biblical term. What about Langer's inclusion of discursive thought under emotivity? Is there something in experience consistent with the idea of a continually articulated, potentially developing common root of all feeling, in Langer's sense? Of course, not *all* feelings can find expression. Feelings only find expression sometimes, and in various ways, for example, in work, science, art, play, sport, and prayer, and the "heart's reasons," though obscure in that root, may become articulated according to the process of feeling that Langer describes.

To explain how this articulation of "Ur-consciousness" arrives at (feeling as) thought while beginning in (feeling as) emotion, Langer offers the following:

> In human beings, nervous sensitivity is so high that to respond with a muscular act to every stimulus of which we take cognizance would keep us in a perpetual St. Vitus's dance. A great many acts, started in the brain by our constant discriminative perception of sights, sounds, proprioceptive reports, and so on, have no overt phase at all, but are finished in the brain; their conclusion is the formation of an image, the activation of other cell assemblies that run through their own repertoire of word formation or what not, perhaps the whole elaborate process that constitutes an act of ideation. One act starts another; a great proportion of such intracerebral events rise to feeling, and, moreover, they are chiefly felt as action, that is, they are subjective [21-22]. . . . The result of this heightened and largely self-perpetuating activity is that we continuously feel our own inward action as a texture of subjectivity, on which such objectively felt events as perceptions impinge, and from which our more sustained and complete subjective acts, such as concerted thought or distinct emotions, stand out as articulate forms. That psychical continuum is our self-awareness . . . [24].

Further, Langer offers a neurological basis or substrate not only for the many differentiations of feeling, but even for the reification that goes by the name of soul:

> The human brain . . . takes up so many stimulations that have to be dealt with mainly in its own systematic way that the need of finishing every started act . . . causes it to have interests of its own, beyond the interests of the organism: the needs of symbolization, expression, ideation, logical thought (achieving order among ideas), and especially communication . . . . We have, consequently, a sort of "inner life," or life of the mind, which makes the mind seem

like a separate being in the body. Since it obviously also
controls the organism as a whole, it is almost inevitably
regarded as a governing agent, the whole man's double or
soul [24].[8]

Langer avoids a mechanistic materialism, therefore, as did
Sartre. Her thesis suggests the origin of many levels of differentiation devolving from an originally undifferentiated core
of affective consciousness, the proprioceptively given whole
person. Further, the brain's asymmetry, commonly given as
left hemisphere for speech, right hemisphere for other "forms
of expression of feeling," could be traced to this need to
manage the overload of stimulation: to handle more than
what one brain can, functioning as a unit, the brain has split
the two "kinds of feeling," namely, sensibility and emotivity,
as she named them, between the two hemispheres, and then
has gone on to develop the ability to use the one dominant
half disproportionately while neglecting, in modern times,
the subdominant half (at least in the verbal, scientific, tech-
nological West). This hypothesis is useful for speculating on
the *need* to split, on the possibility of specialization once lat-
eralization occurred (one specialization being the *conscious*
soul), and on the resulting difficulty of verbalizing the right
lobe's kind of feeling.

As a bridge to Ricoeur let us note the problem of an adequate language of feeling. We expect head to speak, to find
words; heart, however, while it may have its reasons, often
cannot express itself in words; hence the perennial problem
with which we are all familiar.[9]

Affection & Feeling

According to Ricoeur, "The 'heart' is at once the source and
symbol . . . of the 'schemata' of ontological feeling" (Ricoeur
1965 [=*Fallible Man*; hereafter *FM*], 157). His *FM* is part of a
larger work on the philosophy of the will and goes back to
1960. Obviously Ricoeur has written much before and since

then. The author and translator both call this a work in "philosophical anthropology" (ix). It is a work influenced by Strasser's *Das Gemüt* (*The Heart*), which we explore in chapter 7. The German *Gemüt* relates to *Mut* (itself related to the English "mood"). In his excellent translation of *Das Gemüt* as *Phenomenology of Feeling: An Essay on the Phenomena of the Heart* (1977), Robert Wood relates *Gemüt* back to Plato's *thumos* as does Ricoeur (*FM*, 123),[10] that is, to the passionate, affective force of life, a force both vital and spiritual, a part of the *soul*, not relegated only to body. It helps to note that *Gemüt* is translated as "heart," the German *Herz* being more appropriate to the less metaphoric physical pump than to the psychic and personal center of affective consciousness and its intentionality.

Ricoeur's general aim in *FM* (as set out in his preface, a methodological preamble to the book) is to explore affection, emotion, and passion as they affect the will, and therefore he analyzes feeling as ground of volitional consciousness (a project similar to that of Pfänder, as we shall see). His more particular aim is to do this under the very aware condition experienced by everyone who has studied and tried to write critically on affectivity, namely, the problem of an inadequate language for affective consciousness. Psychologists have even coined a clinical term, "alexithymia," to mean "without words for moods and feelings" (Windle 1990). Bellah et al. made it a major theme of their *Habits of the Heart* (1985) that lack of an adequate language as an alternative to the dominant language of individualism hinders us not only from *expressing* affective consciousness but even from *experiencing* it for what it distinctly is.

Ricoeur has in mind to explore symbolic language, the myths of religion, for example, of the Fall, of evil, and so on, and speaks of a "symbolics" of evil, of fallibility, and the like. His primary symbol is the heart and his rich Preface attempts to justify his method.[11] He says "symbols are what give rise to thought" (*FM*, xxi); symbols really make us think, and philosophy's role, as I see it here, is to do the tough headwork of understanding what heart expresses, lived not only, of course, in the tendings, leanings, and strivings that are affectivity, but also in the language of myths and symbols that move us a step closer to interpretation.[12]

Affective Intentionality: Feeling Is a Union of an Affection & an Intention

Let us now consider an important text from *FM* for analysis of feeling, one that sets the scene and tone for what follows in Ricoeur's exposition. Referring to Plato's *Republic,* book 5, Ricoeur writes:

> Then the soul appears as a field of forces undergoing the double attraction of reason called "that which urges" and of desire which is characterized as "something which holds back" (439c). That is where the third term, the one Plato calls *thumos* becomes enigmatic. It is no longer a "part" in a stratified structure, but an ambiguous power which undergoes the double attraction of reason and desire. Sometimes it battles along with desire in the form of irritation and fury; sometimes it takes the side of reason in the form of indignation and endurance. "Anger" or "courage," the *thumos,* the heart, is the unstable and fragile function *par excellence.* This ambiguous situation of the *thumos* evinces, in a static representation of the soul, all the myths of immediacy. In a static representation the intermediate is a "mean," it is "between" two other functions or parts. In a dynamic representation it will be a "mélange" [*FM,* 15].

Here we have Plato's familiar tripartite soul: heart (*thumos*) is a third kind of consciousness, a third way of being and moving (intending), an ambiguous, mixed kinesis—a mixture of *affection* (passivity as autoaffection, as a being-affected, as a receptivity to otherness) and *intention* (a going out to otherness). Besides the cognitional consciousness of reason (*logos*) and the volitional consciousness of desire (*eros*), there is mélange, a mixed consciousness between them. Feeling can give rise to thought, can empower reason with that of which and for which reason reasons, *and* can be the stuff that the will blesses or resists and from which *it* arises. Heart as *thumos* is thus here an unfixed and volatile mix, both a consciousness that streams up, out, forward, and a dynamic primal force, rooting down and back into flesh and blood, evidently not merely a nonspiritual or material, organic, bodily something outside the soul and consciousness, but very soul itself, experienced in affective consciousness as affective intentionality (feelings, moods, symbols) and also as available to cognitive consciousness through reason and to volitional consciousness as will.[13]

It is the mixed aspect of this third consciousness that captures Ricoeur's attention and that dominates his interpretation in *FM*. The heart's betweenness makes it a kind of ground of mind and will (similar to Langer and Heidegger), as a symbol that gives rise to thought and as ". . . the affective rootedness of the will" (78n). In the same note Ricoeur quotes ". . . Aristotle's excellent formula: 'The will moves through desire.'" How does he see in this "mixed" idea a matrix or fund of mind and will emerging from *thumos* as the cognitional and volitional consciousnesses, as evolutions from the more immediate, direct, and spontaneous affectivity? Ricoeur seems to suggest that the affective mix is first a being "mixed up," a confused fusion that is a con–fusion, a fusion of two before they are distinct; and there are three because the later two never fully emerge or evolve out of the earlier, primal heart, so as to leave it behind; so the three always endure. He says, for example:

> I posit actions only by letting myself be influenced by motives. I advance toward . . . (toward the "to be done") only by supporting myself upon . . . (upon the lovable, the hateful, etc.). A human freedom is one that advances by means of motivated projects . . . . Inclination is the specific "pas-

sion" of the will. Only an inclined, aroused will can also
determine itself. Its activity is imbued with this specific
passivity . . . . Shall we say that the human will is finite by
the very fact that it is not pure act but a motivated project,
action-passion? . . . Are we finite because we have to receive our objects in order to form them? . . . Sensory receptivity reveals first its openness and that finitude is the
narrowness of this openness, namely, the perspectival aspect of our way of being affected [*FM*, 80–81; his parenth.].

Thus human action is the unity of a consciousness that
phenomenological analysis shows to be threefold, the three
consciousnesses existing in a relation of dependence of action on passion, revealing human finitude in both knowledge
and freedom, and hence revealing the fragility of human
nature. To advance in knowledge and freedom—which is asymptotically to "overcome our finitude," in time—is to recognize our affective roots by becoming *cognitively* conscious
of *affective* consciousness and by taking up our affective
intentionalities (as motivations) into our *volitional* consciousness, or resisting that taking up. To ignore or deny the third
consciousness is to be a head that knows nothing of whence
come its images, symbols, ideas, urges, motives—is to be a
head in the clouds, without its feet on the ground.

But more than a philosophy of *action* finitely grounded
in affection, Ricoeur's is a philosophy of *habit* as *perfection* of
action: we try to *overcome finitude through habitude*, and this
habit is human (second) nature. The best, most valid meaning of triadic consciousness as the operational synthesis of
affection, cognition, and volition, as we shall see in detail later,
is habit as virtue, that is, as affectively toned (attuned) understanding and affectively grounded (entrained) freedom which
has the spontaneity, immediacy, and directness of action that
has in time become and now is "second" nature, habit.

> *Habit is possible because living persons have the admirable power*
> *of changing themselves through their acts . . . . [B]y learning, I*

> *affect myself,* my subsequent power is no longer in the situation of being but of continuing; life goes on . . . . Thus there arises, *through this continued affecting of myself, a kind of human nature, that is, an imitation of the native, of the innate, by the habitual.* What is learned is acquired (*habitudo*) . . . . This tendency of life . . . bids us to look for the *new mode of finitude* in a primordial inertia that is intermingled with the spontaneity of life and will . . . [*FM*, 87–88; my ital.].

Ricoeur has here enunciated an interpretation that anticipates what we shall be developing later (in chap. 8–10). We note it now and leave until then its full exposition. The key idea is that by the symbol of the heart is meant not a third separate *faculty,* alongside mind and will as *separate faculties;* rather, to speak of head and heart is to use words symbolically, conveniently, synecdochically (thus uncritically and invalidly if taken literally). Heart here actually means a kind of ability or skill, a felt manner of self-presence and self-possession, within the complex that is triune consciousness. What is affirmed is that cognition and volition, mind and will, can be actualized to higher levels of knowledge and freedom only by uniting with affection to operate through connaturality, itself explained through habit as virtue, that is, with a nondiscursive quasi-intuitive knowing and a nondeliberative spontaneous loving. A text from de Finance (to which we return later) makes this clear:

> But to know means more than simple [acts of] knowledge. Knowledge can be momentary, occasional, transitory: it is an act. For knowledge really to *remedy my limitation* and let me conquer the alterity of the object more completely, it must fix itself in me: acting must sediment in being [must settle into my being]. In other words, knowing must become a *habitus.* For *habitus* is a sort of *middle term between being and acting, an acting stabilized in being,* a being in *tension toward acting* and *bearing the structure of that action in its being.* Fixed in *habitus,* the act loses its alterity in relation to the subject in losing its casual character. Insofar as I do not

have the *habitus* or habit, the success of my deed . . . remains chancy, *depending on the other:* there has to be a con-
junction of several elements, of which the knot is *outside
me. Habitus* puts this knot in my hands. If it is perfect, there
is *no need of effort,* as though to capture an elusive prey in
flight. The act is in me and I can at will make it happen
[literally: I can deploy it into actuality] . . . . Knowing is a
habitus: it is knowledge that has *passed into the structure of the
spirit* [1973, 97; my tr. and ital.].

If we take this insight as a motif, namely, that *habit installs
between being and doing*—as a kind of having, an "owned property," proper to a person as a subject of acts, perfecting one's
being for the sake of doing—then the synthesis of head and
heart may be understood as *the highest actuation* (namely, virtue qua good habit) *of an incarnate spiritual being in the direction of acting,* on behalf of the actions it performs in order to
fulfill itself most specifically *as* an embodied spiritual being
(where spiritual means self-transcending, self-appropriating,
self-determining). This fulfillment comes from being able to
know and love self-transcendentally, especially in the two primary areas of intersubjectivity, the ethical and the mystical,
as well as in æsthetic action. Actions transform their agent by
depositing a "sediment," by engraving their lineaments in the
supple tissue of human potential. Ricoeur here gives us the
guiding motif, the clue to what is to be worked out later.

Feeling Is Affective Intentionality

The previous section served as preparation and prelude to
the fourth chapter of *FM* wherein Ricoeur presents the core
of his concept of the heart in terms of affective intentionality.
Two important parts must be grasped in order to make sense
of his careful analysis: (1) feeling as *affective intentionality* and
(2) *affective connaturality* as habit (virtue). Here again Ricoeur
anticipates our later hermeneutics. First, there is the duality
of *feeling as both affective and intentional.* This is crucial. The
full range of human feeling is experienced (1) as a rooting

downward and backward into embodiment, (2) as a kinetic extending outward and forward (horizontally) by intending into the world of "the material singular" (proper object of *ratio*), and (3) as upward (vertically) beyond the material world into the intersubjective world, the world of the personal other, both ethical and mystical, both human and divine. Second, there is the concept of "Like is known by like," older than Plato (who cites it as though it were ancient even to him), a concept also axiomatic to Aristotle in the form "As someone is, so does the end appear to him or her," and central to Aquinas's rich teaching on ethical and mystical experience and on knowledge and action by *connaturality.*

In this concept of connaturality we will find the best explanation of the way affective intentionality works, that is, of why the dual movement of the "out" of *intention* and "in" of *affection* are felt as attunement of one's *being* (or nature—hence the term "connaturality") with the other, deeper than only as a relation to one's *knowing.* The "in" (the being-affected) plus the "out" (the affective response) form a wave, a harmonic or dissonant vibration, whose wavelength can be and always is constantly being tuned (*Befindlichkeit,* attunement, *tonalité affective*) by the continual self-affecting actions that create our habits. Ricoeur uses both affective intentionality and connaturality to great advantage. Here is an important text on the first of these points.

> Here we encounter Plato's valuable idea on the *thumos,* the median function *par excellence* in the human soul. The *thumos* is the living transition from *bios* (life) to *logos.* At one and the same time, it separates and unites vital affectivity or desire (*epithumia*) and the spiritual affectivity that the *Symposium* calls *eros.* In the *Republic,* Plato says that the *thumos* sometimes battles on the side of reason, in the form of energy and courage; sometimes it enters the service of desire as an enterprising power, as irritation and anger. Can a modern theory of feeling come back to that intuition of Plato? If that is possible, the third step of an an-

thropology of fallibility is the "heart," the *Gemüt*, Feeling.
In advancing step by step from consciousness in general to
self-consciousness and then to feeling, or in other words,
from the *theoretical* [cognition] to the *practical* [volition] to
the *affective*, philosophical anthropology would progress toward a point which is at once more inward and more fragile. . . . The "heart," the restless heart, would be the fragile
moment *par excellence*. All the disproportions that we have
seen culminate in the disproportion of happiness and character would be interiorized in the heart. But the question
is whether a philosophy of the "heart" is possible? It must
be a philosophy which is not a relapse into the *pathéthique*,
but which is brought to the level of reason . . . [that is, as
triune consciousness] [*FM* 123–24; my ital. and brackets].

Figure 3 may help us visualize these forces and directions.

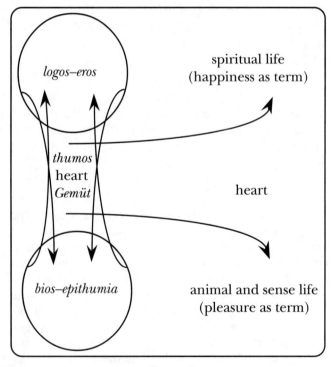

Figure 3

Ricoeur expresses here the heart's dual structure, its mix. It is both a mediation of and a mélange of *bios-epithumia* and *logos-eros,* as both depth of inwardness (affection) and transcendence outward (intention), drawn into the presence of the other. This mélange is the human mystery par excellence, that "the self is an other" (Rimbaud). It is essentially the experience that all human consciousness is finite, a *conversio ad phantasmata* (in the words of Aquinas, *Summa theologiae* 1, q.84, a.7, following the lead of Aristotle, *De anima* 3, elaborated by Rahner in *Geist in Welt*) that is never perfect, always emergent, temporal, kinetic, becoming, radically inadequate to itself insofar as incapable of complete self-knowledge and self-possession. We approach such knowledge and freedom as moving toward a nonobjective horizon that is never grasped but always touched by anticipation (*Vorgriff*) (Tallon 1982a).

What Ricoeur calls heart is the union of the "*bios-epithumia + thumos*"-heart and the "*logos-eros + thumos*"-heart, which is a higher operational synthesis of these two, as explained later. Ricoeur's explanation of the heart in all its finitude is first expressed in terms of affection and intention. In the next text these pivotal categories together explain the experience of feelings. One of two central texts in *FM*, it joins the first part of Ricoeur's philosophy of heart with the second, the idea of connaturality.

> The significance of feeling appears in the *reciprocal genesis of knowing and feeling [head and heart].* Taken outside of this mutual genesis, feeling is no more than a word that covers a host of partial functions: affective regulations, disturbing emotions, affective states, vague intuitions, passions, etc. Put back into the movement of their mutual promotion, *feeling and knowing "explain each other."* On the one hand, the power of knowing, by hierarchizing itself, truly engenders the degrees of feeling and pulls it out of its essential confusion. On the other hand, *feeling indeed generates the intention of knowing, on all its levels.* The unity of *sentir,* of *Fühlen,* of feeling, is constituted in this mutual genesis. . . .

> *Feeling,* for instance love or hate, *is without any doubt intentional:* it is a feeling of "something"—the lovable, the hateful. But it is a very strange intentionality which on the one hand designates qualities felt on things, on persons, on the world and on the other hand manifests and reveals the way in which the self is inwardly affected. This paradox is quite perplexing: *an intention and an affection coincide in the same experience,* a *transcending aim* and the *revelation of an inwardness.* Moreover, in bearing on qualities felt on the world, feeling manifests an affectively moved self. The *affective* aspect of feeling *vanishes as soon as its intentional aspect fades away,* or it at least sinks into an inexpressible obscurity. It is only thanks to its aim, overspilling itself into a felt quality, into an affective "correlate," that feeling can be expressed, said, communicated, and worked out in a cultural language . . . . *We cannot void the intentional moment of feeling, therefore, without at the same time voiding the affective moment* of the self [*FM* 126–27; most ital. added; my brackets].

This is a key text for Ricoeur's phenomenology of the heart; he calls it "the corner-stone of our whole reflection" (*FM* 130). It analyzes feeling into two components, one inward (affection) and one outward (intention). Ricoeur does not mean to deny the objectivity of feelings in saying, for example, that love and hate are meant "on" things, but rather he means to identify them technically as *values,*[14] for it is precisely the *intersubjective nature of value,* rather than its merely subjective or merely objective nature, that is essential to his second key concept, that of affective *connaturality between* knower and known, agent and deed, as we have already begun to see.

But what must be emphasized first is the *intentionality* of feeling. Before Ricoeur did, Husserl, Scheler, Heidegger, and Levinas, to name a few, had already made us aware that affective consciousness is as intentional as cognitional consciousness and volitional consciousness. But Ricoeur has been clearer than any of them in his analysis of feeling into its two elements, affectivity and intentionality. The essential point of this text is that *feeling is both affection and intention, an affective intentionality,* both a being-affected-by-the-other and an intending-of-the-other; indeed, feeling is an intending of the other *as* a being-affected-by, a receptive intention, a primacy of the other (as Levinas also would put it, that is, essentially an ability to respond to one's being affected, an essentially ethical response-ability). There is a basic and fruitful ambiguity here in that the *affective* tone (state, mood, disposition) of the subject is an intrinsic ingredient in the experience of the *other.* No one denies the subjective side of feeling, but some overstate it to the point of denying its intentionality or objectivity. For Ricoeur, fears have their basis in reality; joys and hopes do point somewhere real; the horizon of our finitude and death is made real and revealed in anxiety. The truth is that feeling's "strange intentionality," as Ricoeur calls it, is intersubjective: feeling is a *self*-affection that is also an *other*-affection, an autoaffection that is also a heteroaffection. That is its irreducible structure, its confused essence, and its irreplaceable function, like Merleau-Ponty's "intercorporal flesh." As Ricoeur affirms so vigorously, to deny feeling's intentionality is to deny its affectivity, that is, to deny that the self is in touch with reality at all.

Habit (Virtue) as Ground of Affective Connaturality

Now, as we have seen, this affective intersubjectivity is best explained by the concept of connaturality. Here is how Ricoeur introduces this second concept of his philosophy of the heart. (We state it here, to complete Ricoeur's analysis, but develop it later as a major theme.)

> While we oppose ourselves to objects by means of the representation, feeling attests our coaptation, our elective harmonies and disharmonies with realities whose affective

image we carry in ourselves in the form of "good" and "bad."
The Scholastics had an excellent word to express this mutual coaptation of man to goods that suit him and to bads
that do not suit him. They spoke of a bond of *connaturality*
between my being and other beings. This bond of *connaturality* is silently effected in our tendential life; we feel it in a
conscious and sensory way *in all our affections* . . . . Now, since
the whole of our language has been worked out in the dimension of objectivity, in which the subject and object are
distinct and opposed, feeling can only be described para-
doxically as the *unity of an intention and an affection, of intention toward the world and an affection of the self.* This paradox,
however, is only that sign pointing toward the mystery of
feeling, namely, the undivided connection of my existence
with beings and being through desire and love [*FM*, 133-
34; my ital.].

If we correctly situate the term "connaturality" we can recognize its value for our discussion; it is offered by Aquinas—
foremost of Ricoeur's "Scholastics"—as an explanation of how
a virtuous person knows the morally good thing to do, without knowing the ethics textbook (or how the mystic can be
touched by God in a way that felt presence evades concepts
and cannot be brought about or dispelled by will acts).[15] For
our purposes, within the limits of this chapter, suffice it to say
that Ricoeur sees in connaturality an opening to being, to an
"ontological feeling" (the most "celebrated" feeling being the
existential or ontological mood of dread, anguish, or anxiety
(*angest* [Kierkegaard], *Angst* [Heidegger]) of beings related
to beings and to Being through felt affective intentionality,
"pre-cognitively and hyper-cognitively," as he put it. Affective
intentionality is connaturality that has become conscious. Conscious connaturality is feeling; the resonances between like
natures enter consciousness as feelings; they *are* feelings. As
we "become," through our own agency, by forming habits,
thereby constituting our "second" nature, so we become better able to feel resonance or dissonance, harmony or dishar-

mony, according to the beings we *are*, according to our acquired (second) nature. This second nature "imitates," as Ricoeur puts it, the immediacy and spontaneity of first nature (almost as though an elicited appetite could act like a natural appetite, as the Scholastics would say). In practice, our actions issue proximately from our habits, our modified nature, and only remotely from our first nature (an idea important to Ricoeur's general project, namely, a theory of the relation of feeling to will and of the role of feeling in relation to affective fragility and human fallibility).

Developmental Continuum of Triune Consciousness

We have now seen Ricoeur's foundations for a philosophy of the heart in affective intentionality and connaturality, with an important reference to the idea of habitude. He has already equipped us with the working concepts we need—feeling as affection and intention, connaturality, and habit—setting the agenda for what we must develop at greater depth in later chapters. He applies philosophy to an analysis of the "human condition," in order to reach a definition of humanity, one true to his recognition of the distinction (not separation) between affective consciousness and its practical irreducibility to either cognitional consciousness or volitional consciousness. What is that definition, and how does he finally reach it?

Part of his method was to distinguish a horizontal from a vertical analysis. To understand Ricoeur's heart-centered definition of humanity we must review this analysis. He begins, as we saw, with Plato's *thumos*, gratefully uses habit theory from Aristotle, accepts connaturality from Aquinas, and makes great capital of the phenomenology of affective intentionality, affirming the irreducibility of affection to representational intentionality. In the following discussion he says practically nothing about will and volitional consciousness, an omission explained by his situating FM in the context of his larger work on the will; if mind forms the "head," in contrast with the "heart," to speak of knowledge is to speak synecdochically of the head in a general way that includes its finality in volition as choice, decision, and action, at least in a common enough way to contrast knowing and feeling. Thus he proceeds to speak of knowing and feeling where we could think of head and heart. Justification for this interpretation emerges from and depends on the texts to be cited.

While trying to include feeling as essential to a definition of humanity, we recall, Ricoeur noted how language, because of its bias toward objectivity, makes a philosophy of feeling difficult to conceptualize and express. He was trying to face predictable opposition to granting any validity to the concept of affective intentionality, which is the necessary condition of a philosophically useful concept of the heart. Whether we call it ". . . affectivity, that is to say, feeling itself inasmuch as it is experienced as a passive modification of the self . . ." or ". . . affective intentionality . . ." (*FM* 181), the problem of understanding and accepting affective intentionality as real keeps arising, time after time; thus we find that even Strasser (1970) and Levinas (1991) occasionally appear to deny the *intentionality* of feeling—against everything they argue in their main theses—in attempting to preserve the *affectivity* of feeling as its distinguishing quality compared with cognition and volition, an extreme move made to avoid being misunderstood by those who falsely equate *all* intentionality with *representational* intentionality; once this mistake is identified it can be avoided, and without denying the reality of affective *intentionality*. Ricoeur's way of uniting a phenomenology with a hermeneutic takes the form of a definition of humanity in terms of the heart:

> Humanity is that discrepancy in levels, that initial polarity, that divergence of affective tension between the extremes of which is placed the "heart" [*FM*, 140]. The "heart" is at

once the organ and the symbol of . . . the "schemata" of ontological feeling. Here we find the interpersonal schemata of being-with as well as the supra-personal schemata of being-for and the fundamental intention of being-in [*FM* 157]. For the *thumos* is properly the human heart, the heart's humanity. We may place the whole median region of the affective life under the sway of this ambiguous and fragile *thumos*, the whole region situated between the vital *and spiritual* affections, or, in other words, all the affectivity that makes up the *transition between living and thinking*, between *bios* and *logos*. It should be noted that it is in this intermediate region that the self is constituted as different from natural beings and other selves. Living and thinking . . . are, respectively, shy of or beyond the Self. Only with the *thumos* does desire assume the characters of otherness and subjectivity that constitute a Self (*FM*, 162–63; my ital.).

But what is this "discrepancy in levels," this "initial polarity"? How is the heart placed between the extremes of *bios* and *logos, epithumia* and *eros*, pleasure and happiness, the vital and the spiritual? If pleasure fulfills *bios-epithumia*—physical life—and happiness completes *logos-eros*—spiritual life— and if both are feelings, both affective intentionalities, what does it say of humanity that we are connatural to both physical life (in a vertical rooting back down) and spiritual life (in a vertical transcendence outward and beyond)? Is this the correct definition of human nature? And what is the heart if, as Ricoeur says, it is between these extremes, and, as Plato said, can side with one or the other?

Ricoeur's answer to these questions, as suggested earlier, is to distinguish a horizontal from a vertical analysis, and to offer the idea of the mutual genesis of knowing and feeling, which is the origin of mind and will from *bios*-heart in order that by knowing and willing we work for the *change* of heart that constitutes the *second* nature we experience in both vital and spiritual life as the *self*. This is how Ricoeur explains how the heart defines humanity, how it mediates *bios-epithumia* and *logos-eros,* how it can be at once the source of sin and fallibility as well as of a happiness that transcends pleasure.[16]

There is a mediation effected by feeling (from out of the vital toward the personal-spiritual, without ever abandoning the vital):

> The universal function of feeling is to bind together. It connects what knowledge divides; it binds me to things, to beings, to being. Whereas the whole movement of objectification tends to set a world over against me, feeling unites the intentionality that throws me out of myself, to the affection through which I feel myself existing" [*FM* 200; my ital.].

The meaning of the "disproportion" of feeling is its being both embodied (*bios*) and spiritual (*logos*) and so the origin of a new mediation:

> The disproportion of feeling gives rise to a new mediation, that of the *thumos,* of the heart. In the order of feeling this mediation corresponds to the silent mediation of the transcendental imagination in the order of knowledge. But whereas the transcendental imagination is entirely reduced to the intentional synthesis, to the project of the object before us, this mediation is reflected in itself in an indefinite affective quest wherein is evinced the human being. It seems, then, that conflict is a function of man's most primordial constitution; the object is synthesis; the self is conflict. The human duality outruns itself intentionally in the synthesis of the object and interiorizes itself affectively in the conflict of subjectivity [*FM,* 201].

Summary

By "heart" Ricoeur means the tension between pleasure, the goal of sense life (human life qua animal), and happiness, the end of spiritual life (human qua spirit).[17] "Heart" also means the union of *bios-epithumia* with *logos-eros,* a oneness prior to distinction and operational conflict.[18] Heart is this union, and so its restlessness (Augustine's *cor inquietum*) is experienced as the conflict between pleasure and happiness at the interior of consciousness (*FM*, 140–41). At the "low end" of conscious beings, animals are content; they coincide with themselves (*FM*, 204); their ambitions match their powers to achieve them. At the "high end," a pure spirit is self-presence (*Beisichsein*), in its way. But the human soul, as a finite spirit, is to be drawn by pleasure, a partial good of the person, *and* by happiness, the total good of the person.[19] But besides this use of the term "heart" for the early fusion of *bios* and *logos*, before their distinction, there is also a later and higher operational synthesis of the now distinct head and heart as triadic consciousness: affection, cognition, volition.

Ricoeur's analysis of the *logos-eros* heart in its relation to the *bios-epithumia* heart contributes an essential insight into the meaning of triune consciousness as the most useful concept for the ethical and mystical, the two areas of intersubjectivity par excellence. Ricoeur says the self is constituted by the mix of animal and spiritual life. Animal life, like symbols, gives rise to thought, synecdoche for rational life (*FM*, 163). One is origin; the other is term.

Feeling as affective *intentionality* shares with *logos* an *eros* that takes it out toward the other, to be known and loved, and happiness is the term of this transcendence.

Feeling as *affective* intentionality is the inward return, the interiority of subjectivity; it is happiness as one's own, as experienced, and a happiness that isn't felt is no happiness at all. *Eros* makes happiness possible, and feeling makes it actual.[20]

Conclusion

Ricoeur has tried to answer Heidegger's lament in 1927 that research on affectivity has hardly progressed since Aristotle, a lament Ricoeur modestly repeated in 1977.[21] He has strongly affirmed a phenomenological dyad of head and heart, knowing and feeling, and even more strongly emphasized the operational triad of these two in relation to the voluntary. And running through all of consciousness is the primacy and transcendental finality of affective intentionality as the best way of defining the finite, fragile, flawed, and fallible essence of humanity. Like Bollnow, Ricoeur addressed Heidegger's provocative placing of the formless and objectless *Angst* at the center of human consciousness, as revealing the human ontological condition. He agrees with Heidegger that "'moods' alone can manifest the coincidence of the transcendent, in accordance with intellectual determinations, and the inward, in accordance with the order of existential movement. The height of the feeling of belonging to being ought to be the feeling in which what is most detached from our vital depth— what is absolute, in the strong sense of the word—becomes the heart of our heart" (*FM*, 160). And so he concludes with more hope than Heidegger (as does Bollnow):

> If being is that which beings are not, anguish [*Angst*] is the feeling par excellence of ontological difference. But Joy attests that we have a part of us linked to this very lack of being in beings. That is why Spiritual Joy, the Intellectual Love and the Beatitude, spoken of by Descartes, Malebranche, Spinoza, and Bergson, designate, under different names and in different philosophic contexts, the only affective "mood" worthy of being called ontological. Anguish is only its underside of absence and distance [*FM*, 161).

One of the main reasons for Ricoeur's research into affectivity in *FM* was to discover why and how we humans are so able to sin, so fallible, so capable of the extremes and excesses, both of sanctity and iniquity. There must be in us something a tradition calls "spirit" that explains our capacity (Rousselot's *capax Dei*, after Aquinas) for acts and habits much worse than the animals' as well as much better. As Ricoeur says: "Indeed, only a being capable of intending the absolute may also confuse a partial value, to which it attaches itself with all its heart, for the absolute" (1977, xiv).

Notes

1. See Heidegger 1966, 24: ". . . [M]editative thinking . . . does not represent . . . does not construct a world of objects." And ibid., 29: ". . . [M]editative thinking consists in becoming aware of the horizon as such . . . ."

2. "[A]ttunement . . . reveals beings . . . . 'Feeling' is neither a transitory epiphenomenon of our thinking and willing behavior nor simply an impulse that provokes such behavior nor merely a present condition we have to put up with somehow or other" ("What Is Metaphysics?" in 1977b, 102).

3. "[P]hilosophy and philosophizing belong within the dimension of man which we call tuning (in the sense of tuning and attunement)" (1955, 79).

4. "Thinking brings something before us, represents it . . . . [I]n representing we think of what is represented and think it through by dissecting it, by taking it apart and putting it together again" (1959, 100).

5. "We must free ourselves from the notion that originally and fundamentally *logos* and *legein* signified thought, understanding, and reason. As long as we cling to this opinion and even go so far as to interpret *logos* in the light of logic as it later developed, our attempt to rediscover the beginning of Greek philosophy can lead to nothing but absurdities" (1959, 104).

6. Except Max Scheler, who seemed to claim too much, at least according to Husserl, who called Scheler's phenomenology "fool's gold" (Spiegelberg, 1964, 1: 230), a judgment with which I heartily disagree.

7. "We usually translate pathos with passion, ebullition of emotion [*Leidenschaft, Gefühlswallung*]. But pathos is connected with *paschein,* to suffer [*leiden*], endure [*erdulden*], undergo [*ertragen*], to be borne along [*austragen, sich tragen lassen von*], to be determined by [*sich be-stimmen lassen durch*]. It is risky, as it always is in such cases, if we translated pathos with tuning [*Stimmen*], by which we mean dis-position [*Ge-stimmtheit*] and determination [*Be-stimmtheit*]" (1955, 83).

When it is said in objection that feelings have no place in philosophy, as though philosophy were all head and no heart, or as though affectivity were not analogous, changing its meaning from low, visceral sensations, like itches, to the highest spiritual passions of the soul, Heidegger objects to such narrow-mindedness in return: "Sentiments [*Gefühle*], even the finest, have no place in philosophy. Sentiments, it is said, are something irrational. Philosophy, on the other hand, is not only something rational but is the actual guardian of reason" (23). "If, on the other hand, we point out the possibility that that upon which philosophy bears concerns us humans in our essential nature and moves us, then it might be that this being-moved has nothing whatsoever to do with that which is usually called feelings and emotions, in short, the irrational [*Irrationale*]" (25). In other words, Heidegger is affirming a major thesis of this book, namely, that at the high end of the meaning of affectivity, when our phenomenology receives its interpretation, affectivity will be seen to be intrinsic to the highest achievement of the human spirit. Heart will then be understood not as a separate and irrational "faculty" alongside the "faculty" of reason, but instead as synecdoche for the higher operational synthesis of affection, cognition, and volition.

8. In a chapter entitled "Emotion and Abstraction," in *Philosophical Sketches*, Langer says: "[O]nly a highly emotional creature could have developed the talent of abstract thought. At some period in our prehuman history the pressure of central excitements must have become so great that if the countless impulses started by the increasing cortical action had continued to commingle and break through to massive overt expression, the animal's behavior would have become disrupted. The only internal adaptation to the overgrowing sensory mechanisms and their dependencies was to spend the emotional impulses aroused by their individuated acts in equally piecemeal fashion; and as it often happens, the very changes that caused the crisis offered the means of surviving it. The separate intellectual processes took up the separate central impulses they evoked, and the extra charge this gave them automatically simplified main forms, and these only, to the psychical level. The conscious processes that resulted—images, gestures, explicit memories, and other mental phenomena—provided the ma-

terial for the final humanizing function, the use of symbols. It is not impossible that humankind has passed through a much more emotional phase than it exhibits at present . . . ." [1962, 81].

9. As Langer continues: "Language, of course, is our primary instrument of conceptual expression. The things we can say are in effect the things we can think. Words are the terms of our thinking as well as the terms in which we present our thoughts. . . . There is, however, an important part of reality that is quite inaccessible to the formative influence of language: that is the realm of so-called 'inner, experience, the life of feeling and emotion' [1962, 88]; . . . the form of language does not reflect the nature and form of feeling, so that we cannot shape any extensive concepts of feeling with the help of ordinary, discursive language . . . . The real nature of feeling is something as such—as discursive symbolism—cannot render" [89].

10. Ricoeur mentions that *Gemüt* (heart) is Kant's word (rendered often as "mind" by Kant's translators): "But it is a theory of the *Gemüt* that is required and no longer merely a theory of finite reason. Kant evokes this theory in the famous apostrophe in the *Critique* [*of Practical Reason*]: 'Two things fill the mind (*Gemüth*) with ever new and increasing admiration, the oftener and more steadily they are reflected on: the starry heavens above me and the moral law within me'" [*FM*, 119].

11. "[M]an reached his own depth only by way of the royal road of analogy, as though self-consciousness could only be expressed in riddles and would necessarily require a hermeneutics" [*FM*, xix]. Worth reading for more insight into Ricoeur is Doran, *Subject and Psyche: Ricoeur, Jung, and the Search for Foundations* [1981a; 1994] and *Psychic Conversion* [1981b]. As Doran says, "Values are primordially apprehended in feelings, and feelings are ascertainable, identifiable, through symbols" [1981a, iii].

12. As Ricoeur put it in his *Esprit* article of 1959, entitled "Le symbole donne à penser," "The task of philosophy . . . is to promote and shape the meaning through a creative interpretation" (Ricoeur *FM*, xxi; from a note by translator Charles Kelbley). Whitmont adds a psychologist's agreement on the value of symbols: "Symbols . . . [are] means of comprehending and making use of the non-rational and intuitive realms of functioning . . . . This symbolic approach can mediate an experience of something inde-

finable, intuitive or imaginative, or a feeling-state of something that can be known or conveyed in no other way, since abstract terms do not suffice everywhere . . . . [R]eliance upon the intuitive and emotional faculties . . . constitutes the fundamentally new character of Jung's approach. Indeed he held these faculties to be indispensable for an adequate experiencing of the psyche, for . . . only by means of all its elements . . . can we attempt to understand the psyche" [1969, 15–16].

13. Guardini interprets Pascal in a way that confirms this bipolar meaning of heart: "What is the heart in the Pascalian sense? . . . [T]he mind [*Geist*] which appreciates and values, that is, . . . the heart. 'Heart' is the mind [*Geist*], so far as it gets into proximity of the blood, into the feeling, living fibre of the body—yet without becoming torpid. Heart is the mind rendered ardent and sensitive by the blood, but which at the same time ascends into the clarity of contemplation, the distinctness of form, the precision of judgment. Heart is the organ of love—of that love from which arose Platonic philosophy, and then, newly fructified by Christian faith, the *Divine Comedy*. This love implies, namely, the relationship of the center of man's desires and feelings to the idea; the movement from the blood to the mind, from the presence of the body to the eternity of the mind. It is what is experienced in the heart [1966, 131–32; my brackets, copied from the original: 1950, 186–87].

14. "[O]ut of a concern for doing justice to the specific intentionality of feeling, we attribute to feeling objects or quasi-objects, which we shall call *values*" [*FM*, 135].

15. Aquinas says there is in such cases a connatural relation between one's *being* or *nature* and the ethical good or mystical Other, even in the absence of a relation between one's conceptual, objective *knowing* (that is, knowing of objects) and the ethical or mystical (hence the "darkness," the "cloud of unknowing," the lack of concepts, the passivity). The core idea is that connaturality is a *felt resonance* between self and other—before, beyond, beneath, beside any objectively known (that is, known as an object) or deliberately willed intention. It is the core of Levinas's ethical "responsibility that precedes freedom" and of Ignatius of Loyola's mystical "consolation without previous cause," the essential element of discernment of spirits (Tallon, 1982b).

16. Ricoeur adds: "That is the working hypothesis. How can we put it to the test? The test that we propose will consist in questioning the affections which terminate the movements of need, love and desire. It can be shown, in fact, that there are two kinds of terminations of affective movements: one of them completes and perfects isolated, partial, finite acts or processes. This is pleasure. It falls to the other one to be the perfection of the total work of man; this would be the termination of a destiny, of a destination or an existential project. This would be happiness . . ." (Ricoeur *FM*, 140).

17. Ricoeur gives a concise summary of his theory of heart in *FM* in *The Philosophy of Paul Ricoeur*, esp. the section on affective fragility (see Reagan and Stewart, 1978, 31–35).

18. "It is this affective mode that Plato called the *thumos* and tried to situate between *epithumia*, sensible desire, and reason whose specific desire is *eros*. This the inner conflict of human desire reaches its climax in the *thumos*. In this sense the *thumos* constitutes the human feeling par excellence" (*FM*, 139). Ricoeur took up the theme of the affective again in *Freud and Philosophy* (1970, 506–09).

19. According to Ricoeur, "Reason demands totality, but the instinct for happiness, insofar as it is a feeling which anticipates its realization more than it provides it, assures me that I am directed toward the very thing that reason demands . . . . However, I could not make out these signs or interpret them as "transcending anticipations" of happiness [here Ricoeur refers to Strasser's *Das Gemüt* 238ff., where Strasser is himself referring to Rahner's *Vorgriff*, "transcending anticipation," which is Rahner's term (in *Spirit in the World*) for Aquinas's *excessus*, the mark of spirit as self-transcendence of all finite goods] if reason, in me, were not the demand for totality" [*FM*,105; my brackets].

20. Ricoeur says that what ". . . distinguishes the happiness intention from the pleasure intention is reason, reason in the Kantian sense, reason as a demand for totality. Happiness has the same breadth as reason; we are capable of happiness because reason 'demands the absolute totality of conditions for a given conditional thing.' . . . On the one hand, reason, as an openness to the totality, engenders feeling as an openness to happiness. On the other hand, feeling interiorizes reason and shows me that reason is my reason, for through it I appropriate reason for myself . . . . In

short, feeling reveals the identity of existence and reason: it personalizes reason" [*FM,* 154–55].

Later we shall see that feeling in Ricoeur's sense of affective intentionality is essential to the highest achievement of the intellectual soul, to the highest kind of knowledge—*intellectus* (not *ratio*)—as defining the human.

21. Ricoeur continues: "[P]hilosophical reflection has fallen behind psycho-physiology, without our understanding of what emotions, feelings, and passions signify having been augmented by a considerably more precise knowledge than that of the classics of the organic and physiological underlaying layers of affective life. Compared to the philosophy of the cognitive functions, or even to the philosophy of action which today is so full of vigor, the philosophy of affects is in a quasi-infantile state" [1977, xii].

Chapter 4

Emotional Presentation & Will

We possess nothing that is not mortal except the blessings of
heart and head.
Ovid (43 B.C. – A.D. 18), *Tristia,* bk. 3, eleg. 7, l. 44. (c. A.D. 10).

A loving heart is the beginning of all knowledge.
Thomas Carlyle (1795–1881).

The stars have not dealt me the worst they could do:
My pleasures are plenty, my troubles are two.
But oh, my two troubles they reave me of rest,
The brains in my head and the heart in my breast.
A. E. Housman (1859–1936).

Summary

We draw closer to the personal center of consciousness by
examining Alexius Meinong's thesis on feeling as substitute
for thought (cognitive intentionality) and the relation of affection to will (volitional intentionality) as presented in
Alexander Pfänder's detailed analyses. The possibility that
affection can in some degree replace as well as complement
cognition and/or volition receives phenomenological foot-
ing. The irreducibility of affection to cognition or volition is
reaffirmed along with its essential relation to them in a single
triadic consciousness.

Feeling as Emotional Presentation

CONTINUING OUR MOVEMENT gradually from the exterior toward the interior: emotion is, as a specification of affectivity, for our methodological purposes, the next occasion of another step in the direction of understanding the heart tradition better. Let Ricoeur build a bridge to this division of our project:

> [F]eeling reveals the identity of existence and reason: it personalizes reason [*FM*, 155] . . . . [F]eeling unites the intentionality, which throws me out of myself, to the affection through which I find myself existing. Consequently it is always shy of or beyond the duality of subject and object . . . . The human duality outruns itself intentionally in the synthesis of the object and interiorizes itself affectively in the conflict of subjectivity [*FM*, 200–01].

Let us ask Meinong to clarify anew the difference between the "presenting" accomplished by feeling and the *re*-presenting performed by images, ideas, sentences, books, and the like, against the almost inertial, entropic tendency in rationalist philosophy to think of all intentionality as automatically representational. In forcefully insisting on presentation, Meinong throws more light on what Ricoeur means by defining feeling's two moments as intention and affection. Without denying that feeling (as affective intentionality) does both, Meinong takes us a step further in grasping Ricoeur's assertion that affection reveals the self (and, in not denying intention, we preserve the insight that self-revelation is never independent of intersubjectivity).

How does Meinong help? By first insisting on the priority of presentation, on both its existence and its nature: "The notion of presentation has its origin in the fact that there are experiences in virtue of which the apprehension of the specific character of an object is rendered possible even though the apprehension may be incomplete . . . . [T]here are ob-

jects . . . which can be apprehended even though we cannot
have ideas of them . . . . [T]here is presentation without any
having of ideas" (1972, 3–4). Ricoeur hinted that self-knowledge, the perpetual human goal of the "know thyself," begins
in the affective component of human fragility, prior to its idea.
Meinong agrees:

> In perceiving inner experiences there is no reason to be-
> lieve that the relation between apprehension and what is
> apprehended is mediated by an idea of the latter. Such a
> mediation is necessary whenever something external to the
> judging subject is to be apprehended through a judgment.
> But why should a judgment not directly turn toward an
> internal event without the mediation of ideas, which, after
> all, are internal to the subject too? . . . Since the function
> of an idea's content is called "presentation," we were justi-
> fied in using the same term to apply to the same thing in
> the case of internal perception . . . . [T]o be "conscious" of
> a feeling does not require an "idea of a feeling" (*Gefühls-
> vorstellung*) . . . [6–7].

The heart's reasons (its meanings) are not ideas. We are
used to calling them feelings, though perhaps we have also
sometimes allowed rationalism to get away with calling feeling irrational; nor does it help to glory in the irrational element in human existence. There is no need for such a tack:
feelings have forms of their own (they do not have to be
given form by reason, pace Piaget) and thus meaning; feelings are rational, but with a rationality unlike the verbal, discursive, conceptual form that uses ideas: ". . . in a self-presentation of feeling, *the feeling takes the place of an idea,* and in a
self-presentation of desire, the desire takes the place of the
idea. However, it is not terminologically permissible to call a
feeling an 'idea' merely because it presents something . . . .
[I]f a feeling presents itself immediately to perception, the
perceptual judgment does not need a special idea as its basis" (7–8; my ital.). Thus Meinong also denies the derivative

nature of feeling from idea, as though feeling were merely
an epiphenomenon riding on the back of representations.

No claim of privileged or exceptional status for feeling is
made here, but instead equal status alongside ideas: ". . . in
internal perception not only intellectual but also emotional
experiences function as presentative factors, so that *emotional*
presentation can be set side by side with *intellectual* presentation . . . . [N]ot only intellectual experiences but also emotional experiences, for example, feelings and desires, are in-
ternally perceived . . . . [T]hese feelings and desires, that is,
the emotional experiences, must be presentative factors" (23;
see also 24: ". . . one does not need an idea of feeling
[*Gefühlsvorstellung*] to be conscious of a present feeling . . . ").
Meinong means here, quite clearly, that feelings are genu-
inely intentional; we touch reality through them. Emotion
presents being consciously in a prereflective presentation.

Now we began consulting Meinong with the relatively
modest aim of extending slightly the sense of the affective or
inward moment of affective intentionality, as the two moments
or elements were distinguished by Ricoeur. A certain
self-knowledge or *self*-revelation seems a conservative yield
from this intentionality. But can we harvest a greater yield?
Can we intend *others* in this way, through affection? Meinong
says yes. Besides *self*-presentation there is *other*-presentation,
which, when we have no other way of knowing someone, may
prove not enough to *know,* but enough to *act.* Meinong states:

> In order to enter into a certain peculiar affect one must at
> least have experienced something similar . . . . I shall say,
> instead of "think oneself into" (*hineindenken*), "feel oneself
> into" (*hineinfühlen*) or "empathize" (*einfühlen*): and I shall
> mean, by that term, imaginative feelings (or, imaginative
> desires) . . . . In such imaginative experiences the means
> are clearly given by which to apprehend in memory past
> emotional experiences, without having to depend upon
> presenting ideas. This is also a case of emotional presenta-
> tion, which is, however, naturally not self-presentation but

other-presentation [25] . . . . When I say "the sky is blue,"
and then say, "the sky is beautiful," a property is attributed
to the sky in either case. In the second case a feeling participates in the apprehension of the property, as, in the
first case, an idea does. And it is natural to let the *feeling be
the presentative factor* in the second case, as an idea is always
taken to be in the first case [28-29] . . . . Under favorable
conditions the feelings *should* function as a content presentative of objects . . . . *[F]eeling can function as a means of
apprehension* . . . . [F]eeling . . . fulfills the task of intellectual apprehension quite insufficiently, whenever, that is, it
is *forced* to assume that function . . . . [E]ven if feelings
were considered to be inferior to the most subjective of
our ideas, they might still, even under these unfavorable
circumstances, present objects. These objects *would remain
inaccessible* to apprehension if presentation were exclusively
confined to intellect [30; my ital.].

Everyday we experience situations when we rely on our
affective intentionalities, when no other way is open to those
most inaccessible of "objects," namely, other persons, who
are free to reveal themselves or not. As we show later, for example with Alquié, faith is just such a situation; faith, trust,
and believing in another human person are not acts of discursive reason or deliberative will, but are a different kind of
consciousness, an affective cognition either led by or sup-
ported by affective intentionality, the being-affected by and
the intending of the other as affecting oneself that are the
defining elements of feeling; it is a knowing by connaturality,
by spiritual empathy. In intersubjectivity, faith is the *best* we
can do, in the best sense of best, and is not secondary or inferior in these cases precisely because it uses *more* of triune consciousness, not less. Meinong provides an approach to faith
consistent with his paralleling emotion and intellect, consistent also with his giving them the status they deserve (114).

If we ask whether emotions can be true or false, we immediately call to mind the parallel question about ideas. Truth

is a matter of *judgments,* not merely of unpredicated ideas, according to the oldest tradition, yet we say that one has a true *idea* because one *can* make a true judgment (for example, a value judgment) using this *idea*; so also, substituting a feeling for an idea, according to Meinong, one can say one's feeling is true if one can make true judgments through this feeling. One can act well, whether in sport, music, art, movement, or life in all its nonverbal complexity, basing oneself on affectively intending, without ideas, concepts, and the like, as the basis of living and acting well. Such a person, not as a schooled and lettered intellectual and therefore not knowing through true ideas, knows connaturally through true feelings as emotional presentation, a knowing not in mind but in heart.[1]

Knowing Others Nonrepresentationally

Strasser's "Feeling as Basis of Knowing and Recognizing the Other as an Ego" (1970) can be cited in passing here for providing additional light on the line of analysis Meinong has opened up concerning the substitutional role feeling plays in certain situations. One such situation is the problem, a pseudoproblem as we saw before, of knowing other minds or recognizing another ego. Let this brief addendum to Meinong serve merely to deepen our grasp of the nonrepresentational character of some intentionality, that nonrepresentationality which presents oneself and other persons without the mediation of image or idea.

Strasser's approach is to say that even if the problem of knowing other minds is a false problem when presented as though based on a temporal sequence including a reasoning process that conditions such knowledge—once again the bias of representational intentionality—there still remains the real problem of describing phenomenologically how that which has already happened, without prior representations, did in fact happen. Strasser's solution to the problem is to invoke the preintentional. Now since we are to examine the ontological structure of intentionality itself in detail later, in fact by way of Strasser's distinction of it into preintentional, intentional, and postintentional, we can be brief at this time. He calls preintentional what others call nonrepresentational, parallel to prereflective and nonreflective.[2] Taking a clue from Merleau-Ponty and Heidegger that prior to objective knowledge of things there is meaningful behavior in the world, he says: "This meaningfulness is, however, not imparted by a mind but by a body-ego" (292). This body-ego is unlike any disembodied Cartesian cogito-ego; for "the body and its emotional equipment . . . 'preconditions of reason' . . . implicitly are rational. They constitute first sources of meaning; they provide the emotional . . . 'physiognomic' character of reality" (304).

Now this pre-intentional (as emotional, embodied, and as precondition of reason) is nonrepresentational, basically an original awareness, a moodlike attunement (*Befindlichkeit*); it is how one "finds oneself" in one's state of being: "The nonintentional, nonobjectifying mode of awareness is genetically the oldest . . . . This 'awareness' has as yet *no objectifying character*" (295). By being nonrepresentational and preobjective is it therefore empty of content, of meaning, not truly an awareness or "consciousness of"? By no means. In fact, for Strasser feeling is the most original form of awareness.[3] Following Plessner, he describes feeling as "direct intimacy" (*distanzlose Sachverhaftung*), as the

> opposite of intentional aiming at something, where a "distance" is always presupposed between the aiming subject and the object at which it aims . . . . "[A]bsence of distance" [means] that no medium and no mediator is situated between the feeling subject and the felt object. This explains why the specific subject-object tension does not, as yet, exist. Thus, the situation may best be characterized as follows: as a feeling subject I feel myself by the fact that I feel my fellow-subject; and reversely, you as the fellow-subject who are felt are present to me the feeling subject by the fact that I feel myself [299–300].

This solution of the problem of other minds, then, re-written not in terms of cognition but in terms of affection, recognizes persons first in a distanceless oneness, an affective presence that is a genuine intentionality—a nonobjective and nonrepresentational intentionality—endowed with meaning and content; the content of this affective intentionality is not the *ego* of the *cogito* or *ich* of the *ich denke*—the self of self-consciousness, the subject-pole of objective representations; rather,

> in the original, nonobjectifying mode of awareness . . . that to which as a subject I am first committed—both in vital and in emotional respects—is my fellow subject . . . . . : "As feeling subject I feel myself by the fact that I feel my fellow-subject." It is not difficult now to understand what direction the further development of awareness takes; what was at first one—feeling one's own state and feeling the other—separates out. As a subject who feels a fellow-subject I begin to realize that I am an autonomous ego . . . [305].

Strasser's contribution to this point is his strong emphasis on affectivity, almost to the disparagement of intentionality, so that distance-less presence nearly replaces affective intentionality, mostly because of a heightened awareness of the nonrepresentational nature of this kind of intentionality. "Our original feeling and emotional mode of awareness . . . rises to the surface whenever the situation appears to the ego in such a manner that I cannot maintain a distance ([which phrase describes the essence of] emotion)"[4] or whenever, in the nature of things, no distance exists ([which is the essence of] feeling). A philosophy of affectivity, not of rational mind alone, of feeling, not representations, then, offers a solution to the "mind-body problem" because feeling is affective intentionality, presence, nearness (Levinas's *proximité*): ". . . [A] philosophy of immanence and reflection cannot provide an explanation for this presence" (1970, 306).

Feeling as Ground of Will

We already broached the theme of feeling's relation to will when considering Ricoeur on motivation. We can now take up this theme more thoroughly, because to do so is to prepare the phenomenological terrain for the insight that intellect's conversion to or dependence on phantasm is paralleled by will's conversion to or dependence on feeling as well as intellect. Spiegelberg (1964, 1: 173–95) has made some of Pfänder's work available and this can be our primary source (Pfänder 1967).

We are asking Pfänder for light not merely on the fact of a distinct heart tradition but for much more, for another small step forward in its essential articulation. We have already seen how affection can be understood as ground of representational intentionality, because of the experiential priority, in embodiment, of affective intentionality as mode of consciousness of the body-subject, and as the mediation of biological life's and spiritual life's desires. Now we turn to the question whether affection relates to the appetitive or to the volitional side in an analogous manner. Something other than will—feeling, motive, embodiment—grounds will. Will is the only form of consciousness that is free, the ultimate *arbitrium* between head and heart, but absolutely dependent on them for everything it does. Head and heart are not free; and will is neither head nor heart. What is will? What is its essence? Is the will the real ego, the core of the self? Von Hildebrand says the heart is the real self. Rationalism says reason is the real self. How do the three modes of consciousness interrelate? The thesis of this book—the irreducibly triadic structure of consciousness—has as a corollary the irreducibility of the three kinds of consciousness to each other: *Triune consciousness is the real self.* Knowing is not feeling or willing; feeling is not knowing or willing; willing is not knowing or feeling. Their distinctness is as absolute as their inseparability as modes of one triunity. The inseparability leads to a cognition based on affection, an affection based on cognition, and a volition based on both. The inseparability of cognition and affection has been partly described above; but is there a phenomenology of the inseparability of volition and affection? In what sense is heart the ground of will?

Pfänder's important contribution may be presented in five points, each building upon the one before it. As a preface we can note Spiegelberg's statement that "willing can never be reduced to representations (*Vorstellungen*) or sensations (*Empfindungen*)" (1967, 3). Nor is willing the same as striving, which is a blend of "the act of *intending* (*meinen*) of something absent which is considered to be a goal . . . and the *feeling* of a pressing or tending toward . . ." (3; my ital.). This intending plus feeling, which is striving, becomes willing when the ego appropriates it as its own, when the will accepts the movement of feeling: "[W]hat converts such striving into willing in the proper sense is that the ego sides spontaneously with such striving" (3). Let these words of Pfänder be our leitmotif: "[T]here is no willing in which thinking and feeling do not constitute essential ingredients. Likewise, in thinking, feeling plays an essential part . . ." (4). Here is head and heart, triadic consciousness, in operational synthesis.

(1) Striving & Ego-body: Entrainment
Trying to regain a nondualistic humanism Pfänder speaks of ego-body and ego-center:

> [T]he strivings and counter-strivings originated in the ego do not always have the same location in it. For the ego has a characteristic structure: the ego-center (*Ich-Zentrum*), or the ego core, is surrounded by an ego-body (*Ich-Leib*). And the strivings can arise in the ego, but outside the ego-center in the ego-body, and hence, in this sense, can be experienced as eccentric strivings. Probably most strivings and counter-strivings in the adult human being have at first this eccentric location . . . [18].

Here the impression given is of a person in a certain situation, prompted by some person, thing, or event that affects her, that touches her, and who then spontaneously responds; affectivity is engaged. There is an affective movement, an intending, but no will-act yet, unless the will has already been brought along (entrained) by the sheer violence or seductiveness felt in the heart:

> [L]ike all strivings, these eccentric strivings have by themselves a centrifugal direction pointing away from the ego [intention]. But at the same time they have a tendency to shift from their eccentric location into a central one, or to seize the ego-center and pull it inside [affection]. This tendency can then more or less quickly reach its goal; the central ego can be quickly seized and held down without its will . . . . The central ego can, without a will and naively, be within the strivings as they arise . . . [18–19; my brackets].

Heart, as affective consciousness, can entrain the will, as volitional consciousness. In Pfänder's language, this describes how striving becomes affective intending, as can be seen by its double structure (also noted by Ricoeur), namely, feeling as constituted by intention and affection, outward and inward. Strasser, as noted above, also had recourse to this double structure to explain the distanceless presence of feeling (as touching and as emotion), a moment of being one with the other prior to the objectification of that other in representational intentionality. Here Pfänder is describing more in detail how that oneness occurs, namely, by an entrainment or drawing in of the central ego along with the ego-body. The point of Strasser's and Ricoeur's recourse to feeling, with its double structure of affectivity and intentionality, was to account for person-to-person encounter as not merely a meeting of body-egos alone (which Strasser feels is all thst Merleau-Ponty's theory of the *corps-sujet* accomplishes [1970, 292-93]).

Pfänder adds an important distinction that further illuminates this experience of entrainment: "[T]he experienced

relation of the eccentric strivings to the ego-center is a phenomenal causing, not yet by any means a motivation. The
fact that the ego-center is drawn into these strivings is by itself no act of willing. The central striving which usurps the
ego is, therefore, not yet a willing" (1967, 19). This is important. We have here an intending and an affection,that is, the
meaningful feeling of striving, a *kinesis,* the ego-body entraining the ego-center, and *still no will-act.* Entrainment is experienced as cause, not yet as motive. This is an affection more as
a passion, a being-affected, moved by the other, prior to my
response. If we think of *affectivity* as divisible into *passion,* as
the most passive form of affection, and *emotion* as the mixture
of the active (response to being affected) and the passive (the
being-affected), and *feeling* as the most active, we can diagram
(Figure 4) the range of affectivity thus, and relate the affec-

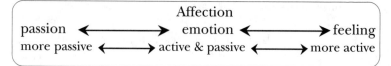

Figure 4

tive to the volitional with a little more precision. The more
active an affection is, the more it involves the subject, the
more of the subject it commits to response, and the more
deeply it reaches from the "outer rings" of embodied consciousness (Pfänder's *Ich-Leib* and *Seelenleib*) into the center
of the ego (Pfänder's *Ich-Zentrum* and *Seelengeist*) and begins
to constitute the self, to become solidary with the self. Recall
again that only feeling has a verbal form, suggesting at least a
prima facie notion of affective development. Cause (as efficient cause) becomes motive (as final cause), we might say, as
passion becomes first emotion and then feeling; this is at least
one provisional way to think about Pfänder's analysis, a way
to follow it with more understanding.

(2) *Willing and Ego-center: Motivation*

Now Pfänder goes on to clarify this important distinction between cause and motive: cause is to striving as motive is to will. The way he presents this distinction is especially illuminating for the meaning of feeling as affective intentionality. To speak of the *four* (Aristotelian) causes of feeling, is to recognize that here, as is often the case, "cause" is falsely taken to mean only efficient causality—which is only one of the four—whereas cause can and should be taken to mean (at least) also formal, material, and final causes, with motive fitting into the last category. The way that striving affects action differs from the way motive does. It clarifies Pfänder's phenomenology to translate his language in this way: strivings act like efficient causes, motives like final causes. That this is Pfänder's meaning is shown by his saying that if we compare the two processes, namely, feeling the affective pressure of some emotion or passion and the process of voluntarily assenting to or willingly going along with or ratifying that striving (that is, the degree of affection as feeling, emotion, or passion, as diagrammed in Figure 4), then the former "process is essentially different from the [latter] process in which the ego lets itself be induced to a certain willing by a motive . . . . The act of willing differs from striving . . . by the fact that it is always central . . . [,]performed by the ego-center itself" (19–20; my brackets).

Here we find the familiar doctrine, similar to the essential spontaneity (nonpassivity) of reason in Kant, that is, reason contrasted with sensibility's receptivity. First we must purge from mind the case of a pure "fantasy will," and of those mere velleities ("wishful thinking") that never result in deeds and never seriously could. Next we need to recognize that

> in performing an act of willing the ego proposes to itself a
> certain way of behaving *of its own*, namely, *to do* something
> or *not to do* something . . . . This proposing issues from the
> ego-center . . . as a particular doing in which the ego-cen-

ter centrifugally, from inside itself, performs a mental stroke. This stroke does more than merely approve . . . . [T]o be a *genuine act of willing*, then, *one's own ego must not be merely thought* about *but* must itself be immediately grasped and must be *made a subject* referent of a practical proposing. Thus willing, but not striving, includes the immediate consciousness of self . . . . It is an act of self-determination . . . [,]an act of self-charging; the ego charges itself with an intent [22–23; my ital.].

Now we must understand how this act of will is grounded in affectivity. First note that "a positive act of willing can be directed toward a project against whose execution the ego feels in itself a counter-striving down to the last moment" (24). Here is the classic situation of the head saying one thing while the heart says something else. The opposite could also be the case (". . . in spite of violent striving toward something, the ego decides against . . ." [24]), or it could be that the heart has already come to rest, so that "there are acts of willing in whose performance neither strivings nor counter-strivings against the projects in question can be discovered. These are especially the cases where, after completely calm and reasonable consideration and insight, one decides for or against something in accordance with this insight" (25).

Pfänder is not saying that the will could act without the involvement of feeling. The human will is never its own ground, any more than the human intellect is ever its own ground, since intellect can never know, as to its content or its very act, on itself, through itself, from itself, and so on, even when it wants to know itself. Here Pfänder presents the experience that motives are the grounds of willing.[5] So now we must see (3, next) how strivings become motives, and (4) how motives become grounds.

(3) How Strivings Become Motives

Pfänder says:

> [T]he relation of the strivings to the performance of the
> act of willing is a phenomenal relation to causing—the ego
> experiences an urging or pulling coming from striving,
> which attacks the ego-center and tries to draw it into the
> striving . . . . [I]t is by no means the case that the strivings
> by themselves simply cause the performance of a certain
> act of willing . . . . [T]he ego itself always appears as the
> agent that performs the act of willing. Never can the per-
> formance of an act of willing be a happening which is suf-
> fered by the ego [25–26].

Thus I may feel love surging up in my heart but not give it life
by assenting to it to the point of action, of acting upon the
ground of that movement of feeling. To say, for example, that
love is from the heart, not the will, is to say that the will's act
is not love but is assent to a striving that transforms it into a
motive: I will that good befall someone (*velle alicui bonum*)
because I love him or her. (See Tallon 1983.) Without action
the love may be let die, as in the Pauline expression "dying to
sin," which means not giving it life, not ratifying it into life,
not enacting its potential to *be me in actu.* One is not yet *fully*
identified or solidary with an *élan* of feeling until one *acts*
upon the feeling as the ground and support upon which the
will depends, and then the striving becomes a motive, a "motif," a motor or mover, moving one to action, to the fourth
level of consciousness.

(4) How Motives Become Grounds

A motive is a ground of willing (*Willensgrund:* motive). Pfänder
is describing how the I appropriates or not the strivings and
thereby constitutes them as motives; to be able to will means
to be able to find a reason or ground (motive) for so doing,
which can come from affection. Pfänder gives several ex-

amples of grounds, repeating every time the phrase "decides *on the basis* [*Grund*] of . . ." (27). The act whereby love is able to become a ground-of-willing—a cause in the sense of basis, support, or motive (a "why" or a "because"), so that I more correctly say "I will because I love"—is capable of still finer analysis, however. It is obvious that not all love leads to will-ing.

Pfänder offers a four-pronged approach. Implicit in his analysis of experience of the interaction of affective and voli-tional intentionality is a doctrine about conversion (change of heart) that shows the will's radical dependence on affec-tion. His first prong is put in dialogal terms. He speaks of the ego-center (will) "listening inwardly or mentally [*geistig:* spiri-tually]. This mental listening contains a questioning intent [*Zielung*] or attitude [*Haltung*] . . . . [T]he ego lives in this practical questioning attitude" (28). The ego-center moves centrifugally out from the center toward the ego-body's feel-ing (listening for the word or demand of the heart), while "into this listening, hence centripetally and, as an answer to the question-behavior going toward it centrifugally, rings out the demand . . . heard by the ego-center" (28).

A second prong goes beyond this "at first . . . merely . . . cognitive acknowledgment, namely, the grasp of a mental pointer toward what I am to do" (28), and moves to a second stage. "At that stage the ego has no longer left the demand standing outside and has no longer merely acknowledged and approved of it, but has taken it in, has incorporated it, and has then, in *falling back upon it*, carried out the act of willing in accordance with the demand and thus fulfilled it ideally for the time being. This *using something as support* in the per-formance of an act of willing is a peculiar mental doing" (29; my ital.), precisely the act whereby motive (*possible* ground) becomes ground (*actual* ground); in other words, an act of will becomes possible on the ground of affectivity. Again, just as the intellect has neither act nor content without *imago (phantasma)*, similarly will depends on affective intentionality distinct from itself within triune consciousness.

The third prong moves a bit further in the direction of a more careful description of this very interesting "falling," and again the contrast of heart and will is very sharp. "The arousal *befalls* the ego; it *touches* or *seizes* the ego. And the ego *suffers* the aroused strivings like a compulsion of nature. By contrast the ego perceives the demands made upon it. It is not conquered by them but confronts them in complete freedom" (31; my ital.). Now obviously the first two sentences are in flat contradiction with the second two—unless *ego* means first *heart* and *then will*. And this is the case. In Pfänder's terminology, "the regions of the soul . . . are different. The arousal affects the 'body of the soul' (*Seelenleib*), as it were, whereas the making of the demand addresses the 'spirit of the soul' (*Seelengeist*) and especially that part of the 'spirit' of the soul which is able to hear the practical demands made by this 'spirit'" (31-32).

The fourth prong, finally, articulates the precise relation of will to "heart":

> [T]he phenomenal cause of the performance of an act of the will is never anything outside the ego-center but is always the ego-center itself. The entire essential nature of this willing would be immediately destroyed if any kind of a phenomenal cause outside the ego-center *caused* the supposed willing . . . . [T]he *grounding* of the will (*Willensbegrundung*) *is no causation* of willing, and *motives are no* phenomenal *causes* of willing.[6] . . . [T]he ego-center *lets itself* be determined. Thus in forming intents before giving them the stamp of will, the ego can let itself be guided by general principles or rules[7] (my ital.).

Pfänder speaks of obeying, subjecting itself, and the like. "This *letting itself* be guided, adapting itself, following, obeying, subjecting itself in willing is each time something special and something which takes place in mental life" (36; my ital.).

We have a nuanced doctrine here, in which the human spirit (*Seelengeist*) becomes fully whole and integrated only when, listening to the demands of the heart (*Seelenleib*), it lets itself be led by affective intentions or does not. Though Pfänder does not suggest here how we try to change a heart whose guidance we cannot follow, he does cover the possibility of such a heart. He does so in the context of restating the relation of motive to willing: "[T]he sufficient motive . . . motivates the performance of the act of willing only when the ego-center *makes it* the support of its willing" (38; my ital.). This "making," like the less forceful sounding "letting" (he repeats: "lets itself be induced" and "lets itself be determined" several more times), means that the spirit-soul integrates itself enough as head (cognition) and heart (affection) through volition to move into action, so that the love in one's heart receives the will's stamp of approval and results in love in deed. *Character* is the term around which Pfänder organizes his conclusion, saying, "In the middle of the character stands the ego-center which wills spontaneously in a certain manner and is the free *doer* and not the *sufferer* of willing" (39; my ital.). The door is open to the possibility that one willingly places oneself in circumstances where a willed arousal should befall the heart (*Ich-Leib, Seelenleib*), after which affective consciousness can supply the strivings that could ground volitional consciousness. The circular structure is obvious, implying a distinction without separation of three consciousnesses dynamically tending toward a triadic operational synthesis.

(5) Heart as Ground of Will

To summarize the interpretation: In Pfänder's description of willing, a doctrine of a distinct affective consciousness stands forth quite plainly as the necessary ground of willing. Thinly veiled names like ego-body (*Ich-Leib*) and body-soul (*Seelenleib*) indicate Pfänder's intention to describe a spirit composed at its center (*Ich-Zentrum; Seelengeist*). The one same self is both composed and yet one, not according to a soul-body separation where soul and body operate independently of each other, but according to a description where the ego or self always acts, with a distinction, *within* the I, among three kinds of differentiated consciousness, differentiated according to three intentionalities: affection, cognition, volition. Instead of separable parts we have degrees of distance from a center; we have a moving analogy, that is, one where motion both centrifugal and centripetal is accurately described, just as we experience it. These feelings (strivings) are myself (as heart), taking myself intentionally toward others and affecting the same self (as will), entraining and drawing that more central, free self after it. The undeniable ambiguity that we experience when heart says one thing and head another must be respected and not blurred by "clear ideas"; ultimately my embodiment is myself, but ambiguously, because I neither solely am nor merely have my embodiment. We need to guard against removing the ego or self from embodiment, so that it becomes only "a" body, for that "body" must not be equated with heart. With Pfänder's analyses we have reached an important stage in a phenomenology of triune consciousness, one that points clearly in the direction of recognizing, in the idea of three essentially interdependent modes of consciousness, a higher operational synthesis of head and heart through will.

Conclusion

Despite the clear advances realized in this chapter through the contributions of Pfänder, I find his analyses only provisionally and temporarily helpful. They are important stages on the way to a complete theory of triune consciousness. But there is something about locating affectivity too much in embodiment that runs the risk of regressing toward the periphery of consciousness rather than progressing toward the center. No doubt, as affection moves from passion through emotion to feeling, affective intentionality itself undergoes changes in its experiential mass and momentum, becomes thinner or deeper, stays on the surface or reaches to the core of one's being. Depth is a crucial category for affectivity. The experience of importances and values, from vital to æsthetic, ethical, and mystical, has been a classical way of talking about depth. Depth is, however, unmistakably a spiritual experience. To move toward values, especially the ethical and mystical, even recognizing their ground in the æsthetic, is to raise the interesting and important question about the "spirituality" of affection. Is only the head spiritual, as a tradition holds that allows only intellect and will to be spiritual? Or is the heart also spiritual? We are facing a conflict of traditions, and its issue will be decisive for the thesis of triune consciousness. The next chapter moves in this direction.

Notes

1. Here is Meinong's text (114–15; my ital.): "[S]omeone has a right or false idea of something, and what is meant by this is simply that by means of the ideas in question one may make a true judgment or a false one. If in fact, under certain conditions, *a feeling or desire is substituted for an idea as a means of presentation* . . . the *justification is also attributed to the emotions* . . . . *[A] feeling or desire is never said to be justified or unjustified per se, but always relative to an object to which the emotion in question is directed,* and which is its presuppositional object . . . . [I]t is quite *appropriate to call a feeling justified* if it presents an object whose designation is the predicate of a judgment and whose presuppositional object's name is the subject."

2. Nonrepresentational is clearer than "preintentional" because all intentionality has a structure of three moments. This structure is discussed in detail in a later chapter but can be stated summarily here. The three moments are: (1) the preintentional disposition or readiness for intending (in affective intentionality this is the affectability of the subject), (2) the actual act of intending, and (3) the subsequent moment of postintentionality or metaintentionality, which is the residue engraved in the subject by the intending, which then becomes part of the predisposition (for example, attitude) and thus the preintentionality of further intendings. In affective intentionality, one's ability to respond (as responsibility) can thus be seen to depend on one's prior capacity to be affected (as affectability); as we shall see in the second half of this chapter, one can voluntarily change one's affectability and thus one's responsibility.

3. Strasser quotes René Spitz's expression "pre-objective apprehension" (297) and also calls it a "nonobjective mode of presence" (298). The term "nonintentional" should be interpreted carefully. Recall von Hildebrand's distinction between mere states, teleological trends, and true intentionality. Despite Strasser's terminology he means here true intentionality, but nonrepresentational, affective intentionality, not objective, representational intentionality; he seems to equate all intending with the intending of objects so that when he has not objects but personal subjects as the term (or "objective") of the intending he does not want to call it an intending;

but there is still, by his own descriptive analysis of emotion (302), a meaningful, affective intending, with an existential, expressive, responsive, kinetic quality. Recall also Ricoeur's distinction of feeling into its intentional and affective elements; Strasser can be interpreted less as denying that feelings are intentional than as emphasizing their affective essence. Strasser is not far from Langer in this understanding of feeling which, he says (306) "leads to the renowned distinction within experience between 'sensation' and 'reflection' and to the division of the world into an 'outer' and an 'inner' world."

4. Strasser 1970, 302; my brackets; he adds: "The 'primordial distance' (*Urdistanz*) which, as noted by Martin Buber, characterizes us human beings as human and enables us to define our attitude towards fellow-subjects, things, and situations, completely disappears."

5. Pfänder adds a sentence that could lead to the mentioned misunderstanding: "I must consider it a prejudice in favor of a false theory of the will if it is asserted that the strivings which one cannot discover here at all are nevertheless present and that the voluntary decision of the will consists in their 'victory'" (25). The point is to rule out all reduction of will to merely a name for a kind of caused, but motiveless and groundless, willing that would be a resultant of strivings and counterstrivings reinforcing or canceling out one another. His purpose, emphasized by underscoring "consists," is to deny that the will could operate without grounding itself in something other than itself, namely, heart, that is, in strivings that have become motives.

6. Ibid., 34. The Kantian sounding "phenomenal" cause suggests that room remains for introducing finality as a legitimate cause, so that we can then say, in an Aristotelian framework, that willing *is* caused because motives are *final* causes. The sense of Pfänder's distinction is preserved since final causes cause by attracting, not by efficiency or formality.

7. Ibid., 36; my ital. Here Pfänder permits an informing of the will where he just disallowed an efficient determination. In both cases, will's action is to accept from its other, heart (as *animus* embraces *anima*), as a form that is an end or exemplar, not "suffering" a determination, but actively appropriating or vetoing the heart's end and/or form.

Chapter 5

Value &
Affective Consciousness

Where your treasure is, there will your heart be also.
Luke, 12: 34 (c. A.D. 65).

There is no good above that of a good heart.
Ben Sira, Book of Wisdom (Ecclesiasticus), 30: 16. (c. 190 B.C.).

C'est le coeur qui fait tout.
Molière (1622–1673).

His madness is not of the head, but heart.
Lord Byron (1788–1824), *Lara*, canto i, sec. 18, (1814).

Summary
A number of sources, beginning with Max Scheler, cluster together as we touch upon the center of the self in terms of hierarchy of values, the order of love (*ordo amoris*), and, with Michel Henry and Ferdinand Alquié, the self as auto-affection (that is, feeling as the living sense of the core of the self), irreducible to object-knowledge.

Spirit through Value-Perception

S CHELER IS ONE OF THE BEST KNOWN PHENOMENOLOGISTS explicitly in the heart tradition, so there is no need to locate his contribution in his many works. We need only identify a certain facet of his doctrine that descriptively advances us another step closer to the center of the person. We examine Scheler's view after Pfänder's because, despite his final ideas on spirit, the way Scheler presents heart (in his writings of an earlier period) as even more closely tied to spirit (*Geist*) than Pfänder affirmed, goes one step further in the direction of eliminating the facile reduction of feeling to a purely physical accompaniment to the psychic, thereby overcoming the Cartesian-split-plus-parallelism that plagues philosophical anthropology.

In studying Scheler there is no surer guide than Manfred Frings (1965/1996, 1997). In Scheler's teaching on value perception we find new insight into the meaning of heart as affective intentionality. For the sake of sharpening our focus, let us suppose that some of the splendid autonomy of spontaneity so forcefully attributed by Pfänder to the will—its almost too spiritual nature, its almost too Kantian purity—were accused of being optimistic to a fault. We should also distrust a separation of head and heart that denied the reality of spiritual feelings. Scheler's last period, when spirit lost its "classical power," as it were, becoming entirely "modern," that is, energy-dependent on materiality, already was influencing his meaning of spirit in earlier periods, so that nothing truly human, no matter how spiritual, ever reached a point, in his view, where feeling, embodiment, and the heart were left behind. If this were established, we would be a step closer to locating heart not at the fringe of the person, at the *Ich-Leib* or *Seelenleib,* but nearer the center. Placing feeling or affectivity at the core of spirit rather than only in body and its senses is emerging from the foregoing analyses as essential to the idea of the higher operational synthesis called triune consciousness. Is feeling a secondary mode of consciousness, not as essential as cognition and volition, and only a form consciousness takes when embodied—or is affection intrinsic to spirit as such, finite and infinite ?

Is there phenomenological evidence for a union of heart and spirit? Langer has shown that feeling originally precedes thought. Ricoeur, Meinong, and Pfänder have described a primordiality of heart over head. The conflict that occurs now is with a classical doctrine that puts spirit alone at the deepest core and center: but can spirit feel? Can feeling be at the center along with cognition and volition, intellect and will? Can feeling be spiritual? Are there spiritual feelings? Scheler suggests that the finitude of the human spirit, in principle granted by the Aristotelian-Thomist tradition, is a more severe finitude than first we thought, to the point of approaching the position of near powerless that Scheler came to hold near the end of his life, a position more consonant with the idea that we are embodied because finite, not the other way around.

Scheler is so explicitly in the heart tradition that it would be easy to miss the insight that he is among the few who have also said something about what heart *means*. He acknowledges Augustine and Pascal as his predecessors in this tradition, trying to make sense of what they meant by "heart." This is clearest in his essay "Ordo Amoris" (1973; see also Frings [1972] and Blankenburg [1972]). There Scheler says:

> Whoever grasps someone's *ordo amoris,* has hold of the person and possesses that person as a moral subject—what crystal form is to crystal itself. You see into this person as far as one can see into one's fellow. You see before you the constantly simple and basic lines of someone's heart [*Gemüt*] flowing beneath all the empirical many-sidedness and complexity. And *heart* deserves to be called the core of the person as a *spiritual* being *much more than knowledge or will.* One possesses in one's spiritual make-up the original

source that secretly spawns everything emanating from human nature [Scheler 1973, 100; Frings 1972, 40]; my ital.).

Scheler's argument for the *spirituality* of the heart rests ultimately upon experience of a hierarchy of values irreducible to the vital (life-values) or sensual (æsthetic in the classical sense). Joy at the conversion of a sinner is an example of a spiritual feeling, as are interpersonal faith, hope, and self-transcending love. As Frings says, "The traditional division of spirit into reason and sensibility (*Sinnlichkeit*), dating from ancient Greek thinking to contemporary philosophy, is for Scheler thoroughly inadequate, because the whole of emotional life must on this premise be assigned to sensibility, including love and hatred" (1965, 50; Frings refers to Scheler 1954, 268). But this restriction ignores that "as a human being, before I am an *ens cogitans* or an *ens volens,* I am an *ens amans*" (Scheler 1973, 110). In fact, "*Love* is always what awakens both knowledge and volition; indeed, it is the mother of spirit and reason itself" (110). The reason for this primacy of love and heart lies in value perception, which resides in feeling; such perception is called "value-ception" (*Wert-nehmung,* literally "worth-taking," taking as worth or value, analogous to *Wahr-nehmung,* true-taking, taking for true). "Everywhere Scheler indicates that value perception precedes any knowledge of being, since without the act of participating, one cannot have *any* part in being. Every conative comprehension of an object presupposes an emotive experience of value . . ." (Frings 1973, 41). Now "love is the original structured foundation of value-ception. For the *ordo amoris,* one's emotive attunement . . . the heart of the person, is a 'structured counterpart' of the world of values" (43).

Ordo amoris refers to an "emotional a priori,"[1] an "affective a priori" (Sweeney 1964), "*the topology of the heart*" (Frings 1972, 48), and is offered as an attempt to make sense of Pascal's "*logique du coeur*": "In Pascal's maxim, 'The heart has its reasons,' what does 'its' connote? And what does it mean that the ranks of values and the laws of preference are as lucid as truths of mathematics?" (44). Scheler's response is that

> the heart is itself a *structured counter-image* of the cosmos of all possible things worthy of love; to this extent it is a *microcosm of the world of values.* *"Le coeur a ses raisons"*. . . . The heart possesses a strict analogue of logic in its own domain that it does not borrow from the logic of the understanding; laws are inscribed on it—as the Ancients' doctrine of the *nomos agraphos* had taught—which correspond to the plane on which the world is constructed as a world of value. The heart can love and hate blindly or insightfully, no differently than we can judge blindly or insightfully . . . . There is an *ordre du coeur,* a *logique du coeur* . . . [1973, 116–17].

There is also a *désordre du coeur,* both possible and usual, thus requiring "a cultivation of the heart as an autonomous concern, completely independent of the cultivation of understanding" (119). For this a priori of the heart is *acquired,* and when order becomes disorder, when one's *ordo amoris* is askew, then a change of heart is needed. But how can one change one's own heart? How can an a priori be acquired, or replaced by a new one? If the "basic lines of our emotive attunement determine for Scheler the what and the how of knowledge and of willing" (56), we seem to be locked in a circle. The early education or cultivation of one's heart, in great part an indirect affair at best, must therefore have within itself some degree of self-presence, of spirit, whereby it can recognize critically its need to change. Without falling into an idealist or rationalist interpretation of heart and affectivity, which would make any change (conversion or *metanoia*) both impossible and unnecessary, we must maintain that feelings change as affectivity matures and develops. We deal next with the problem of explaining how this occurs under the theory of an "affective a priori." A sorely needed critique of feeling seems to lie beyond any system, whether Pascal's or Scheler's, that holds for too much independence of heart from reason or heart from will. In other words, the closer we approach to the center of the person, the harder it becomes to maintain these separations—pushing feeling out of the same consciousness as cognition and volition—and the more artificial it is to play off one against another. One begins to detect a somewhat reactionary tone, as though one is protesting too much against a tradition deemed inadequate, and so is led to an exaggeration of one's own position. Frings is aware of the problem. He acknowledges that what Scheler emphasized and continued brilliantly he also left unfinished. The last chapters of his book, *Max Scheler,* bear out this view.

Michel Henry's phenomenology of affectivity may be compared with Scheler's, for they are in one respect so radically opposite to one another that comparing them must be instructive (Henry 1969, 1973, 1975; Racette 1969). The reason for this comparison is to pursue the question of the spirituality of affectivity, for unless we find phenomenological evidence that affective intentionality is as spiritual as cognitional and volitional intentionalities, there can be no higher operational synthesis of head and heart, no surviving concept of triadic consciousness. A phenomenology of affectivity that began with embodiment and made such a strong case for the reality and distinctness of affective intentionality over against the intentionalities of cognition and volition now seems to run the risk of losing its anchor in embodiment in the ambition to being considered as spiritual as these latter two kinds of consciousness. Can we have it both ways? Can affection be both the flesh of the world, our most vital experience of being, and the source of consciousness's depth, and also be as spiritual as knowledge and freedom?

Self as Affectivity: The Affective A Priori
Our mention of Henry will be transitional, since his position on affectivity can be understood either as revolutionary or as

the next logical step in the recovery of the true meaning of affection, and that question constitutes his contribution. His use of "affectivity" has a paradoxical relation to the ordinary use of the term; in fact, by "affection" he means being's *experience* of its self-presence, that is, the self-presence of *spirit* (*Beisichsein*), the experience that *pure* being (infinite being, not finite being) is and has in its nondistance from itself, wherein (Pure) Being is by definition self-presence (*Sein ist Beisichsein*) and this perfect self-presence is knowledge (*Beisichsein ist Erkenntnis*). Usually *Beisichsein*, in the Hegelian usage that, for example, Karl Rahner follows (Tallon 1971, 1974, 1979, 1982a), refers to the nonintentional knowing enjoyed by pure spirit, whereas *finite* spirit, lacking self-presence, becomes self-present only by first becoming and being self-absent (*Aussersichsein*) in embodiment (*conversio ad phantasma*). Henry's usage seems to want to locate a nonintentional affectivity in the heart of all spirit as spirit, infinite or finite.

To begin, let us cite Sweeney's excellent essay on the "affective a priori," which can initiate our reflection on Henry:

> With Michel Henry we find a counter position—virtually an antithesis—to all approaches to the affective a priori which emphasize intentionality . . . . Feeling, as such and in general, according to Henry, is nothing but a blind and brute fact, except for this self-revelatory power, this "self-tasting." Henry would therefore de-emphasize affective intentionality, seeing it only as a contingent, occasional concomitant of the basic function of affectivity which is to be revelatory of the self and its being, that is, its ontological meaning in the mode of immanence [1972, 87].

It is more common to say that because of the *deficiency of immanence* characteristic of *human* consciousness as *finite* spirit (that is, its lack of self-presence) human existence (and consciousness) *must* be intentional (that is, must become self-absent in order to return to itself [*reditio in seipsum*] in achieved self-presence); and because it is intentional, it must be em-

bodied; affectivity, on that reading, is this finitude first experienced as embodiment.

Racette puts this in the clearest terms: "[I]t seems at times
that a revaluation of interiority brings with it a devaluation of
intentionality. Or that the importance given to self-presence
brings a lack of appreciation of the presence of self to others,
or others to self" (1969, 93). Were human beings to enjoy
perfect interiority and self-presence, which we do not, no intentionality would be necessary. But Henry seems to make
human being "divine" and then rereads everything in this
light. Instead of following the tradition whereby spirit is self-
presence, Henry seems to be saying that *body* is self-presence.
Now while it is true that human (finite) self-presence is embodied, that of pure (infinite) spirit would not be. "For Michel
Henry it is ipseity, immanence, primordial embrace of self by
self that make up the structure of being, of all being" (91).
Perfectly true. "Rich and complex, this notion of being is structured. What is first in being is the presence of self to itself.
Immanence founds transcendence, interiority precedes intentionality, apperception of self is at the source of objective
knowledge" (92). True again, but true about "being as such,"
infinite being, that level of being that is already one with itself in perfect self-presence and self-possession. Can we call
this human being? What can Henry have in mind? Henry lo-
cates our human self-presence not in spirit or soul, but—trying admirably to overcome Cartesian dualism—in body:

> The subjective relation of the "I" to its own body is nothing
> else than the original relation of this body to itself. There
> is not an "I" on the one hand and a body on the other with
> the various powers which constitute it, but the being of
> each of these powers consists in the auto-affection whereby
> this power is present to itself without any distance whatso-
> ever. Such an affection as auto-affection, as affection of
> movement and of sense, but not as a being-affected-by the
> content which they develop in exteriority, by a foreign con-

tent, but an affection of movement and sense by themselves; such an affection is ipseity [1969, 112].

What Henry has done here is clear: since all knowledge is self-presence—absence of distance from self, luminosity, and so on—then insofar as the "body" knows, it is self-present, and to the degree that it is self-present, it is interiority, ipseity—a self. But Henry does not use analogy; he moves immediately to the conclusion that "perhaps this is also what we can call our soul" (112). This way of presenting the body-soul relation makes soul but a name for body's self-presence, its affectivity (experience of itself, autoaffection), and this precisely in conscious activities. This is the body-subject and "flesh" of Merleau-Ponty revisited from the other direction. But does dispensing with intentionality result in solipsism? Is a human being its own proper object?[2] Is *human* self-presence enough for itself, as though we were infinite spirits? Does this reaction against intentionality end by dehumanizing the properly human? Knowledge and love of neighbor seem in jeopardy in this philosophy, and Levinas's primacy of the other, where ethics precedes ontology, seems the polar opposite of Henry's position. Is there a way to read Henry that ends not in stalemate but with insight into a better understanding of affection not as different from cognition and volition (as the spiritual "faculties" of intellect and will) by being *embodied* but as different just by being a *different kind of consciousness*, pure and simple, and therefore as a different way of being, living, and experiencing self-presence? If this were so, Henry will have done a great service in emphasizing, almost to the point of contradiction, what is a paradox and contradiction only to a tradition that has already decided that only cognition and volition are spiritual. The corollary would be to recover the *embodiment of cognition and volition*, of course, thus finally overcoming all Cartesian views of consciousness.

With Scheler we began to reach the spiritual center of the person, but with Henry we might seem to have lost that forward momentum. Can we find a space-time center, a still point, in the dispersal of embodiment? Is consciousness just *postulated* as that center? Must we read Henry that way? It has been said that the body is in the soul, not the soul in the body. Henry has made affectivity his entire philosophy and equated it with self-presence, taking the classic *Bei-sich-sein* of spirit and naming that body (or, he allows, "perhaps . . . soul"). Yet his insistence that embodiment is self-presence correctly provides what a non-self-present spirit needs in order to *become* self-present. It seems possible, then, to read Henry as affirming a most radical nondualistic concept of human nature, one that affirms that nonintentional self-presence (of soul) is given in affective consciousness (of body), but that makes it difficult to explain presence to others. The spirituality of affection has found an expression, but not its final one. Henry has forced us to recognize that we have reached a limit in a certain way of thinking about consciousness, that we need a new model.

To conclude these two sections, then, we have contrasted two philosophers who both root affectivity in being's very self-presence, not in a sensuous body (emotion, passion, and affection, as mere accompaniment to representational intentionality) but in being's spiritual essence. But do we have yet an emerging sense of what "spiritual" means? Can we suspend talk of immateriality and immanence and so avoid defining spirit and the spiritual until fully ready, faithful to the phenomena? If our phenomenological sources have taken us to the center of the person and descriptively presented the heart as the experience of a center, analytically distinct but operationally inseparable from both cognitional and volitional consciousnesses, then we need a major paradigm shift at this juncture. If we are at the center and identify heart with neither representational cognition nor volition, then we must *stop thinking in terms of faculties* of mind and will; we must *shift away from a cognitive (or volitional) model* to a (nondualistic) *response* model, taking response to mean an *operational* relation of whole being to whole being. Replacing the faculty model with the response model may succeed in making heart talk more intelligible, defensible, arguable. Beyond a faculty psychology we must turn to affective consciousness and to the response model, that is, to a fully dialogical, intersubjective, interpersonal paradigm. A paradigm shift to a response model leads to triune consciousness.

Affective Consciousness

As a transition to the response model and to description of the affective response, we can with profit pause briefly to ask whether affective intentionality has emerged sufficiently clearly in the argument developed so far to claim the status of a secure concept, identifiably distinct enough to warrant our expecting it to carry the freight of the meaning of feeling. Has a prima facie case become more plausible for a distinctively isolatable phenomenon to be named "affective consciousness" as a distinct mode of consciousness coequal with cognition and volition? Alquié's *La conscience affective* (1979) goes a long way (some might say too far) toward establishing the specificity of affective consciousness. An *operational* psychology (as distinct from a *faculty* psychology) allows an analysis of consciousness that is aware of three strands or modes of consciousness streaming together in a fusion, a fusion that is perhaps experienced as a con-fusion until eventually it is differentiated into its constitutive moments.

Since Alquié is our bridge from Scheler and Henry to von Hildebrand and Strasser, it is appropriate to note his agreement with Henry: "Affectivity is the very essence of the self" (1979, 20; all translations mine). Affectivity has its own intentionality, an intentionality more basic, more at the root and origin of precisely human experience (18), which at higher levels flows from it: "[A]ffectivity, 'constituting the essence of original ontological passivity,' is the 'ultimate foundation of all reality'" (20–21).

Alquié affirms that at the least "there are . . . two distinct consciousnesses, each one having its own structure and its own laws" (23), and also declares that his task is "to establish the irreducibility of affective consciousness to intellectual consciousness" (21). Alquié clearly distinguishes affective consciousness and its own affective intentionality from representational intentionality, which is the form proper to intellectual consciousness. "By the intellectual I think being as object. In the affective I live my relation to being so intensely that I cannot think it. And these two consciousnesses are not only irreducible but opposed. The power of each diminishes when that of the other increases" (23). Affective consciousness is not a derivative of cognitive consciousness; indeed, it is the other way around, Alquié argues, when he uses the terminology of "representational" in opposition to that of affectivity:

> Sensation becomes representational only by ceasing to be affective. The senses richest in affectivity are the least objective. Taste and smell are never affectively neutral, but remain very nonrepresentational. Already more objective, touch is less penetrated with affectivity: those parts most apt to provide tactile representations, such as the fingertips, are the ones where the threshold of pain is highest. Reciprocally, the most sensitive parts are the least capable of delivering objective information about what stimulates them. Finally, the sensations of hearing and sight, representationally the richest, are in themselves strangers to affectivity: there is no pain properly speaking auditory or visual, but only pains of ear and eye, which is a different thing [23].

At the very origins of the two consciousnesses, in sensation, they are already differentiated (23). More interesting, however, is the way this distinct consciousness develops upon humanization, that is, upon integration into higher human forms of actions. Alquié's second chapter, then, understandably moves into the circle of dialogue, into the intersubjective. "[A]ll thought must be ruled by the possibility of being inserted into a dialogue" (28); "[H]uman consciousness being first affective consciousness, perfect dialogue cannot help appearing as an ideal" (28). Here we find inextricably linked three things, namely, thought, dialogue, and affectivity, and linked in such a way that dialogue emerges as both beginning and end of human consciousness. Dialogue is clearly more than thought, since thought is a part of dialogue and exists only to become part of dialogue, while this same dialogue, as communion of persons, is the goal of affective intentionality. That part of dialogue called thought remains under the criterion of participation in dialogue, that is, of a degree of self-transcendence and generalization, as in language, requisite for any dialogue.

As long as knowledge is defined as "knowing objects," affective consciousness seems nonobjective (Marion 1980, 436). Nonobjective, of course, does not mean untrue. If affective consciousness is as basic and distinct from rational or representational consciousness as Alquié says, then this fact should appear in other ways and places in our experience. We need only attune ourselves to their perception and be open to recognize what our experience means. One such telling experience is mentioned in the third chapter of *La conscience affective*. There Alquié points out the usually ignored fact that we normally love ourselves *without offering reasons* (thus "irrationally") to justify our self-love, and without feeling a *need* to do so. We just do, without reason, for "no reason." And then, in an inversion of the love command, he wonders: since what we really would like is for others to love us just as "irrationally" as we love ourselves, why is it that they do not? The whole scene escapes reason. The whole experience apparently transpires before reasoning can catch up and decipher the code. Prerationally, prevolitionally, and naturally loving oneself, in the best sense of the word, one suddenly and coldly encounters someone who does not ratify one's relation to oneself. It is as though one were wordlessly thrown back upon oneself, without really knowing why, since one's loving self-relation was itself from the heart before "intellect" offered its reasons and before "will" made its decisions. Loving the neighbor as oneself can thus also be understood to mean *loving the other without "reasons"* (of the head), just as one loves oneself, that is, to mean *loving the other from the heart*, as one loves oneself spontaneously and without deliberative will-acts. Alquié's explanation throws new light on the love-command: one is told to love one's neighbor as one loves oneself, that is, by sublating the headwork of thinking, judging, deliberating, and choosing—just as one does in loving oneself immediately and spontaneously.

"For the first time my self ceases being only the center and subject of representations: it is subject for another. The loving relation is no longer, like the intellectual relation, a relation of subject to object but of subject to subject, consciousness to consciousness. By this fact it escapes reason, which knows only by objectifying" (1979, 40). The contrast is not with meaninglessness (nor should it ever have been) but with a kind of knowing or reasoning based exclusively on representational intentionality. Alquié immediately makes the context clear when in the next sentence he says: "But love must abandon the way of logic in order to commit itself to that of faith" (40). Not divine faith but human faith is meant here, as is clear from context and sequel. "The faith that love demands is not only religious faith. All love supposes some faith" (40). Here Alquié means to contrast, at the human level of dialogue and intersubjectivity, "knowing" another person with believing and "believing (in)" another person. This is the meaning of Alquié's statement that "The consciousness of another, directly intended by love, is never attained by knowledge except indirectly" (40). Believing (in) the person is the whole of which knowledge indirectly and subsequently gleaned is a part; such knowledge, like all objective knowledge, is false if it does not also leave room for the unobjectifiable subjectivity of the person, which can only be touched, not grasped—believed in rather than objectively known—and which depends on my being able to be affected by the other, not on my deciding what the other's meaning will be (41-42).

Faith is an *affective response* to the *whole person as a ground* on which appear *figures* that can be *known as objects.* Faith can seek understanding, *fides quaerens intellectum,* as we try to make sense of what we believe. To have *faith* in someone, to *love* someone, to *hope* for that someone's future, are *responses* (quasi-operations: partly passive) to the person as a whole , as a "field" or a ground on which appear, as against this background, all the "figures" or forms grasped by objective knowledge. Such faith and hope are affective responses that intend the *person* as such rather than intending factual knowledge *about* the person. If we can believe Kierkegaard, in *Works of Love,* love, like believing in someone, is a response that enables or empowers the other person to *be* faithful and loving, that brings forth from the other the acts believed to be connatural to that other but which would be otherwise impossible. Alquié says: "Affective consciousness can believe. It cannot know" (43), which means its "reasons" are affections, not the cognitions which are reason's reasons.

Before leaving Alquié, however, whose work we have hardly exhausted, let me cite a few of his observations that reveal the meaning of the heart. Alquié shows that love (like faith and hope) is an affective consciousness that grounds and yields acts of will rather than consists in them. We will (the good of another) *because* we love the other *before* reasons and will-acts.[3] Further, distinguishing (at least) two kinds of intentionality, he holds the familiar thesis that representational intentionality is linked to a visual bias or preference.[4] Merleau- Ponty, in his *Structure of Behavior,* had already emphasized the distortions resulting from such bias, and Sartre exemplified that bias in several ways. Alquié relates representation to abstract space (and eventually to time) and affirms that affective consciousness "refuses" such space and time, thus withdrawing to a "confusion" (128, 139). The language here must not put us off. The active ring of the word "refuse" is fine, since in true Gestalt perspective we do in fact have to refuse to reduce ground to figure, or, in Buber's terms, reduce I-Thou to I-It. Saying that a person-to-person relation is '"ground-to-ground," not "figure-to-figure," indicates a radically different way of relating. This way is not objective if one would restrict objectivity to the sharp delineation and definition associated with placing a figure against a ground, beginning, of course, with the natural grounds of the senses, space and time. The French *confusion* need not be pejorative, but can suggest an original oneness, a fusion-with, regained and retrieved, a unity preceding separation into figures, qualities, and the like: not the person's blue eyes, cultivated manner, and so on, Alquié suggests, are the intention of affective (non-representational) consciousness, but the person as a whole, a ground on which appear and emerge all such figures, those figures and forms that *can* be known objectively, even to the point of ignoring the person as a person, who is always more than any collection of (objectively knowable) qualities.

Finally, parallel to his notion of the *love* without reason(s) that we feel for ourselves, Alquié speaks of an obscure (not clear and distinct) self-*knowledge*, which like obscure self-love, is often rejected because it is obscure, unscientific, unobjective. The point is the same: the heart has its reasons and, in both self-knowledge and self-love, reason doesn't know them as ideas or concepts; the heart's reasons are feelings, affective consciousness. But another point is made: the heart doesn't know reason's reasons. The heart intends the whole person as ground; reason intends the parts as figures on the ground. Focusing on one we may ignore the other. A holistic, triadic response unites affective, cognitive, and volitional consciousnesses together (169). This sheds light on those aberrations where one sinks into affectivity to avoid clear thinking and responsible decision making, a motif Sartre explores in his theory of emotion; that the heart as affective consciousness admits of abuse is not news. We could call this a "lower" synthesis (recalling Ricoeur's *bios-epithumia* heart) rather than a higher operational synthesis of triune consciousness. Thus it makes sense to describe the heart as affective consciousness based on an affective intentionality that arises from a synthesis of "lower" and "higher" energies and that can in different intersubjective encounters be a lower or higher operational synthesis.

Notes

1. Ibid., 40; he adds: ". . . the emotional a priori of love and hatred is the fundament of any other a priori, that is, of any knowledge of being or any willing of contents."

2. Racette notes this also: "One can also regret that a philosophy so deeply spiritual at times seems to articulate itself in a solipsistic atmosphere. This is especially so when Henry wants to define affectivity and feelings without any reference to an object [without intentionality, affective or otherwise]. Also, there is hardly any mention of relations to others, of knowledge of others, of reciprocity of consciousness, or of intersubjectivity" (1969, 93; my brackets).

3. "Aimer conduit à vouloir le bonheur de l'autre" (ibid., 46). Love is from whole (person) to whole (person). It leads us *to will* the good (happiness) of the other (*velle alicui bonum*). "Aimer, dit Leibnitz, c'est trouver du plaisir dans la félicité d'autrui, *felicitate alterius delectari*" (46). This "finding pleasure in another's happiness" is an affective response based on connaturality and is just as prerational and prevoluntary as (con)natural self-love; both loves are affective responses (like faith and hope) that come from the deep center before mind and will. Love is not an act of the will but rather love entrains the will naturally to produce such acts.

4. "The primacy of the intelligence is linked to that of visual representation. To arrive at an irrational grasp of things, therefore, one must attack this representation" (ibid., 128). "Irrational" here means prerational.

Chapter 6

Affectability &
Affective Response

My heart leaps to my mouth.
Homer (fl. 850? B.C.), *Iliad*, 22. 452.

Out of the abundance of the heart the mouth speaks.
Matthew, 12: 34 (repeated in Luke, 6: 45.).

Unhappy that I am, I cannot heave
My heart into my mouth.
Shakespeare (1564–1616), *King Lear*, 1.1. 92 (1605).

My heart flew into my mouth so suddenly
that if I hadn't clapped my teeth together I should have lost it.
Mark Twain (1835–1910), *Life on the Mississippi*, ch. 9 (1874).

Not all who know their minds know their hearts.
La Rochefoucauld (1613–1680), *Maximes*, no. 103 (1665).

Summary
Dietrich von Hildebrand furnishes insights into the structure of affective intentionality first as an affectability (an
ability to be affected) and second as an affective response.
His concepts of cooperative freedom, important to the head-
heart dialectic, and of the spirituality of affection are also presented. The response model replaces the faculty model.

L ET US TURN NOW TO VON HILDEBRAND's important contribution. No one has analyzed affectivity better than von
Hildebrand, especially in his *Ethics* (1953), but also in
Metaphysik der Gemeinschaft (1955), and *The Heart* (1977).
Three points remain (to be treated in ch. 6 and 7) before we
turn to connaturality and habit (in ch. 8–10) as the ontological underpinnings of triune consciousness, and for them we
depend first on von Hildebrand (and, in ch. 7, on Strasser):
(1) The existence and nature of affective *response*; (2) the concept of affectability, or the reality of one's ability to change
how one is affected (and thus how one responds: this leads to
the idea of response-ability as the possibility of being responsible for one's affective responses); and (3) the ultimately spiritual essence of affectivity. The last two points are also central
to Strasser (1977) and we will treat them in the next chapter.
At first it may seem that Strasser only systematizes and gives
structural clarity to von Hildebrand's points. Actually he does
more: while von Hildebrand, after establishing the reality of
changing one's affectability, only briefly suggests how it happens, Strasser carefully elaborates that change. Both address
the structure of change of heart, the phenomenology of affective conversion, a concept of major importance because it
is in the dialectic of change that head and heart interact to
move to the higher operational synthesis which is triune consciousness. Finally, whereas von Hildebrand establishes the
spiritual essence of affectivity, Strasser advances the phenomenology another step toward the point where the next move
belongs to hermeneutics. What Pfänder outlined in terms of
a faculty model (the relation of will to feeling), von Hildebrand fleshes out, within an operational response model, in
terms of freedom's relation to affective response.

Affective Response

Here is how we might outline where intentional acts fit within
consciousness in general and how responses differ from cognitive acts.[1] The idea of *affectability* relates to that of the *circular*

structure of intentionality; since one's responses begin to condition and even determine one's perceptions, we must note an interdependence of responses and cognition. The larger question then becomes one of understanding this being-affected and its structure and how to break into it. Von Hildebrand addresses the question of affectability by distinguishing three responses, those of cognition, volition, and affection (recall Figure 2 on p. 33, above):

> In the realm of responses we are confronted with three different basic types. First, there exist responses such as conviction, doubt, expectation, which we can term "theoretical" responses. Second, there is willing in the strict sense of the word, which we can term the "volitional" response. Third, there are responses such as joy and sorrow, love and hatred, fear and hope, esteem and contempt, enthusiasm and indignation, which we can term "affective" responses . . . . In theoretical responses, for instance conviction, we add, as it were, the voice of our minds to the object's gesture of self-affirmation; we complete it with the "word" of our mind as the expression of our outspoken embrace of the such-being and existence of the object . . . . These responses are not "free" in the full sense of the term . . . not free in the sense that the will is free: for it is not in our power to be convinced or unconvinced when facing a datum of our knowledge. On the contrary, knowledge itself prescribes what response we should give. As soon as we have grasped something, our conviction of it arises organically [1953, 198–99].

Thus freedom and responsibility reside in this "as soon as we have grasped." How one grasps something depends upon oneself as a free participant even in theoretical responses. The question must arise whether and to what extent one can and routinely does affect one's ability to perceive. Clearly a circle of intentionality at the interior of triadic consciousness is implied: if past responses have affected present biases, prejudices, preferences, and so on, to the point of conditioning our present perceptions (a fact most easily noticed in æsthetic and ethical preferences), then we have constant input into how our convictions arise. In a word, the human organism is reflexively and circularly at work upon itself at all times and thus implicated in how convictions "arise organically." But since we treat this point in the following section, let us go on to volitional responses.

> In speaking of the will in the strict sense, we mean the re-
> sponse which is directed toward something not yet real,
> but endowed with the possibility of being realized . . . . The
> will alone is able to command intentionally our bodily ac-
> tivities, to instigate freely and voluntarily a chain of causal-
> ity . . . . Only through willing can we change something in
> the world around us as well as something in our person
> . . . . The will is in our immediate power . . . [I]ts immedi-
> ate issuance from our spiritual center is the only case of a
> fiat in our human existence [200-01].

Putting aside the question of immediacy, we can take as established a second distinct kind of response, the volitional. Von Hildebrand has much more to say about the will when comparing it with affectivity. His point here is to note the way we can voluntarily change our ability to be affected, and thus our ability to respond; so he turns to affective response.

> We come now to another fundamental type of responses:
> the affective responses . . . . Affective plenitude . . . is char-
> acteristic of these responses and . . . . absent in the will.
> While affective responses are voices of our heart, while in
> them our entire person is involved, the will has a one-dimen-
> sional, linear character, certainly committing our entire
> person, but being in itself exclusively a position of our free
> personal center . . . . The will alone is free in the strict sense
> of being in our immediate power, whereas affective re-
> sponses are not free in this sense. We never can engender
> any affective response by a fiat, nor can we command it by

our will as we can any activity. Love, for instance, is always granted to us as a gift [202-03].

Consider the alternatives proposed here. If love is an affective response of the heart, not the will, then we cannot "command it by our will as we can any activity," by the will's *fiat*. We need to be *given* love, and yet, as response, its plenitude is in oneself; it is one's "word," a Yes said to the other; it is one's own response, yet to be *able* to respond is to be given a gift: one rejoices to find someone to love. The notion of *affectability* and its intentional structure or circularity thus leads to a more differentiated meaning of heart. As in the case of theoretical responses, there is indirect or mediate access to one's affectivity and thus a degree of remote freedom in affective intentionality, a *cooperative freedom*, as von Hildebrand says.[2]

Before asking, in our second point, just how affection and volition cooperate, for example, in being "drawn by delight" (Pfänder's "entrainment") or in being moved to action by perception of and sensitivity to evil—which is the question of affectability and one's responsibility for being-affected—let us state exactly what the controlling problem is and how our present context offers a solution.

From the beginning we have been asking not merely about the existence and nature of something called a heart tradition, in general, but, more specifically and practically (in ch. 2), about how probing this heart, beyond unexamined everyday usage, reveals the meaning, possibility, and methodology of *change* of heart, of affective conversion (especially with a view to the role of feeling in ethics), comprehensible only on the ground of triune consciousness. Now in the present context we focus on the relation between feeling and freedom as they cooperate in the move from one's being unaffected to being affected, which then grounds the possibility of a new (changed) affective response; this is a move involving freedom and responsibility, including the *affective* responsibility of affective responses (for example, faith, love, and hope) (see Tallon 1986).

Affectability & Being-affected

If affective conversion as change of heart is possible, then it must be described and eventually explained so that it can be an experience we can recognize and promote in ourselves and others (and to the extent that philosophy itself methodically excludes affectivity from the triad it needs an affective conversion). At issue is the relation of head and heart now that their distinction has been established. Von Hildebrand situates his discussion within an ethical treatise. He uses the circular structure of habit formation (as acquisition of virtue) to exemplify the reciprocal influencing of cognition and the three kinds of responses. Understanding that structure is essential for understanding change of heart. Responses presuppose one's being affected, and being affected presupposes one's being *capable* of being affected, of being *able* to be affected, that is, presupposes one's affectability. Being affected is the centripetal moment preceding the centrifugal response. This going into and out from the center is spatial imagery suitable to the idea of the heart as the core or center. "In one case the other bestows something on me; in the other case, I, by my response, impart something to the other. Thus, in being affected, the direction is from the other to me; in the response, from me to the other. It has here a character analogous to perception, where likewise the other speaks to me" (von Hildebrand 1953, 209). (Here again we have the attunement of connaturality, the vibration of the in and the out, of affection and intention, the waves of the resonant frequencies between self and other.)

Thus another analogy is speech or dialogue: "We are, as it were, *speaking* to the other [in our response], whereas in being affected we are only receiving the 'word' of the other" (209; my brackets). These two analogies are only analogies, since von Hildebrand does not equate knowing with being-affected. Response need not await *explicit* or full cognition; response must, however, follow being-affected, which is *like* knowing and *like* verbal dialogue (which has a cognitive component), which means that some *implicit* knowing is part, and only part, of being affected, but not the whole of being-affected, as a quick reading of von Hildebrand might suggest. This becomes clear when von Hildebrand adds: "Being affected presupposes, first, a knowledge of the other who affects me. So long as I do not *know* of the compassion someone feels for my suffering, I cannot be consoled. So long as another's hostile attitude is neither perceived nor known indirectly, it cannot create a wound in my heart" (208). Clearly, nothing akin to thorough, explicit, exhaustive knowledge is required; a mere glimmer or hint is enough, and the merest nonverbal communication, for example, someone's look or touch, can speak volumes. We must be wary of reading von Hildebrand as mistakenly reducing all intentionality to representationality. As we shall see later, one's affectability depends on connaturality, which is more a relation to one's whole *being* than to one's knowing.

Where does this leave us, then, with respect to the dependence of response on something prior? What are the a priori conditions for the possibility of response? In von Hildebrand's ethical context, analysis of being-affected begins with a phenomenology of value response, where "value" is a better term than "knowledge" to identify the a priori presupposition for response. Value includes more than cognition; "something else" in the known other is added to the event of cognition and it is this something else that affects oneself and engenders a response. I am not just affected by knowledge but by knowledge *plus* an *affecting relation*, which is the other's ability to touch me, the other's "affecting presence" (Armstrong 1971). Nothing could be more obvious: not all knowledge stimulates action, but only knowledge that touches the heart, that is not only interesting but important (von Hildebrand 1953, ch. 3: "The Categories of Importance").

Rather than saying "knowledge precedes response," then, and trying to avoid reducing response to cognition, let us say rather that being affected by the *value* aspect of a person, object, or event is the precondition for response, such that knowledge is *part* of what value means, namely, the relation of interest-*plus-importance* that someone or something has to oneself, even though one may not yet know *why* that person or thing is felt as important, as value. We are now ready to describe this value response:

> We have now to elaborate in detail the nature of the value response, including its difference from any affective response which is not a value response. The first decisive mark of the value response is its character of self-abandonment. In enthusiasm, veneration, love, or adoration, we break open our self-centeredness and conform to the important-in-itself. Our interest in the other is completely based on and completely nourished by the intrinsic goodness, beauty, and preciousness of the other, and the mysterious rhythm of its intrinsic importance . . . . In a response motivated by the merely subjectively satisfying . . . there is no transcending of the frame of self-centeredness . . . [214–15].

This "self-abandonment to the other" as value consists in a transcendence of ego-centeredness or self-interest. Von Hildebrand admits that we can act on the basis of objectively good values or on the basis of things that are merely subjectively satisfying, and by mixtures and combinations of goods and pleasures (214). Self-transcendence means intending the *objectively valuable* rather than the merely *subjectively satisfying*.

In affective response to value, one's heart is touched, captured, stolen, given away. Unlike the teleological trends, which remain self-immanent, value draws us out, leading to self-transcendence, that is, to preference for values because of their goodness in themselves rather than for their relation to one's self-interest.

> In all immanent trends to unfold our nature, our attitude
> has the character of *self*-affirmation [I affirm *myself.*];
> whereas in every value response our attitude has the basic
> feature of self-*donation* [I give myself away in self-*transcen-
> dence.*] [220]. In being affected by a value, we are *broadened
> [deepened] and elevated above ourselves*; in being affected by
> the merely subjectively satisfying, we are rather made nar-
> row and in no way elevated above ourselves. In being af-
> fected by values we also experience the unifying power of
> the values: we become internally more unified, more rec-
> ollected [228; my ital. and brackets].

The whole person is integrated by a double movement when
value affects us at the core of our being and the response
comes from that deep center. Heart thus means the capacity
to be so affected and names our ability to respond with our
whole being.

Clearly, then, we should most earnestly *will and desire to be
affected by values and thereby to be empowered to respond,* for in this
dialogue with values we undergo the *radical conversion* that is
the comfort and purpose of time, which is life as movement,
and advance to the higher synthesis of triune consciousness.
Von Hildebrand says: "First, it is quite possible that we may
perceive the value without being affected by it. We may wonder why a piece of music, which had once moved us deeply
does not move us at all at another time, though we really
perceive its beauty and do not merely recall having perceived
it before. For one reason or another the music does not pen-
etrate the deeper stratum of our soul wherein we are actually
affected" (234).

Here, in the first moment of analysis of being-affected,
von Hildebrand confirms that the response depends not so
much on perception or knowledge in general, or even on
perception or knowledge of the *value* capable of engendering the response, but on *ourselves* as relating to that value in
some way irreducible to cognition. Why are we not *always* affected or always affected in the *same way,* if not because while

the one pole of the relation remains the same, the *other* pole, *myself, has changed?* To what extent can one contribute to one's own affectability? Von Hildebrand answers: "Secondly, in the value perception as such, I am, so to speak, void; and the content is exclusively on the other side, that is, in the value of the other. In being affected, however, there is a content *in my soul* (for example, the specific experience of *being moved*) . . . . The value acts on my heart in a deep, meaningful manner, in melting it, in piercing through the crust of my indifference and bluntness . . ." (234).

Here the contrast between perception and being-affected is sharper yet. We are meant to recognize that something in us, a certain content that is like a response by being on the side of the subject (unlike perception), and yet is not yet response in the full sense of response. There is a potentiality to respond, *in actu primo proximo.* How should we translate this phrase? It suggests a leaning or disposition that is already a response begun, an incipient tilting toward, a predisposition; but even more seems to be meant; more than disposition, we have here an initial degree of response that while *insufficiently appropriated* by me as *active* subject is *still me somehow as affected* subject. "I was moved before I caught myself." "I was in love before I knew it." Such expressions point to this second preresponsive moment: meaningful encounter, irreducible to clear and distinct ideas, is already empowering my response. This is my being-affected as the necessary condition for my affective response.

More than perception, yet less than response, not solely in the other nor solely in me but (as Buber says) *between* us. We should not underestimate this ambivalent moment. As von Hildebrand says:

> We rightly *desire to be affected* by beautiful music or by the beauty of a landscape; we desire to *be affected* by the value of a spiritual gift bestowed on us, such as another's kindness; and we are regretful when we are not able to go *be-*

yond the mere perception of the value. The very fact that, in perceiving those values without yet *being affected* by them, we desire to be affected testifies to the *new and higher level of union* which being affected represents. Similarly, we pray that we may *be touched* by the divine . . . : that our hearts may be melted so that the irradiation of this infinite sanctity may *transform our nature.* Again the fact that we expect still another and deeper influence on our personality from a *being affected* by the values than from a value perception alone reveals the intimacy of the union in *being affected* [234; my ital.].

Recognizing that one's heart has lost what Gabriel Marcel calls the "paradise" of immediacy, that is, what we might call "Heart 1" (the heart of a child, before innocence is lost at the "age of reason"), we strive by acts of will to "become like little children again," not literally, of course, but insofar as spontaneity, immediacy, and like qualities also characterize the changed (converted, instructed, or "headed" heart), transformed precisely by the mediations of reason and will, that is, by cognition and volition. We might call this new, converted heart, after the headwork, Heart 2, the heart of triune consciousness. Head and heart coexist and interact, or, putting aside this way of speaking in "faculty psychology" language, the three currents of the stream of consciousness, affection, cognition, and volition, while distinct intentionalities, constitute, *in action*, the triad that is their higher union in mature adults. This insight is implied in affective conversion and merely becomes explicit in explaining the theory underlying change of heart: there is no change of heart without willed, voluntary headwork. Von Hildebrand calls this "cooperative freedom." Let us turn to it now.

After distinguishing direct and indirect freedom, so that the "zone of indirect influence includes our affective responses as well as our virtues and even the responses and virtues of other persons" (314; "direct freedom" refers to volun-

tary acts proper), von Hildebrand mentions accepted under-
standings of the limits of such indirect freedom:

> In the case in which an other lies in the zone of our indi-
> rect influence, we realize from the very beginning either
> that we can only prepare the path for its coming into exist-
> ence or else that we are in a situation where we could say:
> I must at least do everything which is in my power toward
> its realization . . . . We can do our share. It may consist
> either in a removal of obstacles (for example, this is the
> purpose of ascetic practices) or in creating favorable cir-
> cumstances [for exmple] . . . in exposing ourselves to the
> right and salutary influence of the irradiation of good ex-
> ample [314].

This recalls the structure of affective intentionality mentioned earlier. The key element for von Hildebrand is ethical
responsibility for our affective responses; he needs to show
that radical conversion is indeed possible by showing *how* it is
possible, dispelling the illusion (and evasion) of being powerless over one's unloving selfishness in order to generate
efficacious desire for ethical conversion.

Von Hildebrand speaks of

> a threefold role of our free influence in this area. First,
> there is the indirect influence in preparing the ground in
> our soul for *being affected* by values. Secondly, there is the
> *free cooperation* with this experience when it is granted to
> us. Thirdly, there is the role *of our freedom* in harvesting
> fruits of this experience. Thus apart from the cooperative
> acceptance of our being affected, there still exist a pro-
> logue and an epilogue to human freedom [318; my ital.].

We cannot directly and freely engender affective responses;
we cannot just give commands, exercise volitional acts, and
thereby immediately *feel* in some way, *respond affectively* in some
way. Since this is not in our power, not wholly within our-

selves, then it must be "in the other"—or in "the between," as Buber more accurately says, that is, precisely in the other's relation to me: ". . . [I]t is this other who must enkindle our response" (319).

But this radical dependence on otherness is not an evil, but a sign of our finite intersubjective nature. Relation to otherness is intrinsic to human nature, and we experience our social nature in a way that verifies its naturalness. To experience as repugnant the very idea of being able to command affective responses is to recognize this phenomenological insight:

> The idea of being able to command affective responses by our will, to innervate them as we innervate a movement of our limbs, would by implication deprive them of their *meaningful relation to the importance of the other*. It would deprive them of *their essential perfection*, which *is that of a response motivated by the importance of the other*, and in addition place them on the level of certain activities without even giving them the specific (although much lower) perfection which these activities possess. No one who realizes the nature and meaning of joy, love, or veneration could even desire that his affective responses should be accessible to the command of the will. For we can see that this would be incompatible with the dignity of these responses [319; my ital.].

Of course, love can be engendered by the need of the person loved as well as by the lovableness of the other, in the sense of the other's being a gift fulfilling one's own needs; ability to respond is still the common element.

> We mentioned before the cases wherein we face an other endowed with a high value and are aware that the other deserves a value-responding joy or sorrow, love or veneration, but nevertheless find ourselves unable to give the adequate response; we then experience as a trial our incapacity to freely engender these responses. What is really

our wish in those moments is to be able simply to *engender* the responses freely; never could we seriously wish to be able to *command* them by our will. We may regret that inso-far as the affective responses are concerned we do not pos-sess the first dimension of freedom, or that they are not free in the same sense as is willing itself. But never—so long as we understand the nature of affective responses—could we regret that they cannot be *commanded* in the same way as any action or movement of our limbs or an act of attention. Here we touch a deep problem closely connected with our creature-hood. The *things which can be commanded by our will,* which we can bring into existence, *are limited in their ontological rank.* The *higher something is, the more it pos-sesses the character of a gift,* which we cannot simply give to ourselves [319; my ital.].

Here again we find confirmed phenomenologically the wonderful and precious difference between volition and af-fection as modes of consciousness, not only establishing their difference on experiential grounds, but also offering insight into the nature of the difference and cooperative relation between them within triune consciousness.

In comparing the volitional and the affective responses, we can easily grasp the superiority which the former pos-sess over the latter: freedom. But we can also see that *affec-tive responses possess a plenitude in which willing is deficient. In affective responses the heart and the plenitude of a human person-ality are actualized . . . . In affective responses I am able to give myself with my heart, with the plenitude of my personality,* but without being capable of engendering them freely . . . [320; my ital.].

"Plenitude" calls attention to the fullness, richness, depth, and wholeness experienced in the heart, compared with the partial, shallow, and thin nature of intellectual and volitional acts. Head and heart need one another; only in an opera-tional union, as a conscious triad cooperating with freedom, is that need fulfilled. The trial, as von Hildebrand calls it, felt in a *partial* response, stems from our human sense of the appropriateness of *whole*-hearted response, so that love for persons as wholes (as grounds rather than as figures on grounds) is essential to the affective response.

Now we may rightly ask how exactly we can engender affective responses, how we can move from theory to practice. In what remains of this second part of our dialogue with von Hildebrand, then, we can sketch out his answer, which essentially comes to the idea of habit as virtue (treated more fully later; I merely provide a few notes here).

He begins by presenting the position that love is an affective response, with indirect ("cooperative") involvement of cognition (the headwork) and volition, by describing naturally good-hearted persons as "tacitly in solidarity with everything which arises in them spontaneously" (321), and other persons, as perhaps not so good-hearted, as asleep or unconscious when it comes to their uncritically following affectivity wherever it leads. For von Hildebrand, such persons are premoral, or morally unconscious, since they have not involved their free personal center in approving or vetoing their responses. He names "the superactual [that is, "more than actual," meaning virtual or habitual] general will to be morally good" (322; my brackets) as the fundamental mark of a moral person.

This general attitude or fundamental option runs into conflict with individual evil affective responses which, having spontaneously arisen prereflectively and prevoluntarily, now present themselves for avowal or disavowal by the free personal center. "In this disavowal I emancipate myself expressly from this affective response and counteract it with my free spiritual center; I withdraw from it in such a way that I desubstantialize the response, 'decapitate' it, so to speak. In this disavowal the free 'no' affects the response from within and takes from it its character of a valid position toward the other" (322). First the heart responds, and then the *will, as*

executor of the heart, assents or vetoes the spontaneous affective response; first the affective response, then the will, in a
temporally secondary moment, breaking apart the whole by
driving a decisive and divisive wedge between heart and will.
One is and feels divided, as St. Paul complained, because one
feels the affective response as truly oneself, just as truly as
(and usually more emotionally than) the volitional response.
Turmoil accompanies this division within oneself, as though
requiring a denial of part of oneself; one desires that the heart
be single, for, as Kierkegaard said, "Purity of heart is to will
one thing."

Love as first in the heart, and then in the will, means that
the "executor-will" spends itself monitoring the heart, never
leading and initiating change of heart. We cannot expect to
effect any true, deep, or permanent affective or ethical conversion by a series, no matter how indefinitely long, of purely
negative, reactionary, consequent vetoes. What then can we
do? "By a long process we can work toward uprooting this
response, or rather toward uprooting the presuppositions of
its becoming. This is the process of a moral transformation
of our nature, and such transformation is the purpose of all
ascetic practices" (323).

One might ask what could cause, or at least occasion, the
reflection back upon oneself implied in any such correction
of one's spontaneous affections. With Levinas we can strongly
affirm that the other, embodied in the face-to-face relation,
is experienced—or, better, "encountered" (to respect Buber's
terminology)—as just this calling into question of my one-way
intentionality, representational and totalitarian, by the two-
way affective consciousness of the infinite value of this other.
The affecting presence of the other occasions both a cognitive reflection and a critique of feeling, questioning the very
meaning of myself as sole source or projector of meanings
(Tallon 1995b). Thus prereflective or prevoluntary "Heart 1"
needs to but may or may not—under the influence of the
head—become "Heart 2," and be a consciousness in solidar-

ity with itself: "The affective response is in itself the position which we take toward an other; thus the sanction, which is the most outspoken conscious position, can join it as its very soul, can go in the same direction as the affective response, can, in melting with it, become one single attitude" (von Hildebrand 1953, 324).

Thus we have two possible head-heart relations, two ways of synthesizing the three intentionalities into triadic consciousness. The heart can lead and the head follow, or, when change of heart is needed, head can lead and heart follow. When the heart leads and head follows, it does so either by becoming one with cognition and volition or disavowing them in the one single attitude. Without such critique of spontaneous affectivity, avowal is presumed: "Affective responses arising in our soul without the direct intervention of our freedom have . . . the character of a position we take toward an other. So long as my free personal center does not disavow them, I implicitly identify myself with them . . . so long as there is no counteraction by the spiritual center . . . . If I make no use of my power to sanction and disavow, I live in undisputed solidarity with my own affective responses" (325). The momentum of feeling sweeps (entrains) all before it: the (e)motion carries. Von Hildebrand thus confirms Pfänder's analyses of chapter 4.

But if the head leads, the strategy adequate to the task of changing one's heart "consists in preparing in our soul the ground from which right responses, rather than wrong responses, will arise spontaneously . . ." (338). This solution is the one descriptively expressed by Pfänder as "preparing the *ground*." Later we express this same notion in terms of an affective connaturality that operates not according to what one *knows* conceptually but according to who and what one *is,* the affective intentionality Merleau-Ponty calls "existence" and Levinas calls "responsibility." As von Hildebrand expresses it, "Affective responses, as well as being affected, depend above all upon that which we call someone's character, one's heart, one's sensitivity to good, and especially one's superactual attitude, one's general inner direction" (338). A change of heart, more than just changing one's mind, implies a change deep in one's being, that is, the change from first to second nature[3] (through habit as virtue). In von Hildebrand's words: "Affective responses . . . and being affected depend themselves upon our character, upon our sensitivity for values, upon our habitual state of being awake, upon our superactual attitudes and responses. Thus our free influence on the coming into being and vanishing of affective responses, as well as being affected or not affected by some good, is only possible through the change of our character" (338).

Nothing less than self-transformation is the goal, a goal we may conceive of as both ethical and mystical. It takes full triadic consciousness, head, heart, *and* will, since "our freedom has a definite role in preparing the ground from which our affective responses arise, and also in forming the way of our being affected . . . the great moral task of transforming our nature . . . the changing of the very ground of our personality . . ." (341); he goes on: ". . . [C]ontemplation embraces not only cognition but also the conscious state of *being affected* by a value . . ." (353).

Affectivity as Spiritual

We now come to the third part of von Hildebrand's contribution. Are we affective beings because we are embodied or because of the very nature of the human spirit as finite? Can we try, still phenomenologically, to gain some insight into the spiritual nature of the heart? Practically this means raising the question whether heart reduces to the "merely sensible part of the soul," or of whether it is itself spiritual. Are there relevant phenomenological data linking feeling with the realm of spirit? The importance of the question whether the heart is at root "spiritual" concerns its rank with cognition and volition. Von Hildebrand has written strongly against the disastrous prejudice [that] is the exclusion of the entire affective life from the spiritual part of human beings. This unfortunate heritage from Greek intellectualism has never been proven and is still less evident . . . . If one considers without prejudice affective value responses such as joy over the conversion of a sinner or deep contrition over a sin, one cannot but state that they possess all the meaningful features and intelligibility which characterize a theoretical response such as the conviction of a truth evidently grasped or an act of will conforming to the moral appeal [1966, 12].

It is as though the very depth and intensity of passionate human love worked against its being considered as spiritual as intellect and will, those angelic powers that make us so "godlike" (as the argument might run). The cost of this very abstract estimation of intellect and will has been to disembody them, of course, to thin them out, so that they have become associated by ordinary folk with the nonhuman, computer-like, emotionless androids of science fiction (like Spock, Data, Tuvok, or the Borg of *Star Trek*). The tradition that denied the spirituality of feeling had to skin love of its flesh and make it a will-act.

As a result, in order to save its spiritual character, love has been deprived of its affective character and made either an act of will, an appetite striving for self-perfection, or a mere movement toward an end . . . . Thus, as one accepted the verdict of the non-spirituality of all affective experiences, the artificial problem imposed itself of interpreting love as something non-affective and as an act of will. The observation of St. Paul's, that if one did not have charity [*agape*] one would still be nothing, though one gave all one's goods to the poor, definitely excludes such an interpretation of love. Since good will is obviously present in someone's desire to give all one's possessions to the poor, love must be more than an act of will [12].

The expression "halfhearted" describes the would-be saint in the Pauline example as someone able to muster only the "will" part of triune consciousness. To be wholehearted means much more. As von Hildebrand puts it, "If knowledge is an '*adequatio intellectus ad rem*,' what happens in an affective response can be characterized as an '*adequatio cordis ad valorem*'" (14). He continues: "Hand in hand with the denial of the spirituality of affectivity goes the thesis that affectivity essentially presupposes the body and is linked to it in a completely different way than is an act of knowledge or of willing. However, this thesis is by no means evident, nor has it been ever really proven" (15). And here he offers at least a suggestion, to take along to the next chapter, for how a phenomenology of affectivity must reveal its spiritual essence in our human experience. He says:

> In fact, this prejudice flows again from the mistake of using the *lowest* type of affective experience as the pattern for affectivity as such. In reality there are several types of feeling which essentially presuppose the body, but this does not apply at all to the *higher* types of affectivity. A headache or the pain felt when one is wounded are bodily feeling in the strict sense of the word. In these cases the feelings are clearly voices of the body, dealing with body, and mostly located in the body. Yet certain affective experiences, which in themselves differ radically from the above mentioned bodily feelings, can also depend upon the body. States of depression, bad humor, or unrest are indeed not bodily experiences, but they are linked to the body in manifold ways. Even though their nature does not make them a voice of the body, they still may be caused by mere physiological processes. The above is not the case with affective *value* responses. *A value-responding joy, or love, or veneration presupposes the body not a whit more than act of will or of knowledge.* There is, of course, the general mysterious relation between the soul and body, but *acts of will and of intellect are no more exempt of this mysterious relation than are affective responses*" [15; my ital.].

Just as we saw, thanks to Ricoeur, two meanings of heart, one "from below" and expressed in embodiment (rooted in *bios-epithumia*), another "from above," the expression of *logos-eros,* so also we will later emphasize, following Lonergan, the differentiation of feeling (that is, of affective consciousness), as it changes its meaning, according to the law of analogy, from the most material to the most spiritual, across the four levels of consciousness, thus supporting von Hildebrand's thesis. Just as analogy applies elsewhere, so does it apply to the concepts of the spiritual and the affective.

There are, then, three levels, at least, sketched above, that one can consider as varying degrees of embodiment of finite spirit depending upon the materialization needed for the kind of intentionality involved. "It is time," he says "to realize that affectivity and spirituality are not incompatible to do justice in an unprejudiced analysis to the nature of these fully affective and highly spiritual experiences. If one examines the nature of an affective value response . . . one must see that this response of one's heart has the same meaningful response character as a response of one's intellect" (14; also see 1960, 180–90).

Appendix
Von Hildebrand on Intentionality: Selected Texts

Here is the first part of the text on which this chapter is based:

> One of the most decisive distinctions to be made in the sphere of our conscious life is that between intentional and unintentional experiences. In saying "intentional," we refer to a conscious, rational relation between the person and an other. Not all human experiences imply such a conscious relation to an other. All pure states, such as being tired, being in a bad humor, being irritated, and so forth, have no conscious relation with an other. They do not imply the specific polarity of the person as against an other. They do not possess the character of transcending the realm of the mind.

We are not tired about something; tiredness is only a state, an experience of something qualitative related to our body, but it does not have any meaningful reference to an other. Of course the state is caused by something. But the objective *causal* relation must not be confused with an *intentional* relation. Whereas our feeling tired in no way presupposes a knowledge of the cause, any intentional experience (such as joy) essentially presupposes a knowledge of the cause of our experience: that is to say, of an other that motivates our experience . . . . Tiredness remains the same whether or not I know its cause. Often we look for the cause of our tiredness, and wonder whether it is due to overwork, disease, or great emotion. The experience of tiredness as such is not affected by an ignorance of its cause . . . . If we compare these states with various experiences of a very different character: for instance, any perception or any response (such as conviction, doubt, joy, sorrow, love, or hatred), we easily see that all these are, despite their thorough differences in other respects, of an *intentional* nature. Perception by its very essence obviously implies the antithesis of a personal subject as opposed to other. It is by its very essence a transcending experience, a *consciousness of* something . . . . In comparing any response to a mere state, the intentional character of the former appears even more evident. Our conviction, for instance, is necessarily *directed toward* something, for there exists no conviction as such; it is always conviction *of* something. It necessarily implies a *conscious, meaningful relation to* something . . . . The conviction itself is a definite *response to* an other; its content is a "yes" to the existence of something [von Hildebrand 1953, 191–93; my ital.] [I've replaced his word "object" with "other" in order to include persons].

Von Hildebrand's distinction between nonintentional states and intentional acts, both cognitions and responses, now being clear, he sharpens our awareness of the intentional essence of responses by contrasting them with "teleological trends." This is done in the second part of the text, which follows:

In order to understand the nature of "intentionality," we have to distinguish intentional experiences, not only from mere states lacking any direction toward an other, but also from all merely teleological trends in human nature. In undergoing an experience such as thirst or a craving for food, we clearly grasp that these are not mere states, for they possess an immanent direction toward something . . . . In place of the static character of a mere state they have a dynamic one . . . a definite tension and direction toward fulfillment, whether this fulfillment consists in appropriating something to us, or in an unloading of vital energies, or in something else.

What matters in our context is the difference between the immanent *trend pushing or leading* us toward something, and the *intentional, meaningful relation to* an other. This instinctive trend also has an element of meaningfulness. As something teleological, it has the element of intelligibility proper to a final cause. Now every final cause presupposes intelligence and will . . . [but t]he final direction is not a personal relation as is the case with intentionality. We experience the trend in our instincts as a blind push toward something. That objectively there is instead a meaningful coordination is something which we may discover only later on "from without" as we do with respect to the finality in a physiological process; but this finality is in no way consciously accomplished in experiencing the instinct.

Intentional experiences, on the contrary, imply a consciously accomplished and *meaningful direction toward* an object; this meaningful direction is a manifestation of our rational personal character. Here the meaningfulness is a personal one; here we act as persons; here a relation exists which is possible only if accomplished by a person. There exists nothing in the impersonal world which could be integrated as intentionality . . . . *Intentionality . . . is a decisive mark of [finite] spirituality.* Teleological relations, on the other hand, pervade the entire nonspiritual world [194–95; my ital. and brackets].

He continues:

> In the realm of the intentional experiences (that is to say, in the sphere of acts) we must make a further fundamental distinction: between cognitive acts and responses. To the cognitive act above all belongs perception in the largest sense of that term. Every time anyone or anything, whatever its nature, reveals itself to our mind a cognitive act is in question. Cognitive acts encompass not only the perception of colors, tones, and in effect, all so-called sense perceptions (such as seeing, hearing, touching, etc.), but also the perception of space, of material bodies, of relations, of other persons, of values, as well as intellectual intuition of essences itself. Imagination and memory belong to cognitive acts despite their decisive difference from perception.
>
> But belief, conviction, doubt, fear, joy, sorrow, enthusiasm, indignation, esteem and contempt, trust and mistrust, love and hatred, all belong to the sphere of responses. *Both cognitive acts and responses have an intentional character. Yet they exhibit a fundamental difference which is expressed in the nature of their intentionality*" [95-96; my ital.].

Finally, von Hildebrand spells out some of the differences between cognitive and affective intentionalities and responses:

> Cognitive acts are first of all characterized by the fact that they are a consciousness of something, that is to say, of the other. We are, as it were, void; the whole content is on the side of the other. When we see the color red, the content (red) is on the other side; we are not red, but we have a consciousness of red.
>
> In feeling joy, on the contrary, the content is on the side of the subject: it is in us; we are not void, but "full" of joy. This content in our soul is directed toward an other. Joy is not a consciousness of something, but is itself a conscious entity, a consciously accomplished reality. The qualitative content is in our act, that is to say, on the side of the subject, not of the other.

Secondly, in the cognitive acts the intention goes, so to speak, from the other to ourselves: the other reveals itself to our mind; it speaks and we listen. In responses as such, the intention goes from us to the other. Language expresses this fact in the words "we are full of joy about something," or "we are enthusiastic over something." In responses it is we who speak: the content of our act is addressed to the other; it is our response to the other.

Thirdly, all cognitive acts have a fundamentally receptive character even though they are not merely passive. We might call it an active passivity or an actively accomplished receptivity . . . . The response, as such, is on the contrary, unreceptive; rather it has a definitely spontaneous character.

The fundamental difference between these two intentional experiences is obvious. But if it is necessary to distinguish between them, it is equally necessary to grasp their essential connection. All responses necessarily presuppose a cognitive act. The other must first reveal itself in its nature, before we can respond to the other.

In this great dialogue between the person and being, cognitive acts form the basis of all other acts and responses. The primary contact with the other is always given by one or another kind of cognitive act . . . . We must first know that our friend will arrive before we can be full of joy about the fact; we must first have a knowledge of a person before we can love or hate her or him. Perception in the largest sense of the term is the fundamental act in which the dialogical situation between person and being is established . . . . All responses necessarily presuppose cognitive acts; they are essentially based on cognitive acts . . . nihil volitum nisi cogitatum (Nothing is willed unless it be thought) [196–97].

Later we see that Lonergan offers two important exceptions, called major and minor, to this Latin maxim, so that sometimes love precedes a higher heart-knowledge.[4] Note that von Hildebrand is attending to the intentional part of affection here, not to the being-affected, to which corresponds the affection of affective intentionality; as Ricoeur has pointed out, it takes both the affection (the being-affected) and the intention (the affective response) to explain feeling.

Notes

1. For the benefit of readers not familiar with von Hildebrand's development of the concept of intentionality, a textual appendix has been included at the end of this chapter.

2. Von Hildebrand 1953, 202–03. Let us conclude this first third of our dialogue with von Hildebrand by reference to Augustine: "St. Augustine . . . touches the very nature of human freedom by stressing in *De libero arbitrio* III, 3 that the will is such a precious good that it suffices to desire it in order to have it present: 'Wherefore nothing is so completely in our power as the will itself. For when we will, immediately, without any interval, the act of will is realized'" [200].

One might comment that this claim doesn't sound very anti-Pelagian, except that only the act of will is realized, not necessarily any consequent action or deed. A second reference to Augustine has to do with love; after he criticizes Aquinas for following Aristotle into making love either a passion or an act of will, von Hildebrand says: "St. Augustine, however, seems to consider love in its full affective plenitude. He sees it as something meaningful, rational, and spiritual; and yet he does not fail to distinguish it from the will. In his famous words: *parum est voluntate etiam voluptate traheris* (*Tractatus 26 in Johannem*: Little is to be drawn by the will, also by delight shalt thou be drawn), he definitely stresses the difference between love and will; and, without denying thereby the spiritual and meaningful character of love, he sees as its essential features affective plenitude, bliss, and the being drawn by delight, features which are lacking in willing" (ibid., 205).

3. Ibid., 362–63: "Thus we see that a virtue requires not only the presence of general superactual attitudes toward a realm of good and their generic value, but also that this intention has victoriously pervaded the entire personality of the virtuous person. It requires that the obstacles of pride and concupiscence have been done away with, and that the general superactual attitude has formed the person's character to such an extent that it has become second nature."

4. For further thoughts on von Hildebrand, see Tallon 1994a.

Chapter 7

The Structure of
Affective Intentionality

> The head is always the dupe of the heart.
> La Rochefoucauld (1613–1680), *Maximes*, no. 102 (1665).

> Tell me where is fancy bred,
> Or in the heart or in the head?
> How begot, how nourished?
> Shakespeare (1564–1616), *The Merchant of Venice*, 3. 2. 63.

> The history of every country begins in the heart of a man or a woman.
> Willa Cather (1876–1947) *O Pioneers!*, pt. ch. 4 (1913).

Summary

Two themes in this chapter conclude presentation of feeling as affective intentionality: the temporal structure of intentionality as identical to that of habit formation and the question about the spiritual nature of affection. Stephan Strasser and Steven Smith are our sources. The essence of spirit and heart's reasons as "sweet" reason are explored.

S TRASSER'S WORK RELATES TO VON HILDEBRAND'S where being-affected or affectability reveals a temporal as well as a causal structure. In his *Phenomenology of Feeling: An*

Essay on the Phenomena of the Heart (1977) *(Das Gemüt)*, he devotes part 3, "The Self-Realization of the Human Spirit and
Its Levels" (181–314), to an analysis of the structure of intentionality and how it reveals the nature of intentionality as spiritual; the chapter titles are: chapter 7, "Heart and Feeling";
chapter 8, "The Pre-intentional Level"; chapter 9, "The Intentional Level"; chapter 10, "The Level of Spirit," wherein
the meaning of the postintentional or metaintentional level
is treated.

The second point where Strasser expands upon von Hildebrand is the spiritual nature of affectivity. Part 4 of *Phenomenology of Feeling* is called: "Happiness: Demonstration of a Phenomenological Typology of Transcending Experience" (317–
79); in an indirect way it addresses the spiritual nature of the
heart, while, as is obvious even from the outline of part 3 just
given, this question is addressed in chapter 10 also. The easi-
est summary of Part Four might be that happiness cannot be
an idea in the mind but must be a reality in the heart; if one
does not *feel* happy, one *is not* happy. It is an experience, not
an idea. One can feel pleasure (the lower *bios-epithumia*) and
still be unhappy, or be happy (the higher *eros-logos*) even when
suffering physical pain. Happiness resides in the deepest (or
highest) "part" of the person and thus must be something
radically spiritual: ". . . [H]appiness is in the affective sphere
. . . for the only way to experience happiness is to feel it . . . .
For knowledge could only have the role of a source of happiness; happiness itself by its very nature has to be felt; a happiness which is only 'thought' or 'willed' is no happiness. Happiness becomes a word without meaning when we sever it
from feeling, the only form of experience in which it can be
consciously lived" (von Hildebrand 1977, 26). And yet happiness is the highest good of the human spirit, thus suggesting
again that heart also means spirit, as finite, that is, as a capacity for happiness, a potentiality not actualized without otherness, without that intentionality which is primacy of and kinesis to otherness and which marks all finitude.

With that brief introduction to Strasser's two points, let us turn to the first, on the structure of intentionality. Wood, in his excellent introduction to Strasser's work, identifies chapter 7, on "Heart and Feeling," as

> the nuclear chapter of the book[:] . . . feelings that permeate the whole of our consciousness: dispositions (*Stimmungen*) [are distinguished into] two senses of disposition . . . an intentional sense—for example, when one is angrily disposed toward someone—and a pre-intentional sense—for example, when one wakes up with an angry disposition. Disposition in the second sense is the pre-intentional ground from which intentional acts spring; but it is also receptive to the reverberations which intentional acts produce. It constitutes the thymic residue of experience that becomes the dynamic matrix of human activity [1977, 27; my brackets].

The ground or matrix from which emanate intentional acts is itself in continual flux and is, in fact, the effect and residual deposit of those acts. The circular (feedback) structure of intentionality accounts for the self-transforming structure of habit formation, and for the way we acquire the virtues and vices that constitute our second nature. The reflexivity of immanent actions also appears here. In immanent acts the agent relates to itself as cause and effect, as affirmed in the idea of freedom as *self*-determination. One relates to oneself as part to whole, insofar as some one specific and individual act that one performs leaves oneself changed and different as a whole, as the very person one is, this impatient, selfish, or loving person. As intentional, these immanent acts are also social and interpersonal, transcending the limits of one's being, moving toward and returning from other beings upon whom one depends, as recipients for one's acts, and upon whom depend the meaning of those acts.

Self-determination means that one determines who and what one is through the circular structures proper to intentionality. The *modified* self then becomes the starting point for subsequent actualizations of oneself. Thus conversion is not a "once in a lifetime being born again"; a basic reflex arc is always at work. The third element, namely, the dependence on others, *may* come to the fore dramatically in some memorable conversion experiences, but conversion as constant change, as *continual development*, whether positive or negative, is intentionality itself, and is a necessity for finite spirit. Thus the question is not so much *whether* to change, since we are always changing, but whether we responsibly take charge of the changes that are always ongoing. Our task is to cooperate, by discernment, with those agents and forces that are at work for our change for the better. Hillman's theory (1961) sees this structure manifested in a psychological phenomenology, where emotion (along with feeling and affectivity), especially love, is intended precisely for the change and transformation of the person who lives that emotion (Tallon 1983). Thus the circle of intentionality, a circular relation where head sometimes follows heart and sometimes leads. As Wood puts it:

> [T]he will-act presupposes the rootage of the full act-complex in a habit of openness, of receptivity and of response that terminates in a kind of spontaneous welling up of feeling in relation to the person to whom one gives such heartfelt thanks or to the task into which one puts one's heart. It is upon such an habitually rooted upsurge of feeling that the will-acts tend to follow as ripe fruit from a healthy tree. Here we meet that "fullness of heart out of which the mouth speaks." On the other hand, in an expression like the liturgical "Lift up your hearts!" it would seem that the will-act is expected to precede and effect the state of feeling [1977, 6].

To turn now to Strasser's second point is to return to the question of the possibility of a double meaning of "heart," a lower and a higher, already suggested by Ricoeur as the *bios-*

epithumia heart (*thumos* rooted in embodiment, aiming as the partial good [pleasure]), and the *logos-eros* heart (*thumos* as spiritual passion for happiness as the total good of the person). Von Hildebrand has also offered arguments for a second, higher meaning of heart. In the coming chapters we meet the thesis of a developmental continuum from the primal heart, through the headwork of reason and will, to the mature higher synthesis of triune consciousness. The principle of continuum through all levels of meaning of heart is affective intentionality experienced as feelings and moods. So we ask, with Strasser: How is feeling spiritual? Classical idealism grants spirituality to intellect and will, to the world of *Geist* (spirit), but not to *Mut* (mood) or *Gemüt* (heart). As von Hildebrand has lamented, affectivity and spirituality have usually been considered incompatible; one does not feel the mind think. In other words, the argument runs, if you can feel something you know by that very fact that it cannot be spiritual. (Thus we get a god who cannot feel and grace that cannot be experienced.) We seem, therefore, in an impossible situation where by definition we cannot feel heart and still claim its spiritual essence. Obviously the definition is too narrow, as Strasser shows by his phenomenology of happiness as goal and term of human self-transcendence.

To generalize about transcendence Strasser prefers the term disposition (*Stimmung*), a word familiar from Heidegger's use of it in *Sein und Zeit* and rendered in French as *tonalité affective*. We sense, perceive, feel, experience, live our finitude affectively (that is, we do more than merely know it in an idea or accept it by an act of will): human finitude is lived in, with, through, by a definite affection, the mood *Angst*, the echo of our finitude felt as temporality, the constant background music of our being-toward-death (*Sein-zum-Tode*). We alone among conscious animals seem to know we will die, so we bury our dead and create art, ethics, religion. Our problem centers on the very meaning of spirit as capable of experiencing the absolute (*capax Dei*): How can such a capacity be

the property of a finite spirit, since infinity seems by very definition beyond, outside, transcendent, and thus thoroughly
refractory to any mind containing it or will's attaining it? As
Strasser put it: ". . . [I]nsofar as human consciousness . . .
experiences something of the absolute, it is spiritual consciousness" (272). There is no stipulation that this experience must
be theoretical or volitional rather than affective; Strasser stipu-
lates no limitation of the absolute to idea or free choice to
the exclusion of emotion. May not affectivity offer as good
access to the absolute? Heidegger's doctrine on mood said it
offered *better* access to the meaning of Being. The *Vorgriff*,
anticipating *touch* of the infinite, puts the finite in our *grasp*.

Strasser offers a compelling illustration of this principle.
He takes from Pradines the comparison of human emotion
or affective responses, pushed to an absolute, with those of
an animal pushed to its limits. Since *the limits are quite different*, the results should show in their behavior; they should be
phenomenologically quite distinct and different.

> Thus from the interior of the organism a surge of excite-
> ment flows which takes visible, expressive form on the sur-
> face of the body, on the region of the boundary and the
> connection between the animal and its environment. In
> this sense, one can very well speak of animal joy, disap-
> pointment, rage, depression, desire, etc., and point out the
> similarity to the corresponding human expressive phenom-
> ena. But there is only one thing one should not overlook
> here: all these feeling-laden manifestations of the life of
> animals belong to their behavior, while the emotional
> breakdown of the meaningful behavior of humans serves
> an end. The animal likewise obeys the adaptive governance
> by feeling with great affectivity; it is then also still "*en route*"
> [on the way] and not "*dérouté* [detoured]." "Even when a
> dog fights in the state of extreme rage, it adapts its efforts
> to its goals, exploits the failings and weaknesses of its op-
> ponent and still watches over it when it flees," notes Pra-
> dines (1946, I, 707–08).[1] On the contrary, human beings,

fascinated by the absolute, run the risk of transgressing the boundaries of behavior. Pradines produces two examples: the excessive desire of love whereby the lover breaks down because of his emotional excitement (1946, I, 732), and the emotional anguish of one who finds herself in danger of death . . . . *Only a being gifted with spirit is capable of violent emotion, of hopelessness, of shame, of remorse, of catharsis*, and so forth [Strasser 1977, 273–74; my ital.].

Only a being capable of the absolute (*capax Dei*), only a being with a heart, in precisely the sense we mean in ordinary language as well as in the phenomenologically descriptive realm of totally "out of bounds" affectivity, thus only a passionate being can lose its reason; only a rational being can be irrational: "Being endangered by emotional breakdown is just the price which we humans have to pay for our reason" (273), meaning that to be a being blessed or gifted with reason is also to be a being capable of totally transcending and thus losing all measure and manner of dealing with the nonabsolute. Only a being with a heart can lose it or give it away. To lose heart in despair or to give one's heart away in love are both "mad" in the "excess" that, as Sheehan (1987) has so well shown, give us "access" to what is truly human, the very finite spirit that is the human soul. Only a being with a heart can believe, love, hope, hate, or despair.

We must rethink the meaning of spirit to fit our human experience of happiness and affective responses, rather than merely apply an idea of spirit that is imported from a metaphysics not drawn from a phenomenology of feeling as a full partner in triadic consciousness, and then mistakenly reject the idea of heart essential to the spirit and core of the person. Only *openness to the absolute*, which is the *meaning and mark of the spiritual*, can explain the atrocious cruelty of torture and terror done to a being, human or animal, by a crazed person whose floodgates of passion have broken down. What else but this spiritual essence of affect can set and then ex-ceed the limits of sacrifice or sanctity in one polarized by the absolute? "That which sets these mechanisms in motion is spiritual experience" (274).

Spirit & Sweet Reason

Stephen G. Smith's *The Concept of the Spiritual* (1988) offers masterful analyses that help us relate the affections of the heart to the domain of the spiritual. Smith presents the meaning of spirit in a book of over three hundred pages. For purposes of this study his distinction between hard reason and sweet reason is especially valuable. Spirit as "macho" force or power had to come on hard times as a viable concept when, as St. Paul says, "What I will I do not, and what I will not, that I do." In other words, a false idea of spirit as invisible force—will to power (*Wille zur Macht*)—has too long beset philosophy. One imagines "the Force" of *Star Wars,* or some other divine or demonic psychokinetic power that can annihilate worlds by pointing a finger, by giving the "evil eye," by casting a spell or waving a magic wand, or by the mere unuttered wish in the mind of some omnipotent being—the stuff of fantasy and bad science fiction. But this is, as Kierkegaard says in a wonderful passage on freedom and omnipotence, a mean and low idea of almighty power.[2]

There is a better idea of spirit than invisible force. Power there is, but conceived on a different model, as in a different order, an interpersonal order, or an "interintentional order," as Smith calls it, that is, an order between persons as persons, not between physical forces. In a section entitled "The Basic Structure of Reason" (1988, 127–40), Smith contrasts, on the one hand, "hard reason," which works its way by requiring assent by marshalling rigorous, irresistible logic, bringing opponents to their knees by sheer force of necessity grounded in noncontradiction, and, on the other hand, "sweet reason." Sweet reason, like Kierkegaard's God, whose very omnipotence liberates us into true freedom, turns the tables on the use of force by being strong enough to live above contradiction and all duality, like Meister Eckhardt's *Gottheit* beyond the gods. This is the spirit of nonviolent resistance, the ethical and mystical might of right.

The great virtue of Smith's idea, drawn from his study of Levinas (1983), is to demythologize a false mechanistic idea of spirit as just an invisible, supernatural, but still ultimately physical force, operating merely by a more subtle body, but still by material coercion. He rightly recognizes that for most of us, until critically examined, spirit is no different from matter, just rendered invisible, inaudible, and so on, like breath or wind; these originary experiences as tornadoes and hurricanes (*ruach, pneuma, spiritus*) can be terribly destructive as well as life giving. But spirit means a totally different ground proper to *persons,* not physical force, appealing to what the most ancient tradition calls heart. Smith invites us to attain *this* meaning of spirit and sweet reason, a reason operating *within triune consciousness:*

> Sweet reason furnishes a place to stand, and when it can, a better place to stand, a place to flourish. Under the aspect of surplus, spiritual demands appear in the first place as opportunities, bonuses to seize rather than shortfalls to avoid. One gives reasons for seizing them in a second moment of turning around and contemplating the alternative of not having done so, which would be a shortfall, so that only the chosen course was right enough. In that sense reason is always "hard" and constraining. But it should be recognized that the constraining aspect can be the correlate of an initially permissive aspect. One's zeal for a more can precede one's fear of a less, and one can give grounds for believing or doing something on that basis. . . .
>
> Hume's dictum that reason is slave of the passions is a skewed but not wholly wrong way of saying that reason is a tool of intention and that it exists in an interintentional context. Praise Hume for at least pointing to this truth. By holding it in view we can understand not only the basic structures of hard reason, which reflect the conditions of the possibility of intending at all; and not only the one

structure of sweet reason, the principle of sufficient ground, which most resembles hard reason; but also the specifically sweetest forms of reason, which might together be called the reasons of *surplus* insofar as they make a proposition right enough by linking it to intentional rewards in excess of what was required of intention or what it looked for. This felicitation of intention counts as reason when it occurs as an explicitated object of affirmation or action, insofar as it leads to the fundamental goods and thus is nonarbitrary. By contrast, in the implicit effect of, say a *work of art*, there is a *surplus of intentional amplitude without any "reasoning"*—although, for *this* reason, it is a *good* thing to experience it, and therefore in the absence of countervailing considerations one *should* experience it [1988, 135–36; my ital.].

An example of surplus is the *otherness* of the other, a manifestation of *spirit* in the *other's irreducibility to my idea* of the other; beyond mind does not mean beyond heart, because while the other may not be knowable in any sense of representational ideas, the other may still be "in" consciousness (that is, intended) under the form of affective intentionality, knowable nonobjectively, that is, coknown (subsidiarily rather than focally, as Polanyi would say) as infinite horizon, as ground against and on which everything known objectively about the other takes place. There is a long tradition about the excess or surplus overflowing consciousness, a surplus incomprehensible (in the sense of uncontainable) by that consciousness even while constantly there in the background; it goes by the name of the infinite:

[A]s both Descartes and Levinas argue, the inadequacy of thought to the Infinite does not count as a privation of the sort that reason is bound to disapprove of; it is rather a *surplus of a sort that reason should glory in.* Descartes claims that he conceives of God more clearly and distinctly than anything else, which is an inaccurate way of putting the point that it is an even greater degree impossible to doubt

God's reality than to doubt his own (Descartes 1911, 1:166, Meditation 3). He is dazzled by brightness rather than defeated by darkness. But Levinas means to criticize the Augustinian appetite for Being that Descartes also represents. The Other is for him not something overwhelming the faculty of knowledge, but something that eludes it. Still, the import of the Other for the life of the self is positive. Living with and toward the Other is an absolute adventure (Levinas 1969, 305).

Now, the notion of adventure is an enticement, even for reason within a narrower horizon than the one we have envisioned. It is a kind of *absolute promise of "more"*—having more happen to one, finding more, getting more. There is an *innate avidity in intention,* from which spring not only the unattractive forms of ordinary greed but also romantic *Sehnsucht* and divine discontent with the world as it is. Sweet reason speaks to this avidity and lures it on but in the end tricks it by placing spiritual conditions on it, so that it becomes zeal for the others and for what is shared with them. Levinas's promise of an idea of the Infinite—a promise that Hegel also makes, with very different results—suggests to thought that it can possess just what it always wanted, an unquestionable relationship with exteriority. And this relationship is delivered, but as the unknowable: justice instead of a truth. Levinas's promise of adventure takes the *essential move of intention, to aim at others and stretch toward them,* and then perfects it into the aimingest aim and stretchingest stretch, a move that keeps going outward without ever heading back for home. This is what one was bound for from the moment one's attention was caught by the others.

The two basic forms of justification by intentional surplus correspond to the two demands of the spiritual concrete, that for the peaceful conservation of plurality and that for its heightening via the amplification of intentions in relationship. They are, respectively, the convergence of different factors which all support a proposition, and the fecundity of a proposition in generating other supportable ones [Smith 1988, 137–38; my ital.].

Smith concludes the section (with an allusion to an example used to illustrate interintentionality) by reaffirming the thesis that while access to others escapes grasping and objectifying (Levinas would say "totalizing") intentionality (that is, the hard reason of the head), there is *in the (sweet) reasons of the heart a different intentionality that is the real meaning of spirit,* conceived on a model different from the emanated physical modality that marks our finitude.

> *A sweet reason is the only kind one can give to another in which the otherness of the other is directly affirmed.* When the girls urge Janet to play dodgeball by saying "It's fun," they lay the proposal before her to accept or reject. This makes them vulnerable, as one properly is before an other. They open themselves to her irrefutable contradiction at the same time that they open a possibility up to her; if she says "No, it's dumb," that could spoil the game. A network of reasoning created in this way is quite a fragile one inasmuch as the assent of all parties to it, which is absolutely contingent in any case, *appears as* contingent, whereas the network of logic requires an obedience from all parties that appears as necessary. *Assent arises in joy,* while obedience is exacted. *The whole being pours into assent,* while nothing is yielded to that which exacts except that which is exacted. And intention cannot be exacted. Freedom is its essence in the self, and imponderability is its essence in the other. So the only way in which intention, the *how* of thinking, saying, and doing, can be directly normed is by sweet reason [Smith 1988, 139–40; my ital.].

Sweet reason is only possible because cognition is warmed by nearness to affection, inside one triune consciousness, as part of the higher synthesis of all three intentionalities in their connatural interintentional contexts, the ethical and mystical (both rooted in æsthetic beauty as our felt harmony with values connatural to us).

Conclusion:
The First Seven Chapters

The existence of a distinct affective consciousness, with its own distinct intentionality—irreducible either to cognition, as it is in a rationalist tradition (which makes feeling at best just another, secondary, way of *knowing*), or to volition, as was a common voluntarist tradition (absorbing affection into *appetitus*, natural and intellectual)—and a question about characterizing its essence as (finitely) spiritual has been raised in these chapters. On a positive conclusion to this first part of our investigation depends the thesis of triune consciousness and the rejection of the thesis of a dyad of intellect and will, where affectivity is relegated to the body dualistically considered as somehow not really part of the human essence, not really part of the "soul," taken as the *forma corporis* and ultimate determining formal cause of everything human. The preparation for this conclusion was seven chapters of contributions from many sources centered on feeling as affective intentionality. Now, to interpret is not merely to repeat, but instead to understand and judge. To do that we need another method. Description, as done by the phenomenological method, may choose never to leave the planes of experience and become hermeneutics through understanding and judgment. But we need insight into our experience before we understand it, and we need to conceptualize it to express it in another language, one that sometimes goes by the name "metaphysics," and by which I mean the causes that form and structure the experience we have been describing. Good phenomenology makes insight possible, easier, likely. There must now be a bridge from phenomenology to hermeneutics and metaphysics, from description to understanding and judgment; heart means not only the deepest physical passion rooted in flesh and blood, but also the highest meta-physical self-transcendence toward the absolute in the ethical and mystical.

Notes

1. Strasser (ibid., 273) adds: "Likewise in the case of humans there are states of excitement which have as their consequence a heightening of psychic and physical capacities for performance. Yet it is easy to demonstrate the intentional character of these powerful feelings—for example, fear, hope, rivalry, etc."

2. This is how Kierkegaard puts it: "The whole question of the relation of God's omnipotence and goodness to evil (instead of the differentiation that God accomplishes the good and merely permits the evil) is resolved quite simply in the following way. The greatest good, after all, which can be done for a being, greater than anything else that one can do for it, is to make it free. In order to do just that, omnipotence is required.

"This seems strange, since it is precisely omnipotence that supposedly would make [a being] dependent. But if you reflect on omnipotence, you will see that it also must contain the unique qualification of being able to withdraw itself again in a manifestation of omnipotence in such a way that precisely for this reason that which has been originated through omnipotence can be independent. This is why one human being cannot make another person wholly free, because the one who has power is captive in having it and therefore continually has a wrong relationship to the person you want to make free. Moreover, there is a finite self-love in all finite power (talent, etc.). Only omnipotence can withdraw itself at the same time it gives itself away, and this relationship is the very independence of the receiver. God's omnipotence is therefore God's goodness. For goodness is to give oneself away completely, but in such a way that by omnipotently taking oneself back one makes the recipient independent.

"All finite power makes [a being] dependent; only omnipotence can make [a being] independent, can form from nothing something which has its continuity in itself through the continual withdrawing of omnipotence. Omnipotence is not ensconced in a relationship to an other, for there is no other to which it is comparable—no, it can give without giving up the least of its power, i.e., it can make [a being] independent.

"It is incomprehensible that omnipotence is not only able to create the most impressive of all things—the whole visible world—but is able to create the most fragile of all things—a being independent of that very omnipotence. Omnipotence, which can handle the world so toughly and with such a heavy hand, can also make itself so light that what it has brought into existence receives independence. *Only a wretched and mundane conception of the dialectic of power holds that it is greater and greater in proportion to its ability to compel and to make dependent.* No, Socrates had a sounder understanding; he knew that the art of power lies precisely in making another free. But in the relationship between persons this can never be done, even though it needs to be emphasized again and again that this is the highest; only omnipotence can truly succeed in this. Therefore if we had the slightest independent existence over against God (with regard to *materia*), then God could not make us free. Creation out of nothing is once again the Almighty's expression for being able to make [a being] independent. The God to whom I owe absolutely everything, although still absolutely in control of everything, has in fact made me independent. If in creating humankind God lost a little power, then precisely what God could not do would be to make us independent" [Kierkegaard 1970, 2: 62–63 (entry #1251; my ital.]. (Thanks to Howard Hong for pointing me to this text.)

Chapter 8

Triune Consciousness

Where my heart lies, let my brain lie also.
Robert Browning (1812–1889), *One More Word*,14 (1855).

God be in my heart, And in my thinking.
Sarum Missal

An honest heart being the first blessing, a knowing head is the second.
Thomas Jefferson (1743–1826), Letter to Peter Carr (1785).

When the heart is won, the understanding is easily convinced.
Charles Simmons

Summary

We move from description to interpretation, from phenomenology (ch. 1–7) to hermeneutics (ch. 8–10), to the thesis of triadic consciousness: only when head and heart are integrated with will in an operational synthesis of affection, cognition, and volition do we have an adequate idea of human consciousness.

Introduction

IN THE INTRODUCTION I sketched out a general structure of the four levels of consciousness focusing primarily on cognition and volition. In order to introduce feeling as a full and equal partner in consciousness, and thereby to establish a higher operational synthesis of all three modes of consciousness called triune consciousness, I have devoted the foregoing chapters to establishing the concept of affective intentionality as the best way to understand the experience of feelings, the heart's reasons. It is time to fulfill the promise of integrating affection into consciousness and to establish the triadic structure of consciousness as affection, volition, and volition.

We have a working analogy that allows us to integrate head and heart, namely: *insight is to truth what feeling is to value.* This formula does not make an emotion or feeling just another form of cognition but recognizes, on the basis of the foregoing chapters, that affection enjoys its *own* intentionality, qualitatively different from that of cognition and volition. Affective consciousness *does not intend knowledge at all*, but since affection *is* a mode of consciousness, there occurs a secondary kind of knowledge common to all consciousness, at least implicitly at the disposition of the subject. If we accept the idea that affection intends value, parallel to and complementing cognition's intending truth and volition's intending action, we are already on the way to an integrated triad. To paraphrase Dame Edith Sitwell, the fire of the heart and the light of the mind will never be one, because, while being forever joined inseparably in the embrace of one consciousness, yet they forever remain distinct; their very irreducibility to one another is what makes them able to *be for* each other and give to each other what they both need to *fulfill their finality in action.*

But it will not suffice to present affective intentionality as the meaning of feeling, nor even to show how the integration of all three modes of consciousness looks in schematic design. We also need to ask another question, namely, *how* exactly does feeling operate at the interior of triune consciousness? *How* does affective intentionality work? If we look at the long history of epistemology, practically coextensive with the history of philosophy itself, we can recognize that explaining how cognition works has occupied philosophers' minds for a much longer time than has explaining how emotions and feelings work. So we need to raise this question. In response I propose—in the three value domains that have been in the background throughout this study, namely, the æsthetic, the ethical, and the mystical—that the concept of *connaturality* provides what we need to understand how affective intentionality works. If connaturality explains affection, we shall have succeeded in the first part of our metaphysical task of grounding and supporting the phenomenology of affective intentionality just presented, and thus advanced closer to the goal of establishing human consciousness as essentially and necessarily a triad. In chapter 9 we will find that there are several parts to an understanding of connaturality. In chapter 10 we will go more deeply into connaturality itself, since to explain this relatively unfamiliar term imposes upon us a final step of taking a new look at the ancient idea of *habitus*. In the end we will find that connaturality is not only the way to understand how affective consciousness works, but also the way to understand how the whole of triune consciousness itself works in its highest mode of operation. Thus, while we begin with connaturality in relation to affection—led by the often-used phrase "*affective* connaturality"—we will come to realize that the term is more properly said not of affective consciousness alone but of the mode of operation of *triune* consciousness itself, in the æsthetic but most especially in the domains of the ethical and the mystical. Affective connaturality, as we shall see, is a synecdoche for triune consciousness.

The most important mediæval text (and Ricœur's main source) that lies at the origin of the modern version of this concept is Aquinas's *Summa theologiae* 2 .2, q.45, a.2.

> We have said that wisdom implies a certain rightness in judging according to divine norms. Now rightness in judging can come about in two ways, through the perfect use

of reason or through a certain *natural kinship* [*propter connaturalitatem quamdam*] with the things one is judging about. Thus in matters of chastity, one who is versed in moral science will come to a right judgment through rational investigation, another who possesses the *virtue* of chastity will be right through a kind of *instinctive affinity* [*per quamdam connaturalitatem*]. So it is with divine things. A correct judgment made through rational investigation belongs to the wisdom which is an intellectual *virtue*. But to judge aright through a certain *fellowship* [*secumdum quamdam connaturalitatem*] with them belongs to that wisdom which is the gift of the Holy Spirit. Dionysius says that Hierotheus is perfected in divine things for he not only learns about them but suffers them as well. Now this *sympathy* [*compassio*], or *connaturality* [*connaturalitas*] with divine things, results from charity which unites us to God; he who is joined to the Lord is one spirit with him [my ital. and brackets].

By using this text we get some working definitions; we see that "connaturality" means a way of acting based more on a felt resonance and felt harmony (or dissonance and disharmony) between one's *doing* with one's *being* or *nature* (hence the term "connatural") *rather than on discursive reasoning and deliberative willing*. My thesis says (1) that what we usually mean by heart (and the higher human feelings associated with it) is a mode of consciousness phenomenologically described by affective intentionality, which is itself explained by the *felt connaturality between a being and its doing*; a nature is and has a law according to which it resonates with its actions, past, present, and future. The thesis further says (2) that connaturality is itself best understood as "first nature's" *attunement by and resonance with second nature* (habit: virtue and/or vice), which plays the most important operative role in consciousness. It is because connaturality is a relatively unfamiliar concept that we will have to dig a bit more deeply (in ch. 9 and 10) in order to uncover its underlying structure. As we saw earlier, Ricoeur also linked connaturality with habit, thus not only giving the clue that refers to those Scholastics he cites as the source for this concept, but also furnishing the further clue that habit is the best way to explain connaturality itself (very clear in Caldera [1980]). Habit, as we saw with de Finance, is the mediating and modifying structure between being and doing, between a nature and its action, where habit is understood as a "having" that interposes or "installs" between nature and action: being (first nature) ——➤ having (*habitus*, second nature) ——➤ doing (action). In its more properly human deployment, connaturality is attunement, *Befindlichkeit*, primarily operative intersubjectively (and only secondarily with reference to things) in the realm of values most important and connatural to persons: æsthetics (the beautiful), ethics (the good), and mysticism (the holy).

How Feeling Fits into Triune Consciousness

For economy and clarity let us focus chiefly on one area of the applicability of connaturality, the *ethical*, which most directly involves our relations with other human persons. We will also comment on a second area, of less direct but infinitely rich philosophical interest, the *mystical*, which involves our relations beyond the human, traditionally called the realm of the sacred, holy, numinous, transcendent, absolute, infinite, divine; we do so not because I wish to do theology, but because (1) our main textual source includes mention of this second area of connaturality, and so requires *some* treatment, and (2) because in the course of that treatment we uncover an *example* of something useful philosophically despite its theological origin. To make use of such an example will not undermine the independent philosophical validity of this study, as will become obvious from the example itself, as well as from our limited treatment of it and from the nature of the conclusions to be drawn from it. As for the third area, the æsthetic, we will not treat it at all; Maritain (1953), Gilby (1934), and others use connaturality in the æsthetic domain.

Feeling Is Analogous to Its Level of Consciousness

To know how feeling fits into the four levels of consciousness requires that we note that *feeling is analogous to the level of
consciousness on and in which it is experienced;* this must be remembered as we ascend through the levels of consciousness
from the lowest level to the highest. In other words, the *meaning of feeling changes* as it occurs on each of the four levels, just
as does that of cognition and volition. Let me now sketch
without much detail how feeling fits into triune consciousness, that is, initially, suggest its changing sense at each level.

1. At the lowest level of experience, in empirical consciousness, for example, in sense experience, feeling can mean
physical, sensible experience, such as simple pleasure and
pain, ordinary physical touch, something as basic as an itch,
heat, cold, pressure, and so on. Obviously some of these feelings are merely the nonintentional states or teleological trends
or tendencies mentioned above.

2. At the second level, that of intelligent consciousness,
the level of understanding, feeling can mean psychological
curiosity (when asking questions), the passion for knowledge,
desire to understand, to reach truth, do research, explore
the unknown; feeling at this level can mean joy, confidence,
interest, doubt—when insights come—and satisfaction, con-
tentment, anticipation, further piqued interest—when the
concepts, ideas, and theories are created as a result of insight, grasped as temporary and possible truths, remaining
to be tested at the third level of consciousness. At this second
level, creative and even daring philosophical or scientific hypotheses are formulated, with all the emotion associated with
them. In an interesting sense, an entire culture, even a civili-
zation of centuries' duration, is an unproved hypothesis about
how to live, and all the affections, moods, and attitudes of a
people in relation to their way of life, especially as their history unfolds and as their ethos comes into contact and perhaps into conflict with other theories of how to be human,
exist as feelings at this second level of consciousness.

3. At the third level, that of judgment, new and different feelings go with digging up evidence to verify the insights of level 2, such as new and heightened curiosity, keener anticipation, perhaps a human kind of faith (or doubt) in one's methods, instruments, data, with renewed commitment and devotion to one's project, and with hope (or despair) for its success, and with respect, even reverence, for nature and its mysteries; these are feelings, even if not always recognized as such. When experiments are planned and executed, in the laboratory or in the field, the meaning of the very experience of feeling changes as consciousness itself ascends to each higher level, building upon the lower levels beneath it. It is here that we begin to refer to such increasingly complex and deeper feelings, such as wonder, compassion, concern, awe, perhaps even when we refer to an elegant and now firmly established mathematical proof or scientific law, as spiritual.

4. At the fourth level, we use the language of faith, trust, love, hope, peace, anxiety, joy, ecstasy, bliss, rapture; these all involve quasi-operations of affective consciousness, and cannot be reduced either to cognitional or volitional consciousness alone. They are the affective acts and states experienced at the fourth level of consciousness, inseparable (but irreducibly distinct) from our deliberations, decisions, choices, and other volitional acts, those voluntary acts (acts of will) that characterize the fourth level of consciousness,; and they are different from though analogous to feelings experienced at lower levels of consciousness.

Developmental Concept of Feelings & Moods

It follows from the above-mentioned analogy ("Feeling is to value what insight is to truth") that parallel to becoming self-transcending subjects of *truth* we are to become self-transcending subjects of *value*. The latter does not automatically follow from the former but instead requires real growth and development in the affective life of the conscious person. Development of feeling is analogous to development of a skill. Like

the insight that feeling is affective intentionality, the insight
that feelings admit of development, analogous to skills, is crucial to the thesis of triadic consciousness.

> No less than of skills, there is a *development* of feelings. It is
> true, of course, that fundamentally *feelings are spontaneous.*
> They do not lie under the command of decision as do the
> motions of our hands. But, once they have arisen, they may
> be reinforced by advertence and approval, and they may
> be curtailed by disapproval and distraction. Such reinforce-
> ment and curtailment not only will encourage some feel-
> ings and discourage others but also will *modify one's sponta-
> neous scale* of preference. Again, *feelings are enriched and re-
> fined* by attentive study of the wealth and variety of the ob-
> jects that arouse them, and so no small part of education
> lies in fostering and developing a climate of discernment
> and taste, of discriminating praise and carefully worded
> disapproval, that will conspire with the pupils' or students'
> own capacities and tendencies, enlarge and deepen their
> *apprehension of values,* and help them *towards self-transcen-
> dence.*
>   I have been conceiving *feelings as intentional responses*
> but I must add that they are not merely transient, limited
> to the time that we are apprehending a value or its oppo-
> site, and vanishing the moment our attention shifts. There
> are, of course, feelings that easily are aroused and easily
> pass away. There are too the feelings that have been
> snapped off by repression to lead thereafter an unhappy
> subterranean life. But there are *in full consciousness feelings
> so deep and strong,* especially when deliberately reinforced,
> that they *channel attention, shape one's horizon, direct one's life.*
> Here the supreme illustration is loving. A man or woman
> who falls in love is engaged in loving not only when attend-
> ing to the beloved but at all times. Besides particular acts
> of loving, there is the prior *state of being* in love, and that
> prior state is, as it were, the *fount of all one's actions*
> [Lonergan 1972, 32–33; my ital.].

Here love is called both a feeling and a *state*; as *acts become habits*, so *feelings become moods*, that is, superactual, virtual, habitual, dynamic states. This "fount of all one's actions" is the feeling that has become the habitual state, disposition, attitude of that feeling, its mood. A mood in this higher sense is a habit of the heart. Even spontaneous action issues from a prior state over which one can and sometimes must exercise cognitional and volitional control (the headwork aimed at change of heart).[1] The idea of development of feelings and moods is the basis of our finding the deeper meaning of connaturality to lie in the idea of habit and to apply beyond affectivity more properly to triune consciousness as operational synthesis. (We definitely have to recover in philosophy this deeper meaning of moods as longer lasting attunements of human nature mediating between shorter duration habits and quasi-permanent character.)

Heart as "what one spontaneously is" is the source or ground of affective responses, different from the attending, inquiring, understanding, conceiving, judging, and deciding operations of cognition and volition. But what one spontaneously is could be other than what one wants to be or should be, and a major role of headwork is to change one's spontaneous responses. Successful working of reason and will upon heart and feeling is part of self-transcendence, which is the necessary condition for an affectivity worth trusting, with all its power to influence cognition and will, as it operates as the heart of triadic consciousness. Self-transcendent affectivity is in touch not just with the subjectively agreeable but with objectively authentic value. As we saw with von Hildebrand, affective conversion changes one's value *apprehensions*, changes one's value *judgments*, and changes one's affective *responses*. Feelings and values then become mutually illuminating and enriching:

Such judgments [that is, value judgments] are *objective* or merely subjective inasmuch as they proceed or do not proceed from a *self-transcending* subject. Their truth or falsity, accordingly, has its criterion in the *authenticity* or the lack of authenticity of the subject's *being* [which is the meaning of connaturality, that is, felt relation to one's *being or nature* rather than to one's *concepts or thinking*] . . . . Judgments of value differ in content but not in structure from judgments of fact. [Hence the analogy: insight is to truth as feeling is to value.] *They differ in content*, for one can approve of what does not exist, and one can disapprove of what does. *They do not differ in structure*, inasmuch as in both there is the distinction between criterion and meaning. *In both, the criterion is the self-transcendence of the subject*, which, however, is only cognitive in judgments of fact but is heading towards *moral self-transcendence in judgments of value*. In both, the meaning is or claims to be independent of the subject: judgments of fact state or purport to state what is or is not so; judgments of value state or purport to state what is or is not truly good or really better .

   Intermediate between judgments of fact and judgments in value lie *apprehensions of value*. Such apprehensions are *given in feelings* . . . . Apprehensions of value occur in a . . . category of *intentional response* which greets either the ontic value of a person or the qualitative value of beauty, of understanding, of truth, or noble deeds, of virtuous acts, of great achievements. For we are so endowed that we . . . *respond with the stirring of our very being* when we glimpse the possibility of the actuality of *moral self-transcendence* [Lonergan 1972, 37–38; my ital. and brackets].

Equipped with a developmental concept of feeling we are now ready and able to proceed with the task of differentiating affective consciousness so as to recognize how feeling operates inside triune consciousness.

Differentiating & Integrating
Affective Consciousness

So our first task is (1) to take the vertical arrow of Figure 1 (in the introduction, p. 18), that is, the undifferentiated line called "feeling ⟶ evaluation," then (2) to differentiate among the quasi-operations or responses of affective consciousness itself, and (3) finally to integrate this newly differentiated affective consciousness, along with cognition and volition, into triune consciousness. We have a clue to follow, mentioned above—which we can now apply to the four levels of consciousness—in accomplishing this task, namely, the analogy whereby *insight is to possible truth what feeling is to possible value*. Figure 5 (see p. 210) summarizes in advance the following discussion.

Thus on the level equivalent to understanding, feeling functions in affective intentionality as insight functions in cognitive intentionality. Feelings put us in touch with what may or may not turn out to be real, actual values. To ascend to truth we need to verify insights by satisfying certain conditions and reaching the virtually unconditioned, at which point judgment becomes the intelligent and reasonable thing to do. The analogous move in the realm of feeling, as would be expected, requires fulfilling conditions so that it would be reasonable and valuable to make the equivalent move in the domain of affective consciousness. *In both cases*, the conditions to be met, taken as a set, are called *self-transcendence*, which means achieving an *objective relation to oneself*: rather than being swayed by self-interest, bias, or prejudice, just as we must conform to the *truth* as it imposes itself upon us, so also we must respond to *values* even when they are not what we want or subjectively prefer. In the realm of affectivity, we might call this objectivity our "being able to trust our hearts," or learning to trust or not to trust our emotions, feelings, instincts, inclinations—the peace and serenity or discord and agitation associated with the discernment of spirits. We might call it having the right "moves" (psychic motions as e-motions), experiencing the right "vibes," having a correct "gut reaction," or "woman's intuition." One classical term used for successful achievement of this posture of objectivity is "conversion," where conversion does not necessarily mean a religious event

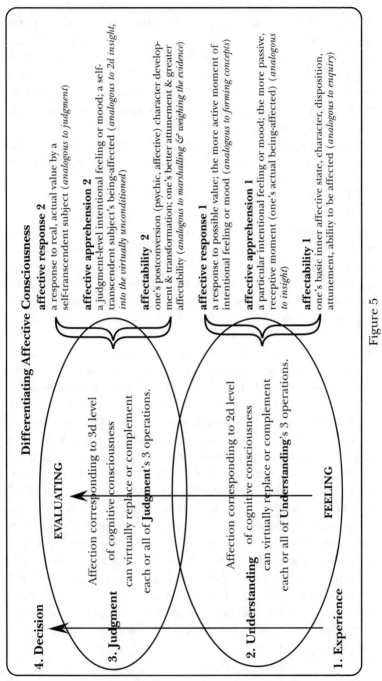

Figure 5

(such as *metanoia* or repentance). There are intellectual conversions, as we become more objective, in the sense of becoming more self-transcendent subjects in the domain of truth. There are affective conversions as we become more objective and self-transcendent subjects in the domain of value, when we transcend our preferences for the merely satisfying in favor of actual value. (See Doran on psychic conversion: 1981a, 1981b, 1990, 1996.) By "change of heart" let us mean success in surrendering to authentic values, allowing them speak to us, touch us, and move us without our distorting them or denying them, in the same way we try to be balanced and objective in seeking truth (see Egan 1976 on "success in surrendering").

In Figure 5, "Differentiating Affective Consciousness," our analogy (namely, "feeling [affective apprehension] is to value as insight [cognitive apprehension] is to truth") relates feeling to insight and indicates where feelings (including passions and emotions)[2] will now fit into the general schema of consciousness: where there was, before this analysis of affective consciousness, a simple undifferentiated line (the vertical arrow between the first and fourth levels of consciousness), we now show a differentiated set of responses that work as quasioperations such that both understanding and judgment have their parallels in affective consciousness. Triune consciousness means this higher operational synthesis of all three modes of consciousness, including some one or more apprehensions and responses of affective consciousness irreducible to either cognitional consciousness or volitional consciousness and integrating functionally with them.

Connaturality as Sublation of Discursive Reason & Deliberative Will

Up to now I have not emphasized what is perhaps the most controversial aspect associated with connaturality, namely, its ability to sublate either or both "normal" discursive reasoning and the deliberations of the will (whether all three operations of a level are sublated or complemented or only one or more levels). Meinong described the conditions under which an emotion could take the place of a concept, allowing someone to act without clear and distinct ideas. But long before him Aquinas, in the quotation above (*Summa theologiae* 2. 2, q.45, a.2) already stated the thesis of a way to reach judgment without the understanding that comes from "use of reason" or "rational investigation." Connaturality as sublation of reason and will is the main topic of the next chapter, but it must be mentioned now because—and this is the central thesis of this book—the proper and optimal functioning of triune consciousness as the higher operational synthesis of affection, cognition, and volition occurs precisely through connaturality, specifically in the value domains of the æsthetic, ethical, and mystical, which means that we love, know, and act because and according to who and what we have *become* and now *are*, not just by what we know. Triune consciousness's native mode of operation (for example, in angels and God) is through connaturality: connaturality underlies all other modes of consciousness. Up to now we have been at pains just to qualify affectivity for membership in "spiritual" consciousness, as equal partner with cognition and volition. Now the new member threatens to supplant the other two! Naturally, caution is advisable here; first things first: the integration of affection into consciousness has been achieved by the foregoing chapters, and that accomplishment is firm, independently of the way we offer now to explain and understand it. To bridge to the fuller treatment it receives in the next chapter, let me offer the following preparatory remarks.

Feeling as value-apprehension, because it operates through connaturality, has the capacity to give us not only nonconceptual, spontaneous *knowledge*, but also to give the equally valid experience of our affective responses sublating *will*-acts: as we *are*, so we connaturally love, with a love that flows spontaneously from the core of our being without need of discursive reasoning or deliberative will. Connaturality operates on the basis of who and what we *are* and have become rather than solely because of what we *think*. Here we can consult Barry Miller:

> [Connaturality is] an *experienced* befittingness, not a mere *known* befittingness; and it is from the former and not from the latter that love arises. Something may be known to be good and befitting to the knower, but it does not therefore automatically follow that it will be loved by the knower. Elicited love does not depend . . . upon what we know, but upon what we ARE. It does not depend . . . upon a known befittingness of the thing loved, but upon an EXPERIENCED befittingness. . . . When what is represented is befitting to the knower, then there is love. But the love does not follow from the "representative intentionality" inasmuch . . . as it is *known*, but only inasmuch as it is . . . *experienced* by the knower. In fact, that the loved be known is so irrelevant to the act of elicited love that there can be love even when the befittingness of the loved is not known. The object may be known as unfitting, but be experienced as fitting to the knower; and this conflict may occur not only between sensitive love and intellective knowledge, but even within the intelligible order—between intellective love and intellective knowledge. The reason is that the knower does not always know himself as he really is, and hence he can quite easily judge something to be unfitting to himself when in fact it is most *befitting* to him, most in *harmony* with him, as he is actually constituted. Love, however, is not subject to the limitations of self-knowledge. *Love flows not from what we know, but from what we ARE* . . . [1961, 147–48; my ital.; his caps].

As we shall see in the next two chapters, two prime examples of connaturality—because they constitute the domains of the interpersonal par excellence—are the ethical, as the human interpersonal, and the mystical, as relation that opens onto mystery. In saying that faith, love, and hope include affective responses beyond cognitional or volitional responses, we use affection and feeling *analogously*. Faith, love, and hope get their fullest and deepest meaning when experienced not in reference to the low end of consciousness ("I hope it will rain," "I love apple pie") but in the realm of personal relations. Love in not a will-act. Love is an affective response; choices, decisions, and actions that come from love remain subject to volition, of course. Faith is not a will-act, but also an affective response, as is hope. No one can force faith or hope by the mightiest act of will. Without reference to the apprehensions of value given in intentional feelings and moods, every philosophical and theological explanation of faith, love, or hope has been pitifully lame and will always remain so.

Now there is strong confirmation of this thesis in the idea that faith—believing in someone, even believing in oneself—is a "knowledge born of love." What exactly does this mean? Consonant with an anthropology from above, which understands human persons as finite spirits (complementary to the anthropology from below, which sees us as the highest animals), there is the experience of a radical transformation of consciousness and of one's very life when one feels loved. The gift of love floods one's whole consciousness and with it one's entire being, also sinking roots deeply into unconsciousness life (Ricoeur's *bios-epithumia*) and connaturalizing a person insofar as the love is accepted. One can begin to experience everything and everyone differently, in a new light, through a new optic; one understands and judges differently, acts and decides differently. Feeling ourselves to be loved makes faith and hope possible responses where formerly despair may have gripped and paralyzed us.

Conclusion

Felt resonance with one's *being* rather than with one's knowing or willing constitutes the feeling that is value apprehension, which is another way of expressing the idea of connaturality. The change that makes one a different person, a being capable of *being affected* differently and so capable of *responding* differently, is a moral change more than a physical change, of course. It is not, however, just a mental change, as though one merely replaced one thought with another, leaving one's being or nature untouched and unmoved. The term "change of heart" always implies being much more profoundly touched and moved, so much so that there is a kind of sinking of roots into the being and nature of the self as agent, a rooting back down through the being's conscious powers as they are themselves rooted deeply in the unconscious neural bases of the nature of the agent, establishing a second nature. As a self-transcendent agent one experiences value judgments as they relate directly to one's ability to change oneself; value judgments should lead one to recognize and appropriate oneself as a moral being, which means becoming authentic or inauthentic.

The change or conversion from being affected (or affected differently) by some values and not others, therefore, begins as value apprehension and leads to value judgment and finally choice: the world of the converted person looks, feels, and is different. So a changed affectability must precede a new affective response; it is an ". . . advance in authenticity, the fulfillment of one's affectivity . . ." (Lonergan 1972, 52). The changed heart lives in a changed world. One's entire consciousness is radically changed from the top down.

Chapter 8 has shown that consciousness is incomplete without a fully differentiated and integrated affective mode. Values are apprehended in and through feelings, our intentional affective responses to the beautiful, to the just and the good, and to the sacred and the holy, comparable to cognitional intentionality's relation to the true. Figure 6 (see p. 216) assembles the previous partial diagrams into a summary map of triune or triadic consciousness. The decreasing sizes of the four boxes suggest that we experience much more than we understand, understand much more than we can ever bring to judgments of truth, and manage to turn into decisions and action still less than we bring to judgments. The

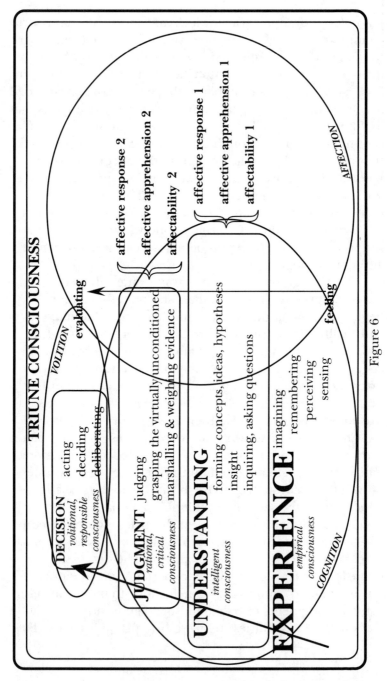

Figure 6

three ovals name the three kinds of consciousness: cognitions, containing the three levels of experience, understanding, and judgment, each level with at least three operations; volition, with its three operations; and affections, with its two levels and their quasioperations (called *quasi-*operations because of the element of response constitutive of affective operations, that is, their mixture of action and passion). Whether we call it triadic, triune (not trine, like the Trinity, for the distinctions are real), spiritual, intentional consciousness is absolutely threefold.

Notes

1. Lonergan continues (1972, 33–34; the parentheses are Lonergan's, from his footnotes): "As there is a development of feelings, so too there are aberrations . . . . . [I]t is much better to take full cognizance of one's feelings, however deplorable they may be, than to brush them aside, overrule them, ignore them. To take cognizance of them makes it possible for one to know oneself, to uncover the inattention, obtuseness, silliness, irresponsibility that gave rise to the feeling one does not want, and to correct the aberrant attitude. On the other hand, not to take cognizance of them is to leave them in the twilight of what is conscious but not objectified. (This twilight of what is conscious but not objectified seems to be the meaning of what some psychiatrists call the unconscious.) In the long run there results a conflict between the self as conscious and, on the other hand, the self as objectified. This alienation from oneself leads to the adoption of misguided remedies, and they in their turn to still further mistakes until, in desperation, the neurotic turns to the analyst or counsellor. (Just as transcendental method rests on a self-appropriation, on attending to, inquiring about, understanding, conceiving, affirming one's attending, inquiring, understanding, conceiving, affirming, so too therapy is an appropriation of one's own feelings. As the former task is blocked by misconceptions of human knowing, so too the latter is blocked by misconceptions of what one spontaneously is.)"

2. Perhaps the term "passion" corresponds to the second level (parallel to understanding), the relatively more "passive" moment of affection (being affected, being moved, and so on), and emotion more to the third level (parallel to judgment), the more active, responsive moment of affection. Relating passion to understanding compares with the experience of how insights come unbidden, flashing into consciousness when the right questions are asked and the right images are available, somewhat the way passions seem sometimes to overtake or even overwhelm, being more like movements one undergoes or suffers rather than actively generates. On the third level, judgments are more one's own productions, just as emotions are more active responses to what one has undergone. Robert Solomon (1976, 185) says that emotions are passions that are judgments, which at least makes some sense in

the overall schema of consciousness: emotions, as more active affections (affective responses), involve more personal responsibility because closer to the center of oneself and would follow upon the preparation laid by the more passive affections called passions.

3. Roldan (1956, 464–68) devotes only a few pages to connaturality, but comes down strongly for the view that affection should be considered a faculty like intellect and will, and thus its acts should be considered operations like the acts of intellect and will, rather than responses. It seems to me that this is a regression to a faculty psychology. Granted it would help the cause of introducing affection into equal status with cognition and volition to be able to describe feelings as operations rather than responses, but there is simply too much passivity in all affectivity, no matter how active feeling is with respect to emotion and emotion to passion, as diagrammed above. As von Hildebrand has so eloquently shown, the spontaneity of responses is their glory, the essence of their authentic expression of oneself; affections that were as directly under our rational and voluntary control as thought and choice would not be human. (See also Bernard 1980, where he discusses Roldan and Alquié, among others.) With Lonergan I call feelings quasioperations because they are the most active of affections and then only at the high end of their performance through connaturality within triune consciousness responding to value.

The literature on connaturality is by no means vast, but it is nonetheless substantial and growing. Aquinas never developed it or explained it himself, and commentators have usually been reluctant to offer explanations of their own, content to quote the master. John of St. Thomas (Jean Poinsot) set the pattern of invoking the influence of love upon knowledge as the simplest explanation, but too often this mistakenly took the form of the influence of will on intellect. There is a certain blindness among some Aristotelians, and even, with less justice but still understandably, among some Thomists, in insisting that love be an act of the will, even to the point of reducing affection and *affectus* to the will, and even further to the point of equating heart with will. One searches in vain for an author who attempts a "mechanics," or, better, a psychological rather than a metaphysical (per faculty psychology) explanation of how connaturality works. One finds a few references or pages, for example (and these are only examples; see the bibliography for more), de Finance (1960, 337–38), Hayen (1954, 122–23), Bouillard (1969, 26, 33–34), D'Arcy (1947, 287–91); or a chapter, for example, Hayen (1957, 238–60), Lebacqz (1962, 113–28), Marin-Sola (1924, 353–92), Maritain (1952, 22–29), Miller (1963), or article, such as Faricy (1964), McInerny (1958), Moreno (1970), Noble (1913), Roland-Gosselin (1938), Simonin (1936), White (1944). There are a few books worth studying, such as Maguire (1069), Caldera (1980), D'Avenia (1992), Kadowaki (1974) and the Keane (1966) and Titus (1990) dissertations.

The most widespread mistake to consider connaturality only as a form of knowledge, and to treat only of knowledge through connaturality. I think this comes in general from so many philosophers (not to speak of philosophically trained theologians) thinking that knowledge about knowledge is their most important pursuit, if not the only important thing, whereas right action should occupy that place of honor. Doing the good certainly takes precedence over merely knowing it. To do the good by connaturality rather than by knowledge results no less in the good being done. The purpose of cognition is action, as it the purpose of affection. Connaturality is not a subset of cognition but of action. It is more correct to approach connaturality as the most fundamental form of consciousness in general, in its full triadic structure, and to ask not about *knowledge* through connaturality but *action* through connaturality, since it is altogether possible and probable that the more skilled the person, the more intuitive and spontaneous he or she will be, and therefore the more likely that the move from experience to action will require less and less discursive reasoning and judging and less and less deliberating and willing.

Chapter 9

Connaturality

Create in me a clean heart, O God; and renew a right spirit within me.
Psalms, 51: 10 (c. 650 B.C.).

I will take away the stony heart out of your flesh,
and I will give you a heart of flesh.
Ezekiel, 36: 26 (c. 590 B.C.).

Nine times in ten, the heart governs understanding.
Lord Chesterfield (1694–1773), *Letters*, 15 May 1749.

OM is the Brahma-sound; going through it we attain the non-sound . . .
so through OM the knowers reach freedom, cross over with OM as our raft
to the other side of space of the heart,
in the inner space, into the hall of Brahman.
Maitri Upanishad (c. 800–400 B.C.), 6. 22. 28.

Summary

Connaturality explains feeling and the mode of operation
of triune consciousness under the influence of affection,
first and foremost in the ethical realm (understood primarily as the realm of human interpersonal relations). Acting
by connaturality means grounding actions more on attunement of our *being* (first *and second* nature) than on discursive reason or deliberative will. Connatural knowledge and
love are the ideal we approach asymptotically. This model
reveals that concepts and judgments are a lower way of
knowing, and deliberate will-acts are a lower way of loving.

THERE ARE FIVE CHARACTERISTICS of knowledge by affective connaturality: it is (1) intuitive, (2) instinctive, (3) experiential, (4) affective, and (5) nonconceptual (Keane 1966, 4). Of these, the most basic elements are affectivity and nonconceptuality. All the other descriptive terms are reducible in one way or another to these two. Maritain defines connaturality solely in terms of these two notions. A flaw in Maritain's otherwise helpful approach to affective connaturality is to present it as secondary to concepts and judgments rather than the other way around; the correct understanding of connaturality depends on a philosophical anthropology from above (which means human nature conceived as finite spirit rather than as higher animal) and holds that connaturality is the mode of triune consciousness and is the *primary* way for humans to know and love one another. Connatural knowledge and love are thus the paradigm; it is because and when one lacks a *converted* heart that one must have recourse by default to concepts, judgments, and will-acts as partial substitutes for full triadic consciousness, for head and heart in an operational synthesis.

Connaturality: A First Definition

"Connatural," as a technical term, can mean any of the following: (1) Used alone, connatural is a synonym for natural; connatural means in this case the same as natural to or for someone. (2) Comparing two terms, connatural means that one nature is proportioned or suited to another; one nature has an affinity to or with another. There are many other words practically and more or less loosely or adequately associated with connaturality, such as attunement, consonance, harmony, congeniality, empathy, sympathy, inclination, affinity, instinct, befittingness, belongingness, and suitability. (3) Comparing a human faculty or power (for example, to know), connatural means that the power or faculty is proportioned or suited to its proper object. (4) Most interesting for the practical world of our human experience—where our powers of affection, cognition, and volition are always continually being modified by learning, habits, and dispositions—connatural applies especially to those powers *as modified by habits, especially* those good and bad habits we call *virtues and vices.* A skilled mathematician has the acquired disposition (the intellectual virtue) associated with training, as does the skilled tennis player or the skilled painter. With Hubert Dreyfus (see Appendix to this chapter) we agree that this also patently applies to *ethical development* (we return to this point in the next chapter, devoted to habit as the explanation of connaturality). Many sources could be cited to make the same point in the realm we have called the mystical, such as the changed world of the Zen meditator (see Kapleau 1980). I could not exaggerate the importance of the idea of habit qua virtue for the theme of connaturality, which is the model for how we humans operate interpersonally, both ethically and mystically. As Lonergan says, "God's gift of love is the cause of our knowledge of God by connaturality."[1]

Thus the importance of this fourth meaning of connaturality lies in the thesis that not only first nature, but *second nature, too,* can ground (and in practice always *does* ground) connaturality: these developments are analogous to skills; they are acquired modifications—the habits and virtues—that are our change of heart, the way we increase our value-affinity.[2]

Defining Connaturality: Knowledge & Love through Feeling

1. The first and least meaning of *knowledge* by connaturality defines it as experiential knowledge or at best knowledge *accompanied by* (and thus not knowledge *through*) inclinations. Simply put, this first explanation of knowledge by affective connaturality reduces to saying that sometimes when we know we *also* feel, and that the feelings, emotions, passions aroused (before, during, and after) give us some added sense of certainty, doubt, or the like. In this first case our affective responses do not necessarily complement in an important way

and certainly do not replace but only *go with* our cognitive intentionalities. This is the weakest sense of affective connaturality. Recall how critical Heidegger was of this minimal meaning of feeling as mere accompaniment devoid of its own intentionality.

2. But knowledge by connaturality can be more than this; it can be consciousness *of* (again, not yet *through*) affectivity. Although still a knowledge primarily of *oneself* instead of the person or thing that is the "object" of the knowledge, a stronger meaning of knowledge by connaturality defines it as knowledge of one's feeling itself. In this second case the judgment would not occur without the feeling, or would be different without it. In the first case (#1 above) the judgment would occur anyway, with or without the feeling; this second case, that is, "in and of feeling," is not reducible to "merely accompanied by feeling." I may be helped to know what to do, for example, because I know what I feel about my projected action; my feeling is a fact I know along with other facts. This is a real form of connaturality because the felt consonance or dissonance of my being with my proposed action is operative and has become conscious. *Self*-knowledge is primary—what I know is *my* feeling—and reference to otherness is secondary; a more or less rapid inference based on feeling slips in between experience and judgment and contributes to the final judgment, which could be different without it.

3. But these first two do not exhaust the meaning of knowledge by connaturality: I may know and ultimately decide what to do *through* affectivity, affinity, empathy, inclination. It does not just mean knowing about oneself and then, through oneself, knowing about another, for example, through one's response to another, which would be an indirect, deductive way. I know and decide *through* this deeper connaturality as based on some shared common nature (first and/or second) with another person or thing (for exmple, my act, some value), that is, *through* and *in* (not just *with* or *of*) my leaning or inclination toward or away from this "object." So connaturality

most properly, in its best sense, means not merely *accompanied* by feelings, nor *of* feelings, but *through* feelings. This is the strongest, most interesting, and most valuable meaning of affective connaturality.

Our focus is on connaturality in matters ethical, that is, on relation to the *human* other. There is also, as often mentioned before, connaturality in matters æsthetic and mystical, that is, in the world of art and in relation to the holy; while we may draw examples from these realms, they are not central to our present study. In all three contexts, connaturality in the tradition of the Thomist text cited above, has meant *judgment* by affective connaturality, for example, æsthetic judgment or taste, ethical or moral judgment, and mystical or religious judgment. Thus, for Aquinas's chaste person, affections are ingredient to and may constitute so high a percentage of the "weight" behind a judgment as virtually to take the place of *concepts*, but not of *judgments*, at least not yet. Thus knowledge by connaturality, in Aquinas's example, usually means a *nonconceptual* judgment where connaturality replaces concepts; we are then said to make ethical judgments by feeling, which means—we are now ready to state definitively—by affective connaturality.

Now while the classical discussion of connaturality usually speaks only of *judgment* by connaturality, in which case feeling substitutes for insight and concepts, we can—in perfect consistency with the principles operative in the case of *judgment* by connaturality—extend the range of connaturality simply by relating it also to the third and fourth levels of consciousness, and we can get quite specific about which of the nine (or more) operations of consciousness, as outlined above (for example, see Figure 6, p. 216) in the general schema of consciousness, is being virtually replaced or complemented. Note that we should by no means take the words "replace" or "substitute" as a total sublation. It should rather be understood that depending on one's development (for example, see Dreyfus's five stages in the appendix to this chapter) connaturality is either the first line of action (for example, of the expert), with reason and will as complements, or, at lower skill levels, and perhaps more usually, connaturality is complementary to and fills up what is lacking in understanding (second level) or critical consciousness (third level) with enough value-apprehension (second level) and value-judgment (third level) to make decision and action (fourth level) possible. (This seems to be Maritain's position.) Our experience shows that affection can virtually substitute for any and all of these levels and operations, depending on a variety of circumstances.[3] The more expert one is, the more heart can and should lead head, that is, the greater role that affection, through connaturality, plays in triune consciousness.[4]

Note again that usually (as with Maritain) "head" is taken as primary and paradigmatic and heart is taken as merely secondary and supplemental to discursive reason and deliberative will. This approach casts feeling into a strictly secondary role. It is my thesis that this approach is incorrect and must be superseded, indeed reversed. When we explain connaturality itself through the even more ancient concept of habit, we will be able to make the case that actually, at the higher levels of human performance, discursive reasoning and deliberative volition show themselves not to be the first line of human agency at all (relegating connaturality to mere backup status), but rather just the opposite: head is secondary to more intuitive knowing and spontaneous love, where the intuitiveness and spontaneity depend, in the three areas of value mentioned, upon affective development and are directly proportionate to it. Here again it is instructive to compare connaturality with skill (for example, as Dreyfus has done) in order to emphasize ethical action, behavior, or comportment rather than ethical judgment as paradigm.

The best way, therefore, to understand knowledge and love by and through affective connaturality is for head *and* heart to mean triune consciousness. To do so is to relate feelings to *all four* levels and *all twelve* operations of consciousness presented in the introduction and chapter 8. Thus knowing in one's heart should be taken as shorthand for triune consciousness qua including, possibly even emphasizing, affection as operating through connaturality; it can mean, therefore, first, that connaturality, at the high end, virtually or completely replaces, or, at the low end, at least complements understanding, enabling one to go to judgment (and eventually to decision and action) without needing one or more of the operations of the second level of consciousness (that of understanding), namely, operations like inquiry, insight, and/or conceptualization. In other words, any *one* of the operations of the *second* level of consciousness could be virtually or completely replaced or complemented, or any two of them, or all three operations on that level could be complemented or even virtually or completely sublated. Thus connaturality can in whole or in part replace asking questions, replace insight, and/or replace forming concepts. Second, "knowing in one's heart" can also mean the above, plus virtually or completely replacing the *third* level (judgment, that is, rational or critical consciousness), enabling one to go to decision without weighing and marshalling evidence, without grasping the virtually unconditioned, without an explicit act of judgment. Any one of these operations of the third level of consciousness, or two, or all of them, could be omitted or (more likely) enhanced and augmented by connaturality to make possible a judgment that cognition could not enable alone or as well. Third, to move to the *fourth* level, *"loving* in one's heart" (we no longer speak only of *"knowing* in one's heart," since we are now at the fourth level of consciousness) can mean that connaturality virtually or completely replaces or complements the fourth level (that of choice and decision), by replacing deliberation and/or the will-act, so that action flows from spontaneous triune consciousness.

The chief confusion about what heart means derives from the capacity of affective connaturality virtually or completely to substitute for or decisively complement any one or all of these numerous levels and operations, and the experience of heart would be *different in every case* because, as we saw above, the *meaning and experience of feeling is analogous to the level of consciousness on which it occurs.*

It would be easy but unnecessarily tedious to give concrete examples of each and every possible occasion when feeling substitutes for or complements each and every operation and/or for a whole level (all three operations, or one or two of the three). Besides examples from the ethical realm, one could cite illustrations from the æsthetic and religious areas. For instance, an artist's insight might happen by the feel of the potter's hands on the clay turning on the wheel, or by the rightness of the color and light together as paint stuggles into life on the canvas; instead of a concept there is the artwork. Again, Maritain (1953) and Gilby (1934) offer many examples from art. Habit, as we shall see in the next chapter, integrates into this schema with relation to *each operation separately or globally,* since one could become very skillful and consequently competent, proficient, or expert in one or other operation without perfecting the rest of the operations on one level of consciousness, or on two levels, again becoming skilled selectively; everyone knows this from experience. In the same way, mood, as feeling that has deepened and endured to become character, could vary at each level and operation, furnishing the foundations of acts connatural to them as their source.

Applying Connaturality 1: Sublation of Discursive Reasoning

At the risk of some repetition, but for the sake of clarity, let us apply the foregoing to human knowing. Connaturality operates, to take the first instance, that is, as triune consciousness's mode of knowing at the second level of cognitive consciousness, as a substitute for or fulfilment of understanding, whether for one operation, for two, or for the entire level, in which case one moves immediately from experience to judgment on the strength of the affective response. Note that love is involved, at least in the general sense of a (positive) affective disposition—an affinity, empathy, congeniality—such that the ground, horizon, and attitude of consciousness are all affected. Note also that the judgment itself is of a *different character* because it is without *conceptual* understanding, and that this difference can be and usually is experienced; it can definitely be felt; feeling is part of the experience, part of a consciousness of *judging without concepts.*

If (to anticipate our explanation in ch. 10), human discursive judgment is, in the first place, a partial and always inadequate substitute for higher intuition anyway (that is, discursive judgments are substitutions for the intuitions we would have if we were less finite spirits, or would have if we were more perfectly attuned to higher skills, higher values, and the like), then connaturality is a "substitute for a substitute." This apparently bizarre expression will be explained in the next chapter; suffice it to say for now that it refers to the hierarchy of spirits according to which the human soul, as a finite spirit, participates in the perfections of the next higher level of spirit by approaching, in its highest mode of operation (intuitive knowing and spontaneous love) the lowest performance of that spirit without fully achieving it. If that higher mode be taken as the ideal toward which we should aspire, then discursive reason and deliberative will can be seen as poor substitutes for the intuitive knowing and spontaneous love of those higher spirits (the angel taken as *Grenzidee*).

Human consciousness is a partial and intrinsically developmental (that is, always subject to improvement or deterioration) asymptotic approximation of the paradigm of human nature represented by those higher spirits. It is a transcending toward, without attaining (as a *Vorgriff*, a reaching-for and touching-without-grasping), the spiritual horizon of spirit as spirit. By connaturality one is enabled to go from experience to judgment without conceptual reasoning, with the corollary that since it is understanding that produces *concepts*, this way of judging is *nonconceptual*, that is, is *without concepts* because the operation of *conceptualization is skipped,* bypassed through connaturality, and so no concept is formed, or one is only partially formed to the extent precisely that conceptual understanding is sublated.

In the key Thomist text (*Summa theologiae* 2. 2, q.45, a.2) cited above, the context is the gift of wisdom, and yet Aquinas himself gives as explanatory examples: (1) connaturality in moral judgment and (2) connaturality in "divine things," or, we might say: (1) connaturality in human relations—in relation to other human persons—and (2) connaturality in relation to God, the divine persons. The value of theologian Aquinas's way of speaking, for our philosophical purposes, is to open the door to our speaking of the interpersonal (human, not divine) virtues of faith, love, and hope.

In the *Commentary on the Sentences* Aquinas distinguishes, in the context of treating the gift of wisdom, between knowing through study and teaching (*per studium et doctrinam*) and knowing through a certain affinity to or with divine things (*per quandam affinitatem ad divina*), or by being affected by divine things (*patiendo divina*), which happens through the gift of wisdom. In the same article, Aquinas says this gift of wisdom has an eminence in cognition through a certain union with divine things (*per quandam unionem ad divina*), which is possible only through love (*per amorem*). In general Aquinas uses language like *propter connaturalitatem, per quandam unionem, per amorem, per modum inclinationis, per modum naturae, patiendo divina,* and *affective* in sharp contrast with language like judgment *secundum perfectum usum rationis, per studium et doctrinam, per modum cognitionis, per modum rationis.*

Recall again the context. Affective connaturality can partially or fully substitute for and/or complement understanding, enabling the virtuous person to judge well through resonance with the *second nature* of *virtue* rather than through theory alone known abstractly or even applied concretely. Knowing in one's heart would mean moving directly from experience to judgment without understanding (or without fully understanding) through concepts. Instead of only cognitional insight into truth, there is also a feeling, an affective apprehension of value, in such a way that the latter is operative, meaning that the judgment could not and should not properly be made without it. Someone might therefore with perfect validity claim to judge in ethics without being able to furnish concepts—without possessing the words to express his or her reasons of the heart—because that middle step has been skipped or transformed by being infused with affection, that is, by affective intentionality as grounded in affective connaturality.

I just suggested that "moral judgment" in the Thomist text be taken to mean interpersonal relations, that is, relation to one's neighbor, justice and love. To analyze the actual instances and examples of affective connaturality in ethical judgment is to turn the discussion toward the difference between speculative and theoretical knowledge, on the one hand, and particular, practical, concrete knowledge, on the other. This is no surprise since any knowledge that skipped or moved ahead without fully formed concepts would not formulate the universals needed for expressing the true knowledge one had in judgments in terms of theories or generalized rules. One might not ask someone who knows ethics by connaturality to write an ethics textbook, although the eventual writer could not do better than to observe what such a person *does*, as Aristotle said long ago.

Judgment without conceptual understanding, therefore, is judgment without explicit speculative or theoretical knowledge. Aquinas contrasts the two knowledges when he says that the judgment by reason or cognition is true with *speculative* rightness, while the judgment by inclination is true with *practical* rightness.

We have, then, a first conclusion, before any further formal extension beyond this substitution for *understanding* to a substitution for *judgment* or *decision*: by affective connaturality the virtuous man or woman judges in the concrete "face-to-face" correctly. That affective knowledge operates in the practical, concrete, face-to-face relation suggests something specific about how persons are present to one another, suggests something of the primacy of otherness for affectivity, and in an indirect way supports the primacy of the other in Levinas's ethical metaphysics.

Applying Connaturality 2:
Analogy with Natural Appetite

Besides the analogy comparing feeling with insight, there is also an analogy whereby connatural knowledge is to rational knowledge what natural appetite is to elicited appetite; or, as Charles Davis (1976) would put it , there is an "*achieved spontaneity*" analogous to a natural spontaneity. By virtue (second nature) we can approximate the spontaneity of first nature. It is by habitude that we are given a way to try to "overcome" our finitude, as we see in the next chapter, that is, by asymptotically approximating our knowledge and love to that of spirits less finite than ourselves. Thus, the specific difference between the headwork and the connatural face-to-face is the affective, the felt "something" that grounds the move from experience to judgment without full conceptual understanding, a consciousness that is more affectively operative because of the face-to-face concreteness of the encounter. This suggests the analogy with natural appetite.

We may think of moral virtues as active forms that influence the movements of the virtuous person's empathy and affinity in much the same way as "the constitutive form of a nature rules the tendencies deriving from the nature" (see Simon 1934, 41–43). A virtue constitutes an acquired tendency toward what is in accord with that virtue, the virtue itself being a modification of a natural tendency, appetite, or affection, like any habit. Face to face with a moral good, or in the performance of a moral action, virtuous appetite or affection should experience a certain empathy or affinity sufficient to reveal that this value or projected action is truly in tune with one's being or nature (that is, connatural to it) and therefore virtuous.

Gilby (1934) speaks of the physical modification that moral virtue works on the being (that is, nature as first nature) of the virtuous person. Taking Aquinas's example, he says that if one is chaste, the virtue of chastity constitutes a certain *esse castum* (chaste being) in oneself so that one cannot fail to respond favorably in the presence of a chaste person, object, or situation: "But if one is chaste . . . one has in addition an instinct which receives, not through the *notion* of chastity, but through the *habit* of chastity. Such knowledge is not formed by scientific criteria, but by a physical modification of one's organism by an *esse castum*; it does not operate through the exercise of one's reasoning powers, but through one's real *inclination* towards chastity" (42; my ital.).

Note the reference to habit as the explanation of how connaturality works. We shall be following this clue in the next chapter. The resonance felt in connaturality is not between action and knowledge in the *mind,* but between the action and one's very *being* (recall the quotation from Miller, in ch. 8). Marin-Sola refers to the "real and objective resemblance" that moral habits confer. We become like what we love. He describes the judgment by affinity which results from this "real resemblance" as an "experiential" judgment and compares its operation to that of the external senses. Just as the external senses perceive exterior objects by "immediate contact," by "simple intuition," without comparison or reasoning, so the moral virtues enable one to judge "experimentally and without reason" of the objects of virtue (Marin-Sola 1924, 1: 355).

Again, let us not be extreme in stating the "substitution" thesis, despite these authors' tendency to take an all-or-nothing approach. Connaturality may be and probably more often is a partial complement rather than a total replacement. With advanced skill and familiarization one would expect the sublation to be primary and more complete. If the good person has an affinity for some value, presumably the even more virtuous person would have a higher affinity. Again, speaking very generally, the saint would be attuned to the holy, the artist to beauty. Connaturality would name a relation between one's being or nature and one's doing, rather than between one's discursive knowing or deliberate will and one's doing. These relationships are not mutually exclusive but occur within the unity of triadic consciousness.

When we try to explain in more depth, in the next chapter, how exactly connaturality itself works, we need to recall this opening discussion of connaturality in relation to habit and natural appetite, for it holds one of the keys to a philosophy of affectivity. Indeed, this analogy with natural appetite recurs in the following section also; it is intrinsic to a thesis that connaturality is explainable best as habit (virtue) understood as second *nature*.

Applying Connaturality 3: As Sublation of Judgment

Although this section, now on the third level of cognition, could have directly followed that of connaturality as sublation of understanding, the second level of cognition, the intervening section on connaturality as analogous to natural appetite or affection makes this section more intelligible. Affective connaturality, as we saw in general above, can also substitute for rational judgment (the third level of cognitive consciousness), not just for conceptual understanding. The aforementioned analogy (natural appetite is to first nature as elicited appetite is to second nature) is relevant. According to Aquinas, "Our reason naturally apprehends as good those things to which we are naturally inclined" (*Summa theologiae*, 1. 2, q.94, a.2). There is a natural affinity between any power and its proper object. Our natural powers are basically natural appetites, that is, orientations, tendencies, dispositions arising from nature, for those goods that are their proper objects (see *De veritate*, 25, 2, ad 8; *Summa theologiae* 1, q.80, a.1, ad 3; *Summa theologiae* 1. 2, q.30, a.1, ad 3 and q. 30, a.3, ad 1). In the presence of their proper objects, our affective, cognitive, and volitional powers naturally and automatically go into action—they *respond* (because of their cor-*respond*-ence with their proper "objects")—and in so doing we experience the befittingness and belongingness that attend the actualization and fulfilment of our potentialities (see *Summa theologiae* 1. 2, q.27, a.3; q.70, a.1; *In III Sententias*, d.26, q.1, a.1, ad 3).

This is, of course, precisely the *ground of the response model*: connaturality is what makes our "faculties" operate with spontaneity, responsive to what is akin to them, befitting them. Our eyes do not need to *know* that light, color, and harmonious form are good for them, but in the presence of the visible they naturally act and experience fulfilment (*complacentia*). Likewise, intelligent and rational consciousness does not need to *know* that being is the good for which cognition is suited, but seeks the truth connaturally and rests in it. It is a small and logical step to say that what is true of the parts of the human person is true of the whole, namely, that we have a natural orientation for other persons as fulfilling our connatural disposition to reach toward ethical life with others in peaceful community and just society. *Experienced* befittingness, affinity, attunement, which is a *felt* (rather than a conceptually *known*) befittingness, explains what connaturality is and why it is the key to triune consciousness as the highest mode of consciousness of the person as a whole.

Summary of Ethical Connaturality

Connaturality naturally operates best in the domain of ethical judgments or interpersonal being, in the face-to-face relation with another person, because as persons we are most connatural to persons (with all due allowance for the concept of the mystical based on an acquired [that is, given gratuitously as "grace"] connaturalization [divinization] of the finite human person to the infinite). Here, above all, triune consciousness as a higher operational synthesis of the whole person can move to judgment without always having to go back to discursive thought and can sometimes bypass rational judgment itself to move to decision and action, that is, can act more intuitively, spontaneously, and nonconceptually. To justify this general practical conclusion we have invoked an analogy with natural appetite, insofar as virtue has changed an elicited appetite, giving it a second nature that is more attuned, befitting, and connatural to persons, who are the natural and proper "objects" of persons. *Triune* consciousness, as "faculty of the *whole person*," operates to enable judgment without requiring an act of conceptual understanding when in the presence of a person. The voice of the heart speaks to the practical only, however, not to the theoretical or speculative; but this primacy of the practical should not be considered a flaw or limit. Connatural knowledge is first and foremost practical and concrete; it precisely is *not* conceptual, speculative, theoretical (the price paid for being nonconceptual). "Heart-knowledge," since it is based on connaturality, does not know ends in the theoretical way of "head-knowledge," that is, by grasping them objectively. To "know" someone "in one's heart" is really more a "know-how," because it is only to know how to relate in loving action to a person, without claiming anything like superior conceptual knowledge of the person. Of course, conceptual, speculative, theoretical head knowledge can eventually come from conceptual understanding and rational judging based on this heart-experience; orthodoxy can come from orthopraxis.

Applying Connaturality 4:
Philosophical Excursus on
Connaturality & the Holy

Aquinas's *Summa theologiae* 2. 2, q.45, a.2 offers a second example, namely, the divine things. How shall we deal with and interpret this *philosophically?* In the guise of the language of faculties, gifts, habits, virtues, and the like, Aquinas is really discussing our connatural relations with persons, only this time the otherness of the Other has about it a degree of activity or agency that exceeds the power of the personal presence of another *human* person: the ethical gives way to and becomes the mystical, the holy, the sacred, the numinous. For the mystic, the touch of God—the Other as gracious—bypasses rational judgment and one finds oneself at the fourth level of consciousness (or even at a fifth, as Lonergan suggests), and one believes, loves, and hopes without having arrived at this faith, love, and hope by conceptual understanding and rational judgment. For faith, love, and hope really are in their greatest part affective responses, rather than intellectual assents to dogmas on someone's authority, or acts of will overriding reason. Faith, hope, and love between human beings are holistic interpersonal responses based on the connatural befittingness of those responses. These human responses have to default back to rational judgment only when affective connaturality between oneself and the other person fails. Aquinas is introducing the case when the Other is God: a mysterious Other, analogous to that of a human person in ethical relations, can conceivably exist and work in one's life with such activity that another empowerment occurs even greater than that of the ethical, greater than *human* love. The purpose of this section is not to import from theology a concept to be used for philosophical gain, but just the opposite: to suggest how the philosophical concept of connaturality and its basis, habit, can furnish an insight into the theological doctrine of grace, which is itself best understood in terms of habit (specifically habit in the form of virtues that are given as gifts: we are gratuitously graced with them; see Maguire 1969). We will then (indirectly) have another analogy in aid of understanding connaturality: acquired virtues are to the ethical what grace (infused virtue, that is, habit given as gift) is to the mystical.

This may seem to be an unexpected shift in the terms of our previous discussion, but it is not. There is an instructive parallel to explore: becoming better at ethical judging, deciding, and acting is something *we achieve,* but holiness (the theologian of grace would say), is received by a connaturality that is done *for* us, given as a gift—a grace, in the terms of theology, that is, a gratuitous connaturalizing of one's human nature to the divine nature by sheer, gratis, divine agency, a salvific *divinizing,* as the Fathers of the Church put it. To use religious language: as adopted sons and daughters of God we are "(con)naturalized citizens" of the "heavenly kingdom," made one with God (in created grace). And the affinity and congeniality (kinship and genus by adoption) are due to this higher agency. A theologian such as Thomas Aquinas, who is also a saint, mystic, and doctor of the church, not surprisingly attributes to the heart this capacity to be touched by God. Before proposing a philosophical interpretation of this mode of speaking, let us note that the gifts of the Spirit, as usually discussed, seem at least initially to be passive rather than operative habits. The gifts are not so much habits perfecting the normal operation of our powers, but dispositions preparing us for further movements by the Spirit.

Philosophically interpreted, then, the doctrine of the gifts of the Spirit is an attempt to restore humanity to a prefallen, preternatural nearness to the paradigm of higher spirits, and the interesting point is that this is done by modifying nature through the gift of new habits; old nature becomes new, first become second, and new actions are now possible. (May we see in this grace doctrine, then, an analogy with human love, with being loved and graced with the life-transforming gift that love brings? Further, may we see, to move a bit "lower," that teaching is also an example of something from above: one is not exactly given the virtue or skill, but without the other's help one would not acquire and possess it.) The same thing happens in consciousness when its full triadic structure is in force: the interplay of all three modes of consciousness

allows us to develop new skills. The idea of grace is philosophically interesting because it facilitates an insight into the
idea of healing and elevating human nature so that we approximate a higher paradigmatic ideal, one that recognizes
that discursive reasoning and deliberating will are *not the best
we can do, if* we fully integrate affection into consciousness.
Because we lack these gifts and yet need them, in a sense we
have an "obediential potency" for them: they are connatural
to us at least in the sense that we can *be connaturalized* to them.
Without them we cannot believe, love, and hope, and so we
must by default descend to rational judgment and deliberate
will-acts. It seems a short step to secularize this language of
divine agency and to suggest that ordinarily it is immanently
in the *human* other that the transcendent Other is met. Edith
Wyschogrod (1990) has asked whether it takes a saint to see
"God in the other," that is, to relate with responsibility to the
other as ground. Connaturalization through habit, analogous
to the gifts of the spirit, is not reserved to the saints; love
seems to be the only condition (*Summa theologiae* 1. 2, q.68,
a.5; 2. 2, q.8, a.4; q.45, ad5). Anyone who loves is disposed to
a change in consciousness that comes "from above," from a
fifth level of consciousness, we could say (meaning the help
of someone who graces one's life with truth, goodness,
beauty), working upon all of triune consciousness from the
top down. Everyone, I hope, has had the experience of the
whole world changing when one is in love; we evaluate and
decide and act differently, we judge and understand our world
differently, and we even experience our world differently.

To sum up what we might glean from this example: The
role of the gifts that come with grace is to connaturalize us to
operate in some sense like those higher spirits who represent
the paradigm of what is possible to us when we do not remain fixed in our first nature but become, through the learning that is habit (virtue), more highly actualized. Analogous
to human development there is the parallel development
through grace, so we can act without needing concepts or

deliberative will-acts: "[S]aints are made by God alone . . . ."[5] The superiority of the new skills lies in the mode of operation. Simplicity, spontaneity, nonconceptuality are the marks of connaturality, and the gifts are virtues that make connatural knowing and loving successful, easy, pleasurable. When it is said that "love floods our hearts because of the Spirit given us," we can see a parallel between grace and human love: now love precedes knowledge instead of vice versa, and judgments are taken up into the dynamism of an affective response, that is, as immediate, spontaneous, direct. To account for the effect of wisdom and love in one's change of heart, therefore, is to account for a move from experience to love without discursive understanding, rational judgment, or deliberative decision; the habit can come from our own *human* agency or (in the theological example) can be extended to include human love, teaching, and beauty from a *higher* agency.[6] The point of using this example is not to import a theological conclusion but solely to note the similar *structure*: in both cases the best way to understand the higher operational acts, the new development and skills, is to see connaturality as habit, as virtue or skill whether acquired or received from another wholly or partly as a gift .[7]

Conclusion to Chapter 9 & Bridge to Chapter 10

If "from affection for divine things comes their manifestation" (*Summa contra gentiles*, 4, c.21; *In Joan.*, c.14, lect. 4, n. 1916), then the heart changed by knowledge, love, and beauty is attuned to the other, and feels the befittingness of possible acts toward and for the other. Aquinas speaks of a visitation and inhabitation or indwelling by which grace changes the soul (*In Joan.*, c.14, lect. 6; *In I Sententias*, d.15, q.4, a.1). A change in being results in a change in action, in one's ability to know and love. The saints who have a fully just heart see God better than those who see God through corporeal effects,[8] because the saints (=virtuous persons) who have justice, charity, and other such effects which are like to God, know God better than others. Connaturality is a likeness that grounds a mode of acting based on that likeness, either a likeness of first nature or, through developed skills, of second nature. Lacking the higher mode of acting through connaturality, one has to have recourse to some other lesser mode of acting. Translated from theological language, a "heart filled with justice" is a triadic consciousness that does not suspend the affective, that is filled with the ethical primacy of the other, transcending one's own ego-centeredness. This is why Maritain uses the expression "love replaces the concept" (1959, 260–63, 450; 1951a, 475) to explain connaturality.

We have been guided in advance by the idea that humans are incarnate spirits—a theme of Chapter 10, to which we now turn. It is of the nature of finite spirits that we need to have recourse to discursive, conceptual, rational, deliberative substitutes precisely because of our finitude and to the degree of our finitude. Habit as virtue is our way of pushing back the limit of finitude. Heart-talk has been taken as a clue to a connaturalized mode of human interpersonal knowledge and love. In the first chapters we have presented some instances of this interpersonal knowing and love through feeling phenomenologically described as affective intentionality. We then offered the concept of connaturality to explain affective intentionality and to begin to show how habit grounds this higher knowing and love. We now turn to the structure of habit as virtue in more detail in order better to understand the nature of connaturality itself. Triune consciousness emerges more intelligibly in the context of finite spirit, and habit as virtue plays the key role in that understanding. To guide us we have the motto: "Habitude, remedy for finitude." The role of habit it to make possible a conception of human nature as lowest on a continuum of spirits, but able to ascend closer to the paradigm through the integration of head and heart in full triadic consciousness.

Appendix
Dreyfus on Five Stages of Skill Acquisition

In an unpublished article entitled "What Is Moral Maturity? Towards a Phenomenology of Ethical Expertise," Hubert L. Dreyfus argues that focusing on ethical comportment (behavior, action) rather than on ethical judgment (reasoning, deliberation) will help us to understand how "most of our everyday ethical comportment consists in unreflective, egoless, responses to the current interpersonal situation" (2). He asks (2) "Why not begin on the level of spontaneous ethical coping?"

To make this point he presents a phenomenology of skill acquisition, using driving a car and playing chess as examples. He aims to demonstrate that ethical behavior shows the same kind of development as acquiring any other comparable skill. There are five stages: Novice, Advanced Beginner, Competence, Proficiency, and Expertise.

With no experience, learning to drive or play chess, for example, requires learning the rules. But that is soon inadequate: "The novice chess player learns a numerical value for each type of piece regardless of its position, and the rule: 'Always exchange if the total value of pieces captured exceeds the value of pieces lost.' But such rigid rules often fail to work. A loaded car stalls on a hill; a beginner in chess falls for every sacrifice" (3). The advanced beginner is someone who is beginning to learn from experience, and flexible *maxims* complement and sometimes supersede and override *rules*. For example:

> The advanced beginner driver uses (situational) engine sounds as well as (nonsituational) speed. He learns the maxim: shift up when the motor sounds like it is racing and down when its sounds like it is straining. No number of words can take the place of a few choice examples of racing and straining sounds. Similarly, with experience, the chess student begins to recognize such situational aspects

of positions as a weakened king's side or a strong pawn structure, despite the lack of precise definitional rules. He is then given maxims to follow, such as attack a weakened king side [3].

Competence comes with more experience, more complex situations, and the need to meet increasingly difficult challenges, such as freeway driving and dangerous road conditions, or, in chess, class A tournament play, where the competition, timed games, and rated levels push one's skills beyond the books. As Dreyfus explains,

> In both of these cases, we find a common pattern: detached planning, conscious assessment of elements that are salient with respect to the plan, and analytical rule-guided choice of action, followed by an emotionally involved experience of the outcome. The experience is emotional because choosing a plan, goal, or perspective is no simple matter for the competent performer. Nobody gives him any rules for how to choose a perspective, so he has to make up various rules which he then adopts or discards in various situations depending on how they work out. This procedure is frustrating, however, since each rule works on some occasions and fails on others, and no set of objective features and aspects correlates strongly with these successes and failures. Nonetheless the choice is unavoidable. Familiar situations begin to be accompanied by emotions such as hope, fear, etc., but the competent performer strives to suppress these feelings during his detached choice of perspective [3].

One difference between a competent and proficient driver or chess player depends on his or her moving from objective plans and strategies—themselves already operative at a higher overall level than merely knowing moves, plays, tactics as pieces of plans, and so on—is that working through a number of plans and strategies has gone on long enough for the driver or player to have lived through enough of them enough times for them to be integrated in his or her repertory "subjectively" or immanently, in the good sense of being readily available with much less attention and much more spontaneity. Since so many situations have been met, there are fewer surprises possible; the world of the driver or player is less "outside" him or her, and there is an integration of self and world in action that becomes increasingly familiar and connatural. Another significant difference is a way of *referencing feelings and emotion rather than suppressing them.*

> As soon as the competent performer stops reflecting on problematic situations as a detached observer, and stops looking for principles to guide his actions, the gripping, holistic experiences from the competent stage become the basis of the next advance in skill. Having experienced many emotion-laden situations, chosen plans in each, and having obtained vivid, emotional demonstrations of the adequacy or inadequacy of the plan, the performer involved in the world of the skill, "notices," or "is struck by," a certain plan, goal or perspective. No longer is the spell of involvement broken by detached conscious planning [4].

Finally the expert stage may be reached. Here the affective dimension has been fully integrated, knowing is more intuitive, action is more spontaneous, requiring little or no deliberation, to the point that reasoning processes, judgments, and even explicit decisions are sublated. As Dreyfus explains:

> The expert driver, generally without any attention, not only *knows by feel* and familiarity when an action such as slowing down is required; he knows how to perform the action without calculating and comparing alternatives. He shifts gears when appropriate with no awareness of his acts. On the off ramp his foot just lifts off the accelerator. What must be done, simply is done.
>   The expert chess player, classed as an international master or grandmaster, in most situations experiences a com-

pelling sense of the issue and the best move. Excellent chess players can play at the rate of 5-10 seconds a move and even faster without any serious degradation in performance. At this speed they must depend *almost entirely on intuition* and hardly at all on analysis and comparison of alternatives. It seems that beginners make judgments using strict rules and features, but that with talent and a great deal of involved experience the *beginner develops into an expert who sees intuitively* what to do *without applying rules and making judgments* at all. *The intellectualist tradition* has given an accurate description of the *beginner and the expert facing an unfamiliar situation, but normally an expert does not solve problems. He does not reason. He does not even act deliberately. Rather he spontaneously does what has normally worked and, naturally, it normally works.*

John Dewey (1922, 177–78) introduced the distinction between knowing-how and knowing-that to call attention to just such thoughtless mastery of the everyday: "We may . . . be said to *know how by means of our habits* . . . . We walk and read aloud, we get off and on street cars, we dress and undress, and do a thousand useful acts without thinking of them. We know something, namely, how to do them . . . . [I]f we choose to call [this] knowledge . . . then other things also called knowledge, knowledge of and about things, knowledge that things are thus and so, knowledge that involves reflection and conscious appreciation, remains of a different sort . . . ." [4-5; my ital.]

Dreyfus then applies this paradigm to the context of ethical action, with very illuminating results for the Kohlberg–Gilligan debate on moral maturity.

Notes

1. Lonergan 1985, 250. The following texts present both the idea of love that changes consciousness from above, and the idea of vertical finality, the subject transcending toward a higher operational synthesis called triune consciousness: "Moreover, in the measure that this transformation is effective, development becomes not merely from below upwards but more fundamentally from above downwards. There has begun a life in which the heart has reasons which reason does not know. There has been opened up a new world in which the old adage, *nihil amatum nisi prius cognitum* (nothing is loved unless first known), yields to a new truth, *nihil vere cognitum nisi prius amatum* (nothing is truly known unless first loved [77].

" . . . [T]he passionateness of being . . . has a dimension of its own: it underpins and accompanies and reaches beyond the subject as experientially, intelligently, rationally, morally conscious. Its underpinning is the *quasi-operator* that presides over the transition from the neural to the psychic. It ushers into consciousness not only the demands of unconscious vitality but also the exigencies of vertical finality . . . . As it underpins and accompanies, so too it overarches conscious intentionality. There it is the topmost *quasi-operator* that by intersubjectivity establishes us as members of community. Within each individual *vertical finality heads for self-transcendence* [29–30].

"For self-transcendence reaches its term not in righteousness but in love, and when we fall in love, then life begins anew. A new principle takes over and, as long as it lasts, we are lifted above ourselves and carried along as parts within an ever more intimate yet more liberating dynamic whole. Such is the love of husband and wife, parents and children . . . . Such finally is God's gift of love flooding our hearts through the Holy Spirit who is given us (Romans, 5:5) [175]. Such a positive orientation and the consequent self-surrender, as long as they are operative, enable one to *dispense with any intellectual analogy or concept* . . . [244; my ital.].

2. My whole thesis of reversing the paradigm, that is, of arguing for the primacy of the heart within triune consciousness as a higher development than the rational and deliberative head depends on the principle of connaturality, and to understand the meaning of connaturality requires a correct understanding of habit, as we shall see in the next chapter. It seems that the fourth meaning of affective connaturality (that is, modification of a "faculty" by habit through love) is both the best and the closest to Aquinas's. Here again a single text of Aquinas serves as a pivot and summary for a position that pervades his entire corpus: what *Summa theologiae* 1. q.84, a.7 is for his metaphysics of cognition, *Summa theologiae* 2. 2 q.45, a.2 is for his metaphysics of affection.

3. Connatural knowledge is nonconceptual because a feeling wholly or partly replaces an insight, as Meinong explained, and thus *no concept is formed*. There may or may not be images for the same reason: if one could go immediately—that is, without medium, without a representation—from experience right to judgment, then no image would be formed. An example of this is imageless mysticism (that is, felt presence, without visions, locutions, or any other extraordinary phenomena). The obscurity of the mind is due to lack of images and/or ideas or concepts, as Rahner notes in his great study of the spiritual senses in the Middle Ages (1979, 104–34, esp. 124–34): when the gifts are given directly to the will, this *leaves the intellect in the dark*.

4. With befitting hesitation, and merely for whatever utility it might have, I offer a very simple notation for analysis of triadic consciousness. Using a, c, and v (for affection, cognition, volition), using caps A, C, V (to represent dominance), and using order to represent which mode of consciousness takes the lead, one could notate triadic interaction. For example, aCv would mean feeling takes the lead but cognition is the dominant mode. In one context, for example, affection may lead, as when one is responding to an insult or to someone's anger or expression of appreciation; thought might come after such being affected with one's affective response, and volition later yet. On another occasion one's reasoning might lead to certain conclusions, which then bring peace of mind or considerable anxiety or sadness, as when calculating the monthly bills and comparing them with income. Anyone can imagine the

finite series of possibilities. In simplest form, given the three modes, *a*, *c*, and *v*, we have three simple, uncombined modes of consciousness and twelve possible sequences, depending on which mode leads, on whether there are two or three other modes of consciousness involved, and the subsequent order of the other modes operative. Thus, if only two modes are operating, we get *ac*, *ca*, *av*, *va*, *cv*, *vc*, again depending on which mode of consciousness takes the lead. If all three modes are in operation, we get the following range: *a* yields *acv* and *avc*, *c* yields *cav* and *cva*, *v* yields *vac* and *vca*. It is easy to imagine examples for each combination; the point is to cover the full range of consciousness as we experience it, as no simpler analysis does. The minimum is three, the maximum always a combination of the three. For example, *cvA* would describe deciding to seek out friendly company in order to feel happy (see Edith Stein: "When I want to stop worrying I seek out happy company" [1989, 23]). Obviously, the complexity can increase, for example, to *acva*, to notate Stein's cognition of the prior affective state of worry as giving rise to the decision to seek company in order to be happy. So *Acv* suggests that affection is not only leading but dominating the triad, while *aCv* suggests that although affection has begun this particular conscious episode, cognition is the dominant mode. Faith might be *aCv*, where affection disposes one to understand and affirm in judgment what might otherwise seem unreasonable; cognition remains the dominant mode. Hope might be *caV*, where affective disposition leads the will; volition remains dominant. In both cases the affective disposition is essential to the analysis of these experiences. Love would differ from charity in that love would seem to be *Acv*, while charity would be *acV*, or even *cV*, if feelings play no part.

And now, throwing caution completely to the wind, let me also suggest even another analogy that some have found helpful. How fanciful is it to compare the light triad with triune consciousness? The light of the mind, *lumen intellectuale* . . . . Take the three colors of light—red, green, blue (for example, the RGB of a computer monitor)—for the three kinds of consciousness. Let R be the heat of passion and the fire of love in the heart; let B be the cold logic of reason; let G be the "green light," the "go" of will, choice, action. Now, just as together RGB constitute white light, but only when all three are present in perfect balance and harmony, so also triune consciousenss.

5. Thomas Aquinas, In Ps., 28: 7: "*Et isti sancti praeparantur per Deum, non per se.*"

6. A few texts of Aquinas: "Wisdom [occurs] through the mode of taste of one experiencing" (*In III Sententias*, d.34, q.1, a.2, n.77). To know what one ought to believe belongs to the gift of knowledge, but to know in themselves the very things we believe, by a kind of union with them, belongs to the gift of wisdom (*Summa theologiae* 2. 2, q 9, a.2, ad 1). Therefore the gift of wisdom corresponds more to charity which unites humans' minds to God (*Summa theologiae* 2. 2, q.9, a.2, ad 1). Thus we could say with Thomas that one cannot judge of the things apprehended through cognition unless one is united to the highest things through affection (*In III Sententias*, d. 35, q 2, sol. 3, n. 150). All the gifts, precisely as habitual dispositions, are rooted in love. They come with love and are receive their unity from love (*Summa theologiae* 1. 2, q.68, a.5). Wisdom and love go together; wisdom is the habit by which the wise person is spontaneously disposed to act with love and compassion.

7. *In Matt.*, c.5, n.435: "*sancti qui habent cor repletum justitia* [a heart full of justice] *vident excellentius . . . .*"

8. To anticipate chapter 10, another doctrine of "substitution" is at work: just as acts of discursive, conceptual understanding and rational, deliberative judgment are substitutes for the intellectual intuition and spontaneous love that we lack as finite spirits, so also the gifts are substitutes for the virtues that would be the spontaneous springs from which would flow the (primarily human) acts of faith, love, and hope.

Shakespeare put in Hamlet's mouth (act 3, scene 2) some famous lines about our exasperating mixture of the animal, the angelic, and the divine: to be the paragon of animals because sharing noble reason and infinite faculty as would apprehend like a god:

"What a piece of work is man! How noble in reason!
How infinite in faculty! In form and moving how
express and admirable! In action how like an angel!
In apprehension how like a god! The beauty of the
world! The paragon of animals!"

Chapter 10

Habitude & Finitude

Sow a thought, reap an act.
Sow an act, reap a habit.
Sow a habit, reap a character.
Sow a character, reap a destiny.
Zen Buddhist Proverb

[G]ive us the virtues
and in place of the statistical law
governing humanity
one will have an approximation to the statistical law
governing the angels.
Bernard Lonergan, *Grace and Freedom*, pp. 44.

No philosophy can afford to be ignorant of finitude,
under pain of failing to understand itself as philosophy.
Maurice Merleau-Ponty, *Phenomenology of Perception*, p. 38.

Summary

The first two keys to the human spirit, intentionality and
connaturality, need a third, habitude, that is, habit as virtue, remedy for finitude, key to triune consciousness as the
higher operational synthesis of affection, cognition, and
volition, especially, in ethical and mystical life.

Introduction

FEELING IS THE WAY OUR BEING RESONATES WITH OUR DOING; our nature has harmonies ("resonant frequencies") with some actions, dissonance with others, according to who and what we are in our being and nature, especially in our habits, our second nature. Connaturality enables a spontaneous nonconceptual knowing and loving, a true affection with a true intentionality, operating at the core of triadic consciousness. To define human nature "from above" is to say it is a *finite spirit*, the least and lowest in the hierarchy of spirits, but a spirit nonetheless, that is, a being capable of self-transcending knowledge and love. Metaphysically speaking, finitude is the reason for embodiment, which is thus something necessary and positive, the sole means, in fact, by which a finite human spirit can act. This definition does not deny that humans are animals, the highest, as we like to think, of that class of being. There is no conflict between saying we are the lowest of spirits and the highest of animals, although there is a certain explanatory advantage in the former approach when the context is ethical intersubjectivity, not to mention æsthetic and mystical experience.

Tradition knows several ways of naming this manner of defining human nature as a diminished spirit, of doing an anthropology from above to complement the usual one from below. One of the oldest is to distinguish (with Aristotle) *nous*—as spiritual, creative, and intuitive intellect—from *dianoia*—as material, receptive, and discursive reason. The mediævals spoke of *intellectus* and *ratio* to cover this distinction, terms that refer not to separate powers or faculties in or of the soul, but to lower and higher *perfections* and *performances* of the one soul's capacity to know and to love. Thus *intellectus* and *ratio* are not to be understood as faculties but as levels of performance (despite the language used since the fifth century B.C., the proliferation of parallel terms, and the rigid longevity of the persistent old "faculty psychology").

For an anthropology from above, the human soul is a lesser spirit (*un ange manqué, une intuition manquée*).[1] According to the hierarchy of spirits, a doctrine going back at least to Plotinus, at our best human level of performance we asymptotically approximate the lowest level of knowledge and love exercised by the next higher level of spirit, but because of our finitude we usually fall back on concepts and judgments as substitutes for that intuition, and fall back on deliberative volition as substitutes for spontaneous love. Let us now turn to that idea, essential to understanding triadic consciousness as our response to and remedy for this finitude.

Human Knowledge as "Intuition Manquée"

We begin with a key modern text:

> Finally, he opposed certain illogical Scholastics of his own century who had inherited the psychology of the twelfth century: these thinkers, of whom the most typical representative appears to me to be William of Auvergne, having distinguished, as was the custom, between the knowledge of science and the knowledge of wisdom, did not know how to relate them to a common principle and so, like the voluntarists of all ages, they attributed to the affective, to the "*heart*," all that was *direct, simple, and profound in the acts of intelligence.* [Rousselot 1935, 37–38; my ital. and trans.].

This opening text means—which may not be obvious at first reading—that Aquinas (and Rousselot agrees with him), *does* trace both knowledges to a common principle, so that heart is but a name for *"all that was simple, direct, and profound"* in the act of *intelligence*—once intelligence is interpreted to mean triune consciousness. The clue for this interpretation is that the Greek *nous* (see Louth (1981), actually means something closer to heart, with *dianoia* (*ratio*, mind, reason) meaning what is *not* "simple, direct, and profound," namely, the "compound, indirect, and surface" in the activities, as the New

Testament Greek (according to Guillaumont [1950, 41–81, esp. 63–64]) distinguished them; *dianoia* is closer to *ratio* ("reason" as "*discursive* reason"). But *intellectus* here, as we shall see later in great detail, is technically but not really separable (though distinct) from *ratio:* the crucial difference between them is that we cannot predicate *ratio* of God and angels, but we can predicate *intellectus* of them, as the highest power of spirit. To speak of intellect and reason, therefore, is not to speak of two faculties but of two levels of performance or modes of operation of one triune consciousness. Seen from above, *intellectus* is the highest form of spirit, and so of triune consciousness; seen from below, *intellectus* is the habit-perfected level of *ratio.*

Having grown up in the Thomist tradition and having read Aquinas for years in light of interpreters like Rousselot, Maréchal, Rahner, and Lonergan, not to mention Ricoeur, I am convinced that to understand Aquinas's use of *intellectus* we must often (but not always, not, for example when explicit contrast with will is made) read it as triune consciousness, not as a narrowly cognitive faculty. In his usage it is asked to cover too much to mean knowledge alone; it is often (but not always) his shorthand for the spiritual soul itself. It makes better sense of his texts on wisdom and of his synecdochic use of expressions like "the intellective soul" and "our intellectual nature" to include the will *and* the *affectus* he took to be its embodiment. It also fits Rousselot's understanding of the term "intellectualism" as describing Aquinas's philosophy. If we keep in mind this suggestion, we can recover the best of a very rich tradition and bring it into dialogue with the contemporary recovery of the affective. The first fruit of this suggestion is to recognize discursive *ratio* as the lower operation of cognitive consciousness, while *intellectus* names the degrees of our participation in intuitive knowing *and* spontaneous loving; recall the texts describing *non*connatural knowing, *all of which* use *ratio*, not *intellectus*. (All this talk of faculties must finally be overcome anyway, as Lonergan has so well said, when a "faculty psychology," based on a priority of metaphysics over epistemology gives way to a contemporary priority of the phenomenology of consciousness over hermeneutics, leading to an operational description of affection, cognition, and volition.)

"Discursive" knowing means going through some or all of the four levels and twelve operations we reviewed in the introduction and chapter 8. "Deliberative" means that if concepts and discursive judgments are substitutes for an *intellectus,* an intellectual intuition that we humans lack, then deliberate will-acts would also be substitutes for the kind of love which, as a fulfilled resting in union with the good, ideally would be the essence of a spiritual being's communion with other spiritual beings. A perfect act that is not spatio-temporally sequential is certainly not our usual human fare, but represents a *Grenzbegriff,* a paradigm and standard against which to compare our "normal," human, discursive and deliberative performance. Thus, were we spirit in fullness, happiness would consist in an immediate and direct communion with others, in comparison with which discursive thinking and deliberative will-acts are substitutes. Likewise, in cognition, lacking an intuitive knowledge, we must have recourse to discursive understanding and rational judgment.[2] How can we make sense of these claims?

I have gathered below (all ital., brackets, and trans. mine) Rousselot's six arguments (with their Thomist texts) for the position that *discursive reason is a deficient mode* of participation in the paradigm represented by the concept of *intellectus* (where *intellectus* is to be taken as a mediæval term for the higher operational synthesis called triune consciousness). Again, human intelligence is itself *not a faculty*, not a separate power, but *triune consciousness connaturalized to truth and value by habit as virtue* (including, for Aquinas as a theologian, the virtues infused by grace as the theological gifts of the Spirit). Thus *ratio* (the "faculty") perfected by habit is *intellectus,* and *intellectus* is here taken as synecdoche [in Aquinas's mediæval intellectualism]) for the intellective soul, that is, finite spirit as intellect in its higher operational synthesis with affection and will. Viewed from below, *ratio* becomes *intellectus* through habit; viewed from above, *intellectus* as participated in by finite human spiritual souls becomes *ratio*.

[1] *Intellect and reason are not two different powers*, but are distinguished as the perfect and imperfect (*Summa theologiae* 2. 2, q.83, a.10, ad 2), intellect meaning intimate penetration of truth, and reason meaning research and discursive reason [*discours*] (*Summa theologiae* 2. 2, q.49, a.5, ad 3).

[2] Reason [*raison*] differs from intelligence as multitude from unity; according to Boethius its relation to intellect is as circumference of a circle to the center, or of time to eternity. It is characteristic of reason to spread itself out around a lot of objects and to make of them a simple knowledge. Intellect, on the contrary, where it grasps knowledge of a whole multitude, sees right away one simple truth: much in the same way does God, by perceiving the divine essence, knows all things. [Connaturality is based on this reference to one's own nature; affective connaturality is its form in finite embodied spirit.] Thus one sees that *reasoning converges toward intellection and terminates therein* and also that *intellection is the principle* [*principium*: origin, source, beginning] *of reasoning* that collects and combines. (*In Trinitate* 6.1.3).[3]

[3] "*Rationaliy is a quality of the genus animal*; it cannot be attributed either to God or angels"(*Commentary on the Sentences* 1 d.25, q.1, ad 4).

[4] "The lower intelligences, namely the human, obtain their perfection in the knowledge of truth by spirit's movement and discursive reason . . . . But if from the knowledge of a principle we were immediately to see and know all conclusions that follow from it, then *we would not be discur-*

sive reasoners [*discursifs*]. Such is the case of the angels, who right from the start, in their first natural cognitive acts, see all they can know. Therefore they are called intellectual beings, since even *our* immediate and natural apprehensions are called intellections. *Human souls, which acquire knowledge of truth by a discursive reasoning, are called rational.* And *it is the weakness of their intellectual light that causes it.* (*Summa theologiae* 1, q.58, a.3).

[5] It is the *imperfection of our intellectual nature that causes knowing by reasoning,* because something known by means of another thing is less known than were it known directly through itself, and because *the knowing subject's nature doesn't suffice for knowing* the first in the absence of the second [the present context is cognition, that is, *knowing* through one's nature, and connaturality is the model for cognition; but connaturality is the model for *triune* consciousness: thus the model for love is also connaturality, that is, spontaneous affection rather than deliberate will-act]. Now knowledge by reasoning uses middle terms, whereas what is known intellectually is known through itself, and the knower's nature suffices for knowledge without mediation of anything external. Obviously, then, *reasoning is a defect* [*défaut*] *of intellect* (*quod defectus quidam intellectus est ratiocinatio*) [reasoning is intelligence's "default" mode of operation, when connaturality is not available] (*Summa contra gentiles* 1, 57, 8).

[6] The certitude of reason comes from intellect, but the *necessity of reason comes from a defect* [*défaut*] *of intellect: fully intellectual beings don't need to reason* (*Summa theologiae* 2. 2, q.49, a.5, ad 2).[4]

Perfect knowledge, according to this anthropology from above, is intuitive; imperfect cognition is discursive. Likewise, perfect love is spontaneous; imperfect love requires deliberate will-acts. We need to reason because we do not possess intellectual intuition; concepts and reasoned judgments are

our discursive substitutes for intuition. We need to will insofar as we have not achieved ("expert") spontaneity through
virtue; deliberation and acts of the will are our volitional substitutes for spontaneous love, love as affective response. In
brief, we have in this concept of a hierarchy of spirits, and
the resulting view of the human soul as a lesser spirit on a
continuum with intuitive and spontaneous higher spirits, the
ontological basis of the heart tradition. Reason is a substitute
for a missing intellectual intuition; we are rational because
the human soul is a *finite* spirit. Connaturality and habitude
are then to be understood as partial *remedies* for this finitude,
specifically as substitutes for the substitutes.

Connaturality and habit (virtue) are asymptotic approxi-
mations of *intellectus* (including, in this usage, *voluntas*), which
I am interpreting, in the spirit of the foregoing intellectualism, as the higher operational synthesis of affection, cognition, and volition we have called triune consciousness. By
intellectus (*nous*) is meant not a faculty but a set of higher
operations; it is the classical name for triune consciousness.
"Heart" is also a name that tradition has given triune consciousness in recognition of the essential role played by feeling; heart is experienced as potential for higher acts than
reason and will alone. We have seen how affective intentionality and connaturality make sense of feeling by integrating
affection into consciousness and showing how this can be understood phenomenologically and ontologically.

Viewed from below, the highest operational level of consciousness is a sublating of the levels and operations (some
or all) of the "head."[5] Viewed from above, affection, cognition, and volition are a single triune consciousness, and our
acquired habits (virtues)—or the (infused) virtues as gifts of
the Spirit, to recall the theological example—are our ways of
improving our discursive reason and deliberate will in vertical finality, in the upward direction toward the ideal.

Connaturality: Substitute for Substitutes

Connaturality brings the whole of triune consciousness to a higher perfection than either discursive reason or deliberative volition represent, alone or in combination. Connatural knowledge is more perfect than conceptual knowledge or reasoning because it includes all three intentionalities in a higher operational synthesis. From this perspective, a deliberate will-act is a substitute for the spontaneous love of a higher spirit; as finite, a nontriadic consciousness lacks a more "skilled" mode of loving (until habits are developed [or given as gifts]) and instead has to have recourse to volition. Once the higher mode of knowing and loving is taken to be the paradigm, our lower modes can fairly be considered substitutes for those higher modes. Insofar, then, as we find ways to overcome the limitations of the lower modes, we may be said to substitute for the substitutes. Connaturality is a traditional name for just such a way to come closer to the intuitive knowing and spontaneous loving of the higher spirits. This approach makes sense because *the heart of connaturality itself is habit,* and because *the role and function of habit-virtue (acquired or gift) is precisely to extend and enhance the range and performance of human nature.* It is therefore a central thesis of this study that we need a paradigm shift in defining human nature. The proper approach to defining human nature is not solely from below, and the norm for defining human nature is by no means discursive reason and deliberative will.

Why define ourselves by our lowest and least level of performance? Why not define human being by the high end of performance, namely, by human nature as perfected by virtue?

From the moment when human interior distention would cease, our representational distention, the distention of our concepts, would also cease. As human I would contemplate [*envisagerait:* look in the face] my essence, my substantial self; I would live my soul, my entire soul; and in the same instant I would know exterior being by a *sympathetic intuition.* All material apathy would vanish into *spiritual sympathy.* No longer having a remainder to be reduced within itself, the soul would also henceforth find no obstacle to its penetrating into objects. In short, *the deep root of conceptual distention and abstraction . . . is the imperfection of our spiritual being. If I as a human person cannot bring my object completely to light it's because I myself am not completely brought to light* [Rousselot 1910d, 488; my trans. and ital.]."[6]

This is the ground of the paradigm shift in defining human nature not from below as rational animal but from above as finite spirit; virtue (*habitus*) is the true meaning of triune consciousness as the higher perfection of human action, especially in the ethical domain.

I have previously (Tallon 1982a) presented a metaphysical anthropology. But it was too dependent on an approach that almost completely ignored the essential role of affectivity. No doubt it showed clearly that the human, finite spirit, as cognitive, must embody itself in order to begin the task of substituting for the missing intellectual intuition with sense intuition. This need for a finite spirit to be material is nearly a universal metaphysical doctrine, first enunciated by Aristotle, developed by Aquinas, held by Kant in the *Critique of Pure Reason*, echoed by Heidegger in his Kant book, and most solidly established by Karl Rahner in his *Spirit in the World* and *Hearer of the Word*, both written in the Thomist metaphysical tradition and in light of contemporary phenomenology.

And yet we must admit that knowing through feeling had already become a neglected idea in Aquinas's time, and had to be reborn in his teaching of knowledge by connaturality, an idea he left quite undeveloped. The primary locus for this idea was ethical and mystical, as we saw above, and was meant as a practical account of moral uprightness in those who lived without benefit of a college ethics course, and of the way humans might experience the presence of the divine in their lives, without the schooling of the masters of theology.[7] To

explain connaturality we continually needed the idea of habit
(as did Ricoeur), so we now have to articulate that relationship in detail. It is a short step from noticing that every time
we try to understand connaturality we find ourselves talking
about habit, to discovery that in fact the meaning of connaturality after all *is* habit. As Rousselot says,

> This theory, so frequently cited by modern Scholastics, who
> so rarely try to explain it, seems to me can be rationally
> demonstrated in the following way. Virtue once acquired,
> that is, according to Thomist principles, and the appetites
> habituated to act by themselves as ordered by reason, there
> is no need, for each particular act, for a reflection that
> goes back to principles: one makes the quicker move of an
> interior glance at one's *tendencies* and *sees* how they react in
> given circumstances. Thus when a habit has been formed
> and known, *one judges about its specific object by the greater or
> less facility of exercise.* A Londoner who could not logically
> classify instances of when to say *shall* and *will,* accurately
> and without hesitation will respond to concret examples—
> at least as long as he listens to how his organs go and doesn't
> get tangled up in reflection. A little child who is still un-
> sure of the use of the words *right* and *left* might get help
> from mechanically making the sign of the cross. Between
> action and judgment an inference as rapid as lightning slips
> in, based on the bond, known beforehand, between the
> action and its habitual term. In this way Thomas's examples
> and formulæ are both explained without prejudice to in-
> tellectuality.[8]

Intellect and intelligence, then, do not at all mean discursive activity first and foremost but rather the radical simplicity of spirit preceding all talk of faculties of cognition and
volition, language that we find necessary to introduce in order to make sense of our lower *human* version of spirit, that
is, finite, embodied spirit. That a spirit's immateriality by its
very nature makes it self-present and thereby already self-aware
and self-possessed is a thesis characteristic of Aquinas (al-

though one denied by other Scholastics [for example, Siger de Brabant] who insist on adding another act [besides the spirit's self-presence through its immateriality] in order to constitute knowledge and love). A finite spirit, because of its lesser immateriality, is material, embodied; embodiment is its very way to *become* spirit, precisely as flesh is integrated with the spirit through habit (virtue).[9]

The above text includes a cognitional and a volitional example. In both earlier examples, the Londoner and the child knew *in and through* the saying and doing; their performance or operation mediated a knowledge, mediated it nonrepresentationally rather than representationally: in the saying, as an action being exercised, the knowing spontaneously arose. The nonrepresentationality of these examples recalls that of the many similar examples cited in the first seven chapters. In the example of the chaste person we have a nonrepresentationality that is also explicitly affective: the chaste person feels something, a kind of resonance, a "connatural harmony"—either a sympathy or revulsion; in the latter case I might say that it "goes against my nature," or against my "*better* nature," against what has become *second* nature to me. This better second nature is habit as virtue. We are well beyond a notion of feelings as mere accompaniments to representations; the guidance is given with the tendency itself: "In given circumstances, as the possessors of such habits, we have merely to glance, as it were, at our inner tendencies to see how to react" (Rousselot 1935, 79). "What is common to all three levels is that knowledge is *per connaturalitatem, per modum naturae,* that is, by the knower's level of being or self-presence, which is the level of one's self-knowledge."[10]

From Connaturality to Habitude

As the key to understanding affective intentionality is connaturality, the key to understanding connaturality is habit, as acquired and as gift. Habit as virtue is second act (*actus secundus*) that actualizes consciousness to some higher degree of development or skill. When love becomes more than *act*, that is, becomes *habit* (virtue), it transforms the nature whose it is, bringing it closer to the limit-idea of a spirit that knows without thinking and reasoning. This is what we have now to understand.

Habit as Acquired

Habit names something installed between being and acting. We first explore the idea of habit as an *acquired* (that is, learned) perfecting of a nature (saving for later the idea of habit as *gift* of virtue, virtues such as faith and hope, resulting from the transformation of consciousness that comes of being loved by another). I again quote de Finance:

> But to know means more than simple [acts of] knowledge. Knowledge can be momentary, occasional, transitory: it is an act. For knowledge to *remedy my limitation* and let me conquer the alterity of the object more completely, it must fix itself in me: acting must *sediment in being* [must settle into my being]. In other words, knowing must become a *habitus*. For *habitus* is a sort of *middle term between being and acting*, an acting stabilized in being, a being in *tension toward acting* and *bearing the structure of that action in its being.* Fixed in *habitus*, the act loses its alterity in relation to the subject in losing its casual character. Insofar as I do not have the *habitus* or habit, the success of my deed . . . remains chancy, depending on the other: there has to be a conjunction of several elements, of which the knot is outside me. *Habitus* puts this knot in my hands. *If it is perfect, there is no need of effort*, as though to capture an elusive prey in flight. The act is in me and I can at will make it happen [literally: I can deploy it into actuality] . . . . Knowing is a *habitus*: it is knowledge that has *passed into the structure of the spirit* [1973, 97; my trans., ital., and brackets].

If we take this insight as a motif, namely, that habit is "installed" or intervenes (mediates) between being and doing—

as a kind of having, a "property," proper to a person as a subject of acts, perfecting a being for the sake of doing—then triadic consciousness may be understood as the highest actuation of a spiritual *being in the direction of acting*, specifically on behalf of the actions that fulfill it *as* a spiritual being, that is, as a being able to know and to love self-transcendentally (especially in the realms of ethical [and mystical] intersubjectivity). Actions change their agent by "depositing a sediment," by engraving their lineaments in the supple tissue of human potential. Note especially this mention of "*less dependence on the other*," an additional sign of approximation to the higher spirits, that is, to a more fully integrated (more immanent) subjectivity. One who has a virtue can expect to act in accord with it in circumstances that are less supportive, more difficult, minimally satisfying, with "no one watching" (whether to praise or to blame). By acquiring virtues one becomes an authentic, autonomous *subject*, a *principle and source* of beneficence, drawing action from within one's more perfectly immanent self-transcendent subjectivity.

According to Gordon Allport (1955), in great part all capacity to learn means acquiring habits as (re)structuring malleable human nature; it is essential to human becoming:

> I refer to certain latent or potential capacities that play a crucial role in becoming. Every young animal, for example, seems to have the capacity to learn. That is to say, there is something *inherently plastic in our neuropsychic nature* that will *make changes in response possible*. If normally endowed, the human infant will in time develop a conscience, a sense of self, and a hierarchical organization of traits. He or she will become some sort of structural system, self-regulating and self-maintaining. What is more, he or she will exert himself or herself to become something more than a stencil copy of the species to which he or she belongs. Such capacities are not instincts in the sense of McDougall or Freud; rather they represent potentialities for attaining adulthood. What we call instincts are primarily means for

ensuring survival: the capacities I speak of are of the sort to ensure growth and orderly structure. They bring about characteristic stadia in human development.

Consider for a moment the capacity to learn. No theory of motivation explains why we learn at all; at best it accounts for the urge but not for the modifiability of conduct. Nor does any so-called "learning theory" tell why we learn, but only how we learn. Everyone knows that we learn, but few psychologists, least of all the Lockeans, seem to wonder about the nature of the underlying disposition to adapt and to modify behavior. Now whatever else *learning* may be it is clearly a *disposition to form structures. Structures include simple habits and sequences of habits;* but they also include more complex and less rigid *structures such as moral conscience,* one's conception of oneself, pre-emptive traits and interests, schemata of meaning, and even one's embracing philosophy of life . . . *Learning . . . leads to the formation of more or less stable structures . . .* [b]ut it would not do so unless these stadia too were *carried in our natures as inherent possibilities.* They likewise comprise a type of "given" in human nature, much neglected in personality theory today ([1955, 26–27; my ital.]).

This fundamental capacity and tendency to form habits is an innate drive to compensate for and overcome our finitude by developing our potential, by trying to approach the horizon of our capacity to be more highly actualized embodied consciousnesses. The goal of learning, at its most personal and interpersonal peak, is to develop triune consciousness. The developed structures of adult personality and character form the unique constellation of dispositions to act spontaneously and with a directness and immediacy that needs neither thought nor will, primarily in ethical face -to-face relations. We approximate the high end of human potential when our actions work back upon and transform our nature, thanks to its native flexibility and plasticity, in order to mold and model it in the direction of those deeds.

Habit & Conversion

It would be pedantic to offer arguments to prove that we acquire virtues from the ground up, from below, and theology has also told us that grace is virtue from the top down, from above (and a philosophical interpretation of grace has shown that these two ideas are complementary). Allport also refers to the idea of "saltatory becoming" (conversion), which relates to the idea of habit as gift. An example might be meeting someone or hearing someone speak who so touches the center of one's being that a rapid conversion occurs. Let us consider this approach to virtue (habit as acquired) as a bridge to the next section (habit [virtue] as gift).

Allport's word for the self is *proprium,* and this needs a brief word of explanation. For Allport, "the person is the *source* of acts" (12). He says that "the person is not [just] a collection of acts, nor simply the locus of acts; the person is the source of acts . . . . To understand what a person is, it is necessary always to refer to what one may be in the future, for every state of the person is pointed in the direction of future possibilities" (12). Furthermore, "personality is less a finished product than a transitive process. While it has some stable features, it is at the same time continually undergoing change. It is this course of change, of becoming, of individuation that is now our special concern (19) [:] . . . the feature of personality that is most outstanding—is its manifest uniqueness of organization" (21). Allport's name for this configuration of the person's unique organization is the *proprium,* from Latin for "self." "The proprium develops in time" (61). Over time, change is a constant rather than an intermittent process, although there are times when change is greater than at other times, namely, upon conversion as a real change of heart. When we refer to the kind of change that touches the self or proprium, such as love that floods our hearts and reorganizes consciousness from the top down, we are dealing with something built into human nature as its most basic capacity and tendency. Its very being, as a finite spirit, is a personal becoming, an interpersonal becoming (Tallon 1982a).

> It sometimes happens that the very center of organization of a personality shifts suddenly and apparently without warning. Some impetus, coming from perhaps a bereavement, an illness, or a religious conversion, even from a teacher or book, may lead to a reorientation. In such cases of traumatic recentering it is undoubtedly true that *the person had latent within her all of the capacities and sentiments that suddenly rise from a subordinate to a superordinate position in her being.* What she had once learned mechanically or incidentally may suddenly acquire heat and liveliness and motor power. What once seemed to her cold, "out there," "not mine" may change places and become hot and vital, "in here," "mine." I mention this phenomenon of *saltatory becoming,* not because it is frequent or typical but because it illustrates the complexity and lability of the organizational process. Becoming is not a matter of forging links to a chain. It sometimes involves the shifting of dominance from segmental systems to comprehensive systems, or from one comprehensive system to another [Allport 1955, 87].

We overcome limitation and finitude by virtue of habitude.[11] To acquire habits is to acquire *oneself,* but now at a higher level of actualization, which is to gain *self*-possession and to appropriate one's *own* nature by relating to it creatively, which one does with the consciousness and volition of intellect and will. The result of using one's head is thus to change one's heart. As a subject I change myself, take more responsibility for myself, *am* myself on a higher plateau.

The Nature of Habit

We need now to deepen our formal analysis of habit itself.

> Habit is something added to a power. Habit modifies action, which is its principal intent, by modifying the principle of that action. This modification is a relatively permanent and *intrinsic perfection of the power,* and so is like *a form* which *gives determination, actuality, and perfection.* Yet habit is not wholly an act, since it is still a potency in comparison to a further act which is operation. In this, habit is something like the power in which it inheres. For a power is an accidental, qualitative perfection of a substance, and so it is an act in comparison to substance; yet a power is at the same time a potency in comparison to activity. A habit, too, is an act or perfection, inasmuch as it is a *qualitative modification* of a power; yet it is still a potency in comparison to activity. However, *a habit is closer to act than the power,* which is a pure potency in the order of activity. To express this perfection of a habit in relation to activity, as well as to power, *habit may be called a first act* [Klubertanz 1953, 285; my ital.].

If we might in this way (Figure 7) represent the simple model of a nature endowed with powers performing an action:

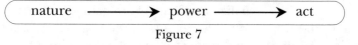

Figure 7

then we might show habit formation thus (Figure 8), much simplified, of course (that is, only one iteration).

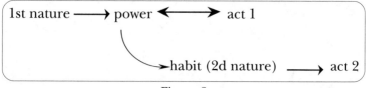

Figure 8

The habit, which is within the power within the nature, is changed by the act; the act changes the habit and thus also the nature whose it is. The act is both within one's nature, so that one changes oneself (one affects oneself) as one acts (this is autoaffection, one's self-transformation as a learning being), and outside one's nature insofar as one affects the world. The act's effect back upon one's nature through the medium of the habit modifies the power, perfects the power and constitutes each habit a second nature.

Habit is simultaneously both the ground of connaturality and the way a finite spirit strives to overcome or compensate for its finitude and become more fully spirit, more spiritual: ". . . *habit becomes connatural,* it adapts the power to itself, it enters into a very close union with the power in which it inheres . . . . *Habit leads to self-mastery,* an increase and concentration of power and effective action . . . . [H]abit is developed by personal activity. Hence it does not depend on an external cause" (287; my ital.). Self-mastery and concentrated immanence mean greater autonomy: the more one's nature improves by habit, the less one depends on external causes.[12]

The best way to point out the increased centering or integration of the personality is not so much in (negative) contrast with passion as in (positive) contrast with reason and will insofar as virtues perfect the person as a spontaneous source of good actions. But we are never so spontaneous that we need *no* other in order to act; we need the *conversio ad phantasmata* that is the hallmark of finite cognition, and the turning to the affections that is the hallmark of finite will. (We should, with Aquinas, call the phantasm the "matter of the cause" [*materia causae*] where intellect is formal cause of knowing, as he explains in the *Summa theologiae* 1 q.84, a.6.) The growth of habits can be seen to be a growth in immanence, interiority, existential subjectivity. This increased interiority of the subject is a direct result of the development of virtue; its opposite is a dispersion of one's efforts, an aimlessness and directionless, a life without a center, meaning, goals, sense of purpose—a *spargi ad multa,* which is precisely the nature of formless matter, not of the self-presence and self-possession of spirit. Habit structurally installs between nature and act, sinks roots into nature, connaturalizing the nature to the acts that form the habit. Connaturality is thus a name for how a nature tends to perfect its ability to act, for example, performing in fewer operations, more easily, enjoyably, spontaneously, immediately, directly; less discursive thought and rational will (deliberation and choice) are needed.

Thus heart does not mean a separate faculty besides intellect, reason, sense, will, and the like, but habituated, connaturalized human nature. Becoming more centered does not mean becoming more ego-centered, because *this* centering and integration is also an ego-transcending adaptation to the world of values that are the other side of the dual nature of a habit, namely, its being both a modification of the subject who is the agent of the act and an adaptation of that modified nature to superior performance of the relevant intentional actions. Since it is *between* being and acting, habit participates in both nature and act, has a foot in both, and so is the structural bridge between them. Thus a centered self is really a self-transcendent subject. The old expression, "remedy for our concupiscence" (grace as gift of virtue), like de Finance's phrase "remedy my limitation," recalls the purpose of habit. By a brief reflection on the concept of grace as virtue, we can now add, in the next section, a final insight into the meaning of triune consciousness.

Habit as Gift

Let us now return to the idea of habit as gift from above. The theological idea of grace as a global reorientation of the whole psyche (the "love of God flooding our hearts") leads to a total effect, a profound change of consciousness affecting one's whole being. Again, this is not an excursus into religion but an attempt to show philosophical insight in an analogous concept. First, let us take grace as a theological word for a human experience (Lonergan 1971). The analogy is that grace remedies sinful human nature in a way similar to the way virtue remedies finite human nature. Grace names the love that comes as a gift from outside ("from above") to transform consciousness. In what follows, as before, we are interested only in the philosophical import of grace as an example of how habit is at the root of connaturality.

The philosophical content of the idea of grace is that *grace is a habit* that exists between the *being* of the human subject and that subject's ability to *act,* specifically to act in a way differently from the way it could act without this addition to or modification of itself. Our line of reasoning relates directly to a metaphysics of connaturality. Beginning with Aquinas's earlier works and moving through them to his later, Lonergan has shown that the concept of habit as gift is a nonviolent (meaning "not unnatural") way to explain the change we call the love that transforms consciousness (and changes our hearts).[13] He has demonstrated that one result of Aquinas's evolved treatment of this relation of interactions between the human nature and the divine was to change the way the gifts of the Spirit were conceived: "unnatural" (violent) evolved into *connatural* (natural). By the time we get to Aquinas's late work, the *Summa theologiae,* the solution there

> . . . is a very adequate answer to the objection that external intervention is violent, or as we should say, unnatural. The moral virtues are of two kinds: those like prudence and justice which perfect the faculties in which they inhere; others like temperance and fortitude which *render the lower faculties spontaneous* in their subordination to higher faculties. Similarly *habits are of two kinds*: the *virtues perfect the individual* that possesses them, but the *gifts of the Holy Spirit make connatural* to the creature the external guidance and aid of the Spirit of *truth and love* [Lonergan 1971, 44–45; my ital.].

Thus an external intervention (an "infused virtue" given as gift of the Spirit) can nonviolently—that is, not *un*naturally but *con*naturally—change its recipient even to the point of being the necessary condition for its being brought from its imperfection to its actualized state of perfection.[14] The philosophical point of this reflection is that the gifts of truth, goodness, and beauty and the power of love that transforms consciousness (called grace in the present context) are, thus, not only acts but also can become habits (virtues), and even become the *deepest marks of someone's character*. In the theological analogy we are using here for our hermeneutical purposes, grace stands for a love capable of connaturalizing the beloved to the lover, just as we can connaturalize ourselves to values. Love perfects both lover and beloved; human nature is raised by gifts, and gifts become virtues, each one a *virtus* as ability to act.

Love as virtue given as gift makes us less finite in the sense that as spiritual creatures we are closer to the next higher level, with cognition and love more connatural, more spontaneous (through the acquired spontaneity of virtue). This large claim has to be guarded with the analogy of proportion, since it is evident that we humans, despite grace, continue to fail at the human rate rather than at the angelic rate; no matter how we admire and strive for the ideal, we are not freed from the labor of concrete life. Still, let us not unduly water down Aquinas's teaching on the transforming effect of grace on human lives: ". . . [I]t would be a grave misinterpretation to ascribe to St. Thomas the view that the supernatural virtues give merely the possibility of a type of action and do not make it *spontaneous and connatural*. His whole exposition is in terms of natural forms and natural inclinations: *a virtue is a second nature . . .*" (46; my ital.). Granted the experience of daily life, if we keep analogy and proportion in mind, we can recall our own experience of being confirmed, loved, accepted and shown truth, value, and beauty by someone, and recall also the way that someone's "Yes" not only changed our lives and our selves, but also made different actions possible and even likely to come forth from us. Kierkegaard's *Works of Love* speaks of how knowing that someone "thinks the world of you" tends to make you be and do your best at least with respect to that person, as though you are led, by being loved, to act in such a way as not to disprove the expectations of someone wise and good enough to love you.

Interaction between persons can be such that connaturally, with an effect almost in the domain of *formal* causality (the power is changed and so through it the nature is also changed) there results a new effect in the domain of *efficient* causality: one becomes capable of actions, through that changed power, that one could not otherwise perform, and they are easier and more spontaneous. Persons have the power to give another a gift that mediates between nature and act by modifying the other's ability to act. Learning is a from-below active acquisition of habits (even when aided by a teacher who is "above" one's present skill level). Being loved is a from-above gift; human love is the prime analogue for such a gift: one person's self-donation changes the life, heart and soul, of another. Out of such an affirming, confirming "Yes" to one's being by another comes faith and trust in that someone, and also hope for one's life to come.[15] The above discussion of grace has been intended to serve not as a foray into theology or religion per se, but as evidence that philosophical insight into the full range of triune consciousness applies both to the ethical and the mystical (per Aquinas's text).[16]

Conclusion

Connaturality has traditionally been presented as an exceptonal, unusual, even ignorable substitute for discursive cognition and deliberative volition, in whole or in part, but we should rethink this idea of substitution in favor of interpreting it more as a natural developental stage in human vertical finality. Recalling Dreyfus's phenomenology of skill acquisition, we might well consider connaturality, especially in light of a thesis of triune consciousness, as the entry of affection into full partnership with cognition and volition rather than as competing with or supplanting them. Connaturality can then become the new paradigm for normality, as the norm rather than the exception in matters æsthetic, ethical, and mystical. Granted that the practical result might appear to be the same: one's knowing is more intuitive, and one's love more spontaneous, but the theoretical cost of interpreting connaturality *exclusively as substitution* is too high. Affection raises head consciousness to a higher level by adding to it rather than putting it out of play.

Appendix
Péghaire on Intellectus & Ratio

Péghaire (1936) has made a thorough study of the important distinction between *ratio* and *intellectus*. I offer here a summary of it. (All translations mine; numbers in square brackets refer to page[s] in his book.) Péghaire says intellect is *not a faculty* at all. Instead he says that the best meaning of *intellect* is that it is a *habit*. Let us first review the part of Péghaire's text that is relevant to our theme. I present a schematic outline of the possible meanings of *intellectus* at the end of this appendix (see Figure 9, p. 279).

The idea of Aquinas's "intellectualism" is based on the frequently cited concept of the Pseudo-Denis according to which there is not only a hierarchy of spiritual beings but a continuum between them such that a lower nature at its most perfect performance *touches* the lowest level of the next higher spirit: ". . . as Dionysius says, in Chapter VII of *On the Divine Names*, a lower nature at its best touches the lowest point of the [next] higher nature; and therefore the nature of the soul in its highest point touches the lowest point of the angelic nature and therefore participates in intellectuality in its [the soul's] highest point" [34]. The terms descriptive of how *intellectus* knows, in comparison with *ratio*, are "immediately," "suddenly," and "without space and time" (*statim, subito,* and *sine continuo et tempore*) [39–40]. Péghaire asks what is the nature of the human intellect: faculty or habit? "(*Nature de l'intellectus humain: faculté ou habitus?*)" [207]. He says: "We have seen that besides *ratio* there exists in humans an *intellectus* whose act is more perfect than that of this *ratio* because despite a certain complexity, whether in what prepares it to act or in itself, it grasps truth nondiscursively" [207]. Everything attributed to *intellectus* can be, should be, and in fact actually is explained in clear texts by Aquinas in terms of *intellectus* being a *habitus*. In three key texts from the *Commentary on the Sentences* Aquinas holds that "it is by a habit that the human soul is called intellectual, and this habit is called *intellectus*" [212]). The primary evidence for this attribution of a minimal degree of intellect to human knowing is, in fact, the "habit of first principles," that mediate knowledge given "without need of thought or judgment" (*sans raisonnement* [213]). "It seems therefore legitimate to conclude that according to the *Commentary* the *intellectus* that one contrasts with *ratio* is, to speak as formally as possible, a habit perfecting *ratio* from the moment that *ratio* becomes present to the first principles" [214].

In the *De veritate* Aquinas asks whether the distinction between *intellectus* and *ratio* is a distinction between two faculties: "*Utrum intellectus et ratio sint diversae potentiae*" (Whether intellect and reason are different powers) [216]. And he says No. Two arguments are given, and they come to the point that *intellectus* and *ratio* accomplish the same thing, but *intellectus* does so without discourse (that is, without thought and judgment), and this accomplishment is, of course, just what habit, as perfecting *ratio*, makes possible [216]. Thus *ratio* and *intellectus* are not two separate cognitive faculties but the latter is the perfect act of the former [217]. But even as the perfection of *ratio,* our *intellectus* is still a deficient human participation in the angelic [215–16]. Quoting liberally from the *De divinis nominibus,* obviously one of his favorite sources, Aquinas argues that there would be a break in continuity in the human soul between *ratio* and *intellectus* if they were two faculties, as though intellect were to participate in the hierarchically higher level of being, while *ratio* did not share in this participation. The simpler and more elegant idea is that *intellectus* is actually *ratio perfected by the virtue* of immediate presence to the first principles (which he explains later to mean presence to being, a nonobjective presence, to be sure).

> We thus come to the same conclusion after studying the *Commentary,* but with a valuable penetration into its [that is, the doctrine of the *Commentary*] metaphysical foundation. If *ratio* and *intellectus* are only distinct in the way an accident is distinct from its subject and not as one faculty from another, and if consequently our intelligence remains basically one and complete, it is because our *intellectus* is but a very weak participation in a higher nature, a participation that *habitus* amply suffices to insure [219–20].

A secondary text from *De veritate* (q.16, a.1) goes over the same ground asking whether *synderesis* is a *potentia* or a *habitus.* What is interesting is the strict parallel between *synderesis* and *intellectus,* both being habits rather than faculties.

In the *Summa theologiae* we find nothing new about cognition: "*Intellectus* is nothing other than the name of a special act of *ratio*" [225]. Aquinas offers another parallel, but one that touches on volition; he says that intellect is to reason as willing is to choosing (*intellectus : ratio* as *velle : eligere*) [225]. In this we have Aquinas's insistence that one same faculty can have qualitatively different acts; one need not multiply faculties to account for performance that is higher, simpler, less discursive—or, in the case of volitional consciousness—less deliberative. We can truly be free and act with the highest freedom (as when loving God, our highest good) and still not exercise choice; the idea of freedom without choice seems less paradoxical when the love comes from the heart (as sublating choice because of participation in the immediate spontaneity of the higher spirits thanks to the virtue of love [and faith and hope] rather than from the head, that is, by deliberate acts of will; here again is someone's "love that floods our hearts," moving us from above.

Finally there are Aquinas's commentaries on Aristotle's works, especially the *Posterior Analytics,* the *De anima,* and the ethics, especially the *Nicomachean Ethics,* Book VI, where *nous* (not *dianoia* or *ratio*) is the evident source of Aquinas's *intellectus.* Even against the strong tide of Aristotle's own des-ignation of *nous* as a faculty—he never once uses habit (*hexis*) for it—Aquinas on the other hand (showing his Platonic side) consistently says of *intellectus* that it is a *habit,* the one that precisely allows our human spirit a knowledge *like that of a pure spirit:* "For precisely this grasp of essences is the proper object of the pure angelic and *a fortiori* divine *intellectus.* As what allows our human spirit a like knowledge it well deserves the name of *nous, intellectus*" [229]. The relation of *ratio* to *intellectus* is also explained in terms of the perfection of rest over motion. It is not necessary to subscribe to Aristotle's full theory of contemplation to recognize the higher perfection of a knowledge needing fewer operations and a love needing less deliberation, of knowledge and love that spontaneously arise in the presence of the other.

What Aquinas has done, essentially, in wedding Aristotle's *nous* to Denis's doctrine of spiritual hierarchy is simply to in-sert habit (the *habitus-intellectus*) to avoid a break in the conti-nuity of the hierarchy [231]. Péghaire goes on for another fifteen pages (the rest of the chapter) to show that first prin-ciples are not abstractions but the relation of all being to the ultimate horizon of Being. One might add that *for a person*

this means ultimately also that the color, tone, and feel of
that horizon or ground as nonobjective co-given with all
knowledge and love *is personal.* For Aquinas, "A human being
[is] a *ratio* ordered to an *intellectus*" [282].

A. beings of whom this faculty is the noblest perfection $\left\{\begin{array}{l}\text{1. Christian angels}\\\text{2. separated substances (Aristotle)}\\\text{3. intelligences (Plotinus, Averroës)}\\\text{4. human souls (rare)}\end{array}\right.$

B. an immaterial faculty $\left\{\begin{array}{l}\text{1. comprising }\left\{\begin{array}{l}\text{knowledge}\\\text{appetite}\end{array}\right.\\\text{2. knowledge only }\left\{\begin{array}{l}\text{opposed to }ratio\\\text{identical with }ratio\end{array}\right.\end{array}\right.$

C. a *habitus* perfecting this faculty $\left\{\begin{array}{l}\text{1. gift of the Holy Spirit}\\\text{2. }habitus\text{ of first principles }\left\{\begin{array}{l}\text{universal}\\\text{particular}\end{array}\right.\end{array}\right.$

D. the activity of this faculty $\left\{\begin{array}{l}\text{1. the operation of this faculty}\\\text{2. the concept elaborated by this faculty}\\\text{3. the object known in this concept}\end{array}\right.$

Figure 9

Notes

1. According to Sheehan (1987, 10; my ital.): "The title of Rousselot's major work, *The Intellectualism of St. Thomas*, which really means 'The Intuitionism of St. Thomas,' and its chief argument, which Maréchal transposes into a transcendental mode, is that *affirmation in human cognition is a dynamic substitute for the immediacy of pure intuition* in angels and ultimately in God. That is, as human by nature I am an *intuition manquée*, a tendency towards pure and perfect actuality (Aquinas writes: 'our intellect in knowing stretches into infinity'), and I know an individual entity by introducing it, as a partial end, into my own finality or movement towards unlimited being. I am thus an analogical (*pros ti*) reference to God: I am a metaphysician (one who knows entities in their being) because in some way I am a theologian (one who is projected towards God in every act of knowledge). In this interpretation, metaphysics is possible on the basis of a theoretical intellect focused on sensible entities, once one has understood the dynamic and not just the formal-synthetic nature of speculative reason."

2. Thus one way that Aquinas explains the likenesses and differences between the human intellect and that of angels and God is to distinguish between intellect and reason, *intellectus* and *ratio*. The following quotation from Rousselot guides my interpretation of Aquinas: "The antithesis between simple intellection and discursive reason [*discours*] is marked by the opposition between *intellectus* and *ratio*: it is impossible to exaggerate the importance of this distinction for Thomist philosophy. According to the Neoplatonic law of continuity, lower beings participate by their highest operation in the simpler and nobler nature of the higher beings, so human intelligence functions as *intellect* in certain acts, but its specific mark is *discursive reason* which shatters the intelligible perfection." (Rousselot 1935, 56; my trans.).

As Sheehan (1987) says, "This doctrine of radical intellectualism (i.e., *nous* not *dianoia*, *intellectus* not *ratio*) establishes what knowing as such is by revealing its normative state. *The proper measure for knowing cannot be the conceptual, representational, discursive knowledge which we call reason . . ."* (64; my ital.).

3. Rousselot issues the following caution: "We are the last and lowest in the intellectual order: faced with what nature unfolds with the greatest clarity, we are as blind as bats in the noonday sun. Thomas's entire noetic is but the development of this primary idea and every aspect of his intellectualism as applied to us is conditioned by it. We must always keep this in mind. Were we to forget this capital restriction and read him implicitly supposing the identity of human intelligence and intelligence *ut sic*, the whole system would at once become puerile and contradictory. When Averroës identified the intelligible in itself with what is humanly comprehensible he said something 'quite ridiculous.'" (1935, 53–54; my trans. and brackets).

4. Rousselot 1935, 66–67; my brackets and ital. Rousselot summarizes this collection of texts: "I thought it was necessary to pile up texts like this because even though the composite imperfection or sensible origin of our ideas is readily admitted as an essential teaching of the Thomist noetic, usually there is *much less insistence on the discursive imperfection.* The exclusive exaltation of simple knowledge might appear more appropriate to a certain type of mysticism such as that of the Victorines than to Aquinas's sober Aristotelianism [*péripatétisme sage*], and yet *it is in intuition that he places the ideal and measure of every intellectual operation.* And it is the distinction we emphasize that allows him to 'Platonize' when he considers the universe as a whole while remaining so Aristotelian in his explanation of the sublunary world. To be able to critique the coherence of his system by the evaluations we are about to undertake, we must therefore *beware of considering the judgment or any number of judgments as more perfect in themselves than the simple idea,* always bearing in mind the doctrine condensed in the formula: *necessitas rationis est ex defectu intellectus"* [the need to reason comes from a deficiency of our intellect] [58–59; my trans., brackets, and ital.].

5. Péghaire has written an entire book on the distinction between reason and intellect. I have summarized this important work as an appendix to this chapter.

6. See especially Sheehan (1987, 55–74) for a masterful inter-pretation of Rousselot's use of connaturality as model of conscious-ness.

7. Rousselot (1936, 70–71, my trans. brackets, and ital.) contin-ues: "If Thomas quite often affirms, as did others, the necessity of a moral preparation for the perception of certain truths, it is easy to see that there is no reason in that to accuse him of a contradiction: as not every condition necessary for the constitution of the know-ing subject comes into play in the very act of knowing.—But an-other doctrine of his would seem opposed to that rigorous cogni-tive [*noétique*] intellectualism which alone conforms to his principles: this is his teaching on *Cognitio per modum naturae*, [that is, connatu-ral knowledge] coordinated with, not subordinated to, rational knowledge.

"[As Aquinas says:] 'One can have rectitude of judgment in two ways: first by the perfect use of reason; second, thanks to a certain connaturality with the things about which one actually has to judge. In matters of chastity, to judge well by the rational method is the deed of someone who knows the moral law; but to judge well by connaturality is the deed of someone who has the habit of chas-tity' [*Summa theologiae* 2. 2 q.45, a.2].

"Elsewhere he says: 'Just as one assents to first principles by the natural light of intelligence, so the virtuous person through the habit of the virtue judges correctly about what is in tune [*convient*] with virtue'" [*Summa theologiae* 2. 2 q.2, a.3, ad 2.]

8. Rousselot 1936, 71; my trans. and ital. Sheehan (1987, 71) adds: "In this primitive transparency of 'life,' Rousselot finds the human experience of imitating the simplicity of angelic knowledge. This is *cognitio per modum naturae* in its anticipation of the unity that draws on human knowledge; and conceptual knowledge has its validity precisely because of its continuity with this pre-predicative cognition. 'Even if from below [such cognition] seems to continue the instinctive knowledge of animals, it also offers, if we look above, an *image of the knowledge of pure spirits, always essential, concrete, and sympathetic*'" [Rousselot, "Théorie des concepts" 592–93; Sheehan's brackets; my ital.].

9. Rousselot continues (1936, 79–80; my ital. and free trans. of the Latin in brackets): "The [72] moralist sets out from pre-exist-

ing moral ideas and makes a deduction; the chaste person *feels sympathy or revulsion and makes an inference.* Which intelligence perceives being better? . . . The moralist possesses a universalized abstraction; the virtuous person sees a concrete *esse castum.* In modern language we should say that the *one has a handy, communicable idea while the other has a 'real' intuition*; in Thomist terms, the first's is an abstract from human sensations, the second's like a piece of angelic idea. So *cognitio per modum naturae* is really the opposite of knowledge of first principles in the form of conceptual judgments; so its opposite is *logical* knowledge not *intellectual* knowledge: *connatural knowledge is higher and more intuitive because it is more personal: est enim aliquid scientia melius, scilicet intellectus.*"

10. Sheehan (1987, 65) continues: "Angels, he [Rousselot] says, 'these models of the intellection in its ideal state,' function as guiding limit-ideas for human cognition, for not only do they *prevent us from identifying intellectual knowledge as such with discursive reasoning* and suppress the opposition between being and idea, but they *show me what as a human being I am to become and therefore why and how I know.* 'One can rightly say that the unknown and most loved end, whose discovery accounts for all our mental dynamism, is the subsistent noumenon which we [potentially] are and will become'" [66–67, quoting Rousselot 1910a, 232 (the word "potentially" in brackets is Sheehan's)].

11. Klubertanz (1953, 275) adds: ". . . [A] habit is . . . a quality, for it *makes one different* from what one was. It is *relatively stable*; once acquired, a habit remains, at least for a while. It *perfects an individual* in a certain way, through not necessarily in a moral way, or even in a desirable way. Finally, it is a determination of an operative power, and so is *ordered to action*. Therefore, a habit may be defined as a stable or permanent quality which determines a power to easy, accurate (sure, steady, consistent) and pleasurable operation under control of intellect and will . . . . [A]s a modification of the nature, habit implies as well a way of 'having myself.' In this way, habit implies possession as well as adaptation" [Klubertanz, 1953, 284–85; my ital.].

12. "Obviously, if we never progressed beyond the first laborious efforts we make to get things done, our whole life would be

taken up simply with our trial-and-error struggles to keep alive—
and even this result would not be assured. Habit is a means of con-
quering difficulties and *acquiring a richer and more meaningful freedom*" (Klubertanz 1952, 291; my ital.). "*Habit does truly connaturalize
power* to a certain object" (Keane 1966, 34).

13. Lonergan (1971, 41–43; my ital.) has written very interesting remarks on this theme: "In estimating human nature Thomas
was a wholehearted pessimist. With conviction he would repeat,
'the number of stupid people is infinite' (*numerus stultorum
infinitus*). And, as one might expect, for this low opinion of human
nature he had at hand a very imposing metaphysical argument.
'One acts according to what one is' (*Agere sequitur esse*): perfection
in the dynamic field of operation is radically one with perfection
in the static order of being. But perfection in the order of being is
measured by the proportion of potency and act: the more refined
the potency and the greater its actuation the more perfect the resultant. Now, since God alone is 'pure act' (*actus purus*) with potentiality at zero and act at infinity, it follows that God alone operates
with absolute perfection. Next stand the angels, existing beyond
time and created in the full development of their natures; com-
pounds of potency and act, for the most part they do what is right.
But humans are essentially creatures of time; at birth our higher
powers are the spiritual counterpart of 'prime matter,' 'raw material' (*materia prima*), and their indeterminate potentiality points at
once in all directions; accordingly, since the good is ever unique
and evil manifold, the odds always are that we will do what is wrong.

"With the human problem so clearly conceived, Thomas has at
once its *solution, a greater actuation of human potency*. . . . . [I]f one
examines the nature of *habits and dispositions*, one finds that they
*constitute precisely the type of internal change required: they make the exter-
nal rule of right action the internal form of the faculty's operation.* A disposition is such a form in its incipient stages, when it is not well
established and may easily be lost. *A habit is such a form brought to
perfection* and, as it were, *grafted on nature. For habits cling to us as does
nature; they give operation the spontaneity and the delight characteristic of
natural action . . . .*"

14. Lonergan continues with this marvelous text (ibid.; my ital.):
"Such appears to be the main line of development in the majestic

sweep of Thomas's thought on the problem of perfecting human nature. It begins with an insistence on the immanent perfection of the *virtues*; it ends with a nuanced theory in which the transcendent perfection of God is communicated to human beings through the double channel of immanent virtues and transient motions. Certain points call for particular attention.

"First, the two aspects of habitual grace, *operans et cooperans*, result from the principle that *actus* is at once perfection and source of further perfection, that *agere sequitur esse*. Because *every habit is a perfection*, the actuation and determination of an indeterminate potency, it will have its immediate effects in the field of *formal* causality and its ulterior consequences in the field of *efficient* causality. The accident, heat, is the ground both of the fire's being hot and of its heating other objects; in like manner grace or any other form as a principle of both *esse* and *operari*.

"Second, the term, proportion, takes on an increasing significance as the *actus* basing the proportion increases. Thus, God, the angels, and humans are all proportionate to the true and the good, for all are rational beings. But in God this proportion is such that divine operations cannot be defective; in the angels it implies only that for the most part operations will not fail; while in us humans it gives a mere possibility with no guarantee of success, so that for the most part we do what is wrong. Nevertheless, *give us the virtues and in place of the statistical law governing humanity one will have an approximation to the statistical law governing the angels* [!]. Endowed with the virtues one becomes a 'perfected agent' (an *agens perfectum*) and, for the most part, one does what is right; thus *a will adorned with the virtue of justice* performs just deeds with the *spontaneity* and the *regularity* with which fire moves upwards.

15. Kestenbaum says of John Dewey's philosophy of habit: "Meanings are experienced by the human organism; they are 'had' by the subject. It is a fundamental postulate of Dewey's theory of experience and theory of meaning that *meanings must be 'had' before they can be 'known.'* . . . [B]eing and having things in ways other than knowing them, in ways never identical with knowing them, exist, and are preconditions of reflection and knowledge [Kestenbaum 1977, 2].

"The basis of Dewey's notion of meanings which are 'had' or 'lived' is his conception of habit. In *Human Nature and Conduct* he says that 'the word habit may seem twisted somewhat from its customary use when employed as we have been using it. But we need a word to express that kind of human activity which is influenced by prior activity and in that sense acquired; which contains within itself a certain ordering or systematization of minor elements of action; which is projective, dynamic in quality, ready for overt manifestation; and which is operative in some subdued form when not obviously dominating activity' [Dewey 1922, 40–41].

"Habits are what Dewey variously calls 'accepted meanings,' 'funded meanings,' 'acquired meanings,' and 'organic meanings.' These habit-meanings or habitual meanings are the motivators of conscious behavior; furthermore, they are the basis of the unity of the organism. Perhaps ever more fundamentally, however, the very *intentional reciprocity of self and world is founded upon habits* since, according to Dewey, '*they constitute the self*'" [Dewey 1922, 5] [Kestenbaum 1977, 3; my ital.].

16. To say with Maritain, after John Poinsot (John of St. Thomas), that "love passes into the condition of the 'object'" (*amor transit in conditionem objecti*, or *affectus transit in conditionem objecti*) is another way to say with Lonergan (after St. Paul) that love "floods our hearts." To know connaturally is to know through a consciousness affected by love, as one in possession of something new; in this new having (*habitus*) of a consciousness changed by being loved, we can understand the doctrine of reversal of the maxim that "nothing is loved unless first known," into "nothing is really known unless first loved." Connaturality depends on the influence of love (affective consciousness) upon the subject (triune consciousness), who is thereby made capable of heart-knowledge, that is, knowledge by connaturality, and, as a result, also of heart-love. Affection then fully integrates into the higher operational synthesis of affection, cognition, and volition that is triune consciousness. As Lonergan says [1971, 44; my ital.]: ". . . [T]he infusion of grace constitutes a *permanent change in the inclination or spontaneous orientation of the will: it plucks out the heart of stone that made the sinner a slave to sin; it implants a heart of flesh to initiate a new continuity in*

justice. . . . Theologians speak of grace as both healing (*sanans*) and elevating (*elevans*), and the result is a condition better than its original condition . . . .

Conclusion

There are three lessons I would write,
Three words as with a burning pen,
In tracings of eternal light
Upon the hearts of men.
J. C. Friedrich von Schiller (1759–1805), *Hope, Faith, and Love,* st. 1 (c.
1786).

Batter my heart, three person'd God; for, you
As yet but knock, breathe, shine, and seek to mend.
John Donne (1571?–1631), *Holy Sonnets* 14.

That prayer has great power which persons make with all their might.
It makes a sour heart sweet, a sad heart merry,
a poor heart rich, a foolish heart wise,
a timid heart brave, a sick heart well,
a blind heart full of sight, a cold heart ardent.
It draws the great God into the little heart,
it drives the hungry soul up into the fullness of God,
it brings together two lovers, God and the soul,
in a wondrous place where they speak much of love.
St. Mechtilde of Magdeburg (1210–1295), *The Flowing Light.*

It is with no doubtful knowledge, Lord,
but with utter certainty that I love you.
You have stricken my heart with Your word and I have loved You.
St. Augustine (354–430), *Confessions.*

If wrong our hearts, our heads are right in vain.
Edward Young (1683-1765), *Night Thoughts,* Night, 6.281 (1745.)

WE NEED A NEW PARADIGM FOR HUMAN NATURE. To complement, not supplant, the dominant anthropology
from below, a one-sidedly rationalistic science, medi-

cine, psychology, and the like,we need an anthropology from above. These two approaches are compatible, not antagonistic or contradictory, because they meet in the concept of triune consciousness, new only in the sense of contemporary methods of arguing for it. The model itself of human beings as the highest animals and the lowest spirits, a little less than the angels, is perennial.

The model proposed here is based on phenomenologically described and ontologically interpreted human experience, however, and is not the result of pure speculation or religious inspiration, although both are sources of examples in aid of interpreting experience, as we saw. Rather, a detailed description of consciousness is the basis of the model. Human consciousness is a triad. Only as a triune synthesis of affection, cognition, and volition is it able to progress operationally along a developmental continuum, in a vertical finality, from *bios-epithumia* through *logos-eros* to the union of head and heart under control of responsible freedom. If any one mode of the triad is too dominant, or slighted, or suppressed, a functional imbalance results, especially in the properly interpersonal worlds of beauty, truth, and goodness, those values that take us beyond our roots as human animals toward the flower of the human spirit in the æsthetic, ethical, and mystical.

This book has taken the form of an effort to integrate heart and head by describing feeling as affective intentionality and interpreting that intentionality through the idea of connaturality. My thesis is that development of triune consciousness toward its higher potential is directly proportional to the increase of connaturality between an agent and its proper action. To explain connaturality I have had recourse to an even older concept, that of habit qua virtue, the middle term between being (nature) and doing (action). Virtue, as the transformation of first nature into second nature, constitutes the ontological basis of connaturality; affection is, therefore, but connaturality that has become conscious, that is, the conscious experience of attunement between human nature and the values corresponding to that nature, both first and second. And the nature that sets the standard for the model is not the beginner but the proficient—the artist, the virtuous person, the saint and mystic—whose nature has become best attuned to value through virtue. The clue that has guided this integration of head and heart as triune consciousness has been affectivity, because the marked increase in intuition in knowing and of spontaneity in response to good and evil is based on, accompanied by, and directly proportional to the degree of affectivity, empathy, compassion, and love operative in consciousness.

An older interpretation of connaturality took it almost exclusively as a substitute for discursive reasoning and deliberative willing, but that approach now seems unnuanced. It was based on a correct model of the human spirit, from above, which saw discursive reason and deliberative will as substitutes for the intuition and spontaneity of higher spirits; but it leapt too quickly to the conclusion that connaturality could constitute a way to substitute for the substitutes, as though completely to elevate human nature out of its lower operational modes, whereas that conclusion would violate the very principle of the continuum of spirits on which it is based. Granted that at the highest level of expert performance in matters interpersonal (that is, especially in the world of the ethical and mystical, and to a lesser extent in the æsthetic), connaturality as felt resonance between one's being (first and, especially, second nature as virtue) and one's doing can virtually sublate concepts (as products of discursive reason) and will-acts (as products of deliberative volition); this level of human action is, after all, the ideal. As such it is at best asymptotically approximated, never fully achieved. But the horizon is there, and it beckons irresistibly.

Calling it the ideal does not undermine its status as paradigm, therefore, since we should define ourselves by our highest and deepest horizon, not by our lowest or shallowest. And that is the point of calling for a paradigm shift, that is, not to ambition an impossible angelism, as a former intellectualism may have been faulted for championing, but to recognize that the role of affection in triune consciousness—a role performed through connaturality as virtue—is absolutely essential for moving toward that horizon. As long as human consciousness continues to exclude or diminish the heart, it must remain less than fully human. And whereas an infrahuman mode of operation might go unnoticed in dealing with the furniture of the world, in matters of personal, social, and political value, only full triune consciousness will yield beauty, truth, and goodness in æsthetic, ethical, and mystical life.

Bibliography

Allport, Gordon W. *Becoming. Basic Considerations for a Psychology of Personality.* New Haven, Conn.: Yale University Press, 1955.

Allwyn, Susan. *Structure in Thought and Feeling.* New York: Methuen, 1985.

Alquié, Ferdinand. *La conscience affective.* Paris: Vrin, 1979.

Anderson, Thomas. Review of *Sartre and the Problem of Morality*, by Francis Jeanson. Translated by Robert V. Stone. *Man and World* 14 (1981) 440–48.

Aquinas, Thomas. *Summa theologiæ*, vol. 35 (IIa IIae 34–46). Translated by Thomas R. Heath. New York: McGraw-Hill, 1972.

Armstrong, Robert Plant. *The Affecting Presence: An Essay in Humanistic Anthropology.* Urbana: University of Illinois Press, 1971.

Baron, Renee, and Elizabeth Wagele. *The Enneagram Made Easy: Discovering the Nine Types of People.* San Francisco: HarperSan Francisco, 1994.

Bauer, Johannes Bapt. "De 'cordis' notione biblica et iudaica." *Verbum Domini* 40 (1962): 27–32.

Becker, Marcus. "Empirical Studies of the Enneagram: Foundations and Comparisons." In *Discovering the Enneagram*, edited by Richard Rohr and Andreas Ebert, 29–69. New York: Crossroad, 1993.

Beesing, Maria, Robert J. Nogosek, and Patrick H. O'Leary. *The Enneagram.* Denville N.J.: Dimension, 1984.

Bellah, R., R. Madsen, W. Sullivan, A. Swidler, and S. Tipton. *Habits of the Heart.* New York: Harper, 1985.

Bernard, Charles A., S.I. "Symbolisme et conscience affective." *Gregorianum* 61 (1980): 421–48.

Birdwhistell, Ray L. *Introduction to Kinesics.* Louisville, Ky.: Louisville University Press, 1952.

————. *Kinesics and Context.* Philadelphia: University of Pennsylvania Press, 1970.

Blankenburg, W. "The Cognitive Aspects of Love." In *Facets of Eros*, edited by F. J. Smith and Erling Eng, 23–39. Translated by Erling Eng. The Hague: Nijhoff, 1972.

Bouillard, Henri. *Blondel and Christianity.* Translated by James M. Somerville. Washington, D.C.: Corpus Books, 1969.

Bollnow, Otto-Friedrich. *Das Wesen der Stimmungen.* Frankfurt: Klostermann, 1943; 2d ed., 1949. French translation: *Les tonalités affectives: Essai d'anthropologie philosophique.* Translated by Lydia and Raymond Savioz. Neuchatel, Switzerland: Éditions de la Baconnière, 1953.

Boyadjian, Noubar. *The Heart: Its History, Its Symbolism, Its Iconography and Its Diseases.* Antwerp: Esco Books, 1985.

Brodie, Fawn. "My Head and My Heart." In *Thomas Jefferson. An Intimate History.* New York: Norton, 1974. Chapter XV: 199-215.

Buber, Martin. "Distance and Relation." In *The Knowledge of Man. A Philosophy of the Interhuman*, 59–71. Translated by Maurice Friedman and Ronald Gregor Smith. New York: Harper, 1965.

Bullock, Helen. *My Head and My Heart.* New York: Putnam, 1945.

Burns, J. Patout. "Spiritual Dynamism in Maréchal." *The Thomist* 32 (1968): 528–39.

Cataldi, Sue L. *Emotion, Depth, and Flesh: A Study of Sensitive Space. Reflections on Merleau-Ponty's Philosophy of Embodiment.* Albany: State University of New York Press, 1993.

Caldera, Rafael-Tomas. *Le jugement par inclination chez saint Thomas d'Aquin.* Paris: Vrin, 1980.

Chenu, M.–D. "Les catégories affectives dans la langue de l'école." In *Le Coeur*, 123–28. Bruges, Belgium: Desclée de Brouwer, 1950.

Cirne-Lima, Carlos. *Personal Faith. A Metaphysical Inquiry.* New York: Herder & Herder, 1965. Translated by G. Richard Dimler.

Condon, William S., "Linguistic-Kinesic Research and Dance Therapy,." In *American Dance Therapy Association Third Annual Conference (Proceedings)* 21–42. Baltimore: American Dance Therapy Association, 1970; Combined Proceedings for Third Annual Conference, Oct. 25–27, 1968, and Fourth Annual Conference, Oct. 31–Nov. 2, 1969).

———. "Neonatal entrainment and enculturation." In *Before Speech. The Beginnings of Human Communication,* edited by Margaret Bullowa, 131–48. Cambridge: Cambridge University Press, 1979a.

———. "The Relation of Interactional Synchrony to Cognitive and Emotional Processes." In *Verbal and Nonverbal Communication,* 1979b: 39-65.

Condon, William S., and W. D. Ogston. "A Segmentation of Behavior." *Journal of Psychiatric Research* 5 (1967) 221–35.

Condon, William S., and W. D. Ogston. "Speech and Body Motion Synchrony of the Speaker-Hearer." In *Perception of Language,* edited by David L. Horton and James J. Jenkins, 150–73. Columbus Ohio: Charles E. Merrill, 1971.

Condon, William S., and Louis W. Sander. "Neonate Movement Is Synchronized with Adult Speech: Interactional Participation and Language Acquisition." *Science* 183 (1974): 99–101.

Damasio, Antonio R. *Descartes' Error: Emotion, Reason, and the Human Brain.* New York: Grosset/Putnam, 1994.

D'Arcy, Martin C. *The Mind and Heart of Love: Lion and Unicorn. A Study in Eros and Agape.* New York: Henry Holt, 1947.

D'Avenia, Marco. *La conoscenza per connaturalità in S. Tommaso D'Aquino.* Bologna, Italy: Edizioni Studio Domenicano, 1992.

Davis, Charles. *Body as Spirit: The Nature of Religious Feeling.* New York: Seabury, 1976.

Descartes, René. *Meditations on First Philosophy,* in *The Philosophical Works of Descartes.* Translated by G.B.S. Haldane and Elizabeth Ross. Cambridge: Cambridge University Press, 1911.

Dewey, John. *Human Nature and Conduct.* New York: Modern Library, 1922.

Dillon, Martin C., ed. *Merleau-Ponty Vivant.* Albany: State University of New York Press, 1991.

Dinan, Stephen A. "Intentionality in the Introduction to *Being and Nothingness.*" *Research in Phenomenology* 1 (1971): 91–118.

———. "Spontaneity and Perception in Sartre's Theory of the Body." *Philosophy Today* (1979): 279–91.

Doran, R. *Subject and Psyche: Ricoeur, Jung, and the Search for Foundations.* Washington, D.C.: University Press of America, 1981a; 2d ed., Milwaukee, Wis.: Marquette University Press, 1994.

―――. *Psychic Conversion and Theological Foundations: Toward a Reorientation of the Human Sciences.* Chico, Calif.: Scholars Press, 1981b.

―――. *Theology and the Dialectics of History.* Toronto: University of Toronto Press, 1990.

―――. *Theological Foundations.* Vol. 1: *Intentionality and Psyche;* Vol. 2: *Theology and Culture.* Milwaukee, Wis.: Marquette University Press, 1996.

Egan, Harvey D. *The Spiritual Exercises and the Ignatian Mystical Horizon.* St. Louis, Mo.: The Institute of Jesuit Sources, 1976.

Emad, Parvis. "Heidegger on Transcendence and Intentionality: His Critique of Scheler." In *Heidegger. The Man and the Thinker,* edited by Thomas Sheehan, 145–58. Chicago: Precedent Publishing, 1981.

Eschmann, E. W., et al. *Das Herz.* Vol. 1: *Im Umkreis des Glaubens,* Vol. 2: *Im Umkreis der Kunst.* Biberach an der Riss, Germany: K. Thomae, 1965.

Faricy, Robert L. "Connatural Knowledge." *Sciences Ecclésiastiques* 36 (1964): 155–63.

Finance, Joseph de. *Être et agir dans la philosophie de Saint Thomas.* 2d ed. Rome: Gregorian University Press, 1960.

―――. *L'affrontement de l'autre: Essai sur l'altérité.* Rome: Gregorian University Press, 1973.

Florival, Ghislaine. "Phénoménologie de l'affectivité." In *L'affect philosophe,* edited by G. Hottois. Paris: Vrin, 1990, 87–110.

Frings, Manfred S. *Max Scheler. A Concise Introduction into the World of a Great Thinker.* Pittsburgh, Pa.: Duquesne University Press, 1965; 2d, rev. ed.: Milwaukee, Wis.: Marquette University Press, 1996.

―――. "The 'Ordo Amoris' in Max Scheler: Its Relationship to His Value Ethics and to the Concept of Resentment." In *Facets of Eros,* edited by F. J. Smith and Erling Eng, 40–60. Translated by F. J. Smith. The Hague: Nijhoff, 1972.

―――. *The Mind of Max Scheler.* Milwaukee, Wis.: Marquette University Press, 1997.

Gilby, Thomas. *Poetic Experience.* New York: Sheed & Ward, 1934.

Goleman, Daniel. *Emotional Intelligence.* New York: Bantam Books, 1995.

Greenspan, Patricia S. *Emotions and Reasons: An Inquiry into Emotional Justification.* New York: Routledge, 1988.

Guardini, R. *Christliches Bewusstsein: Versuche über Pascal.* Munich: Kösel, 1950.

———. *Pascal for Our Time.* Translated by B. Thompson. New York: Herder, 1966.

Guérin, Michel. *L'Affectivité de la pensée.* Arles, France: Actes Sud, 1993.

Gumnior, Helmut. *Die Subjekte der Tugenden unter Berücksichtigung der Connaturalität nach der Lehre des hl. Thomas von Aquin.* Munich, Germany, 1962.

Guillaumont, Antoine. "Les sens des noms du cœur dans l'antiquité." In *Le cœur,* 41–81. Bruges, Belgium: Desclée de Brouwer, 1950.

Hall, Edward T. *The Silent Language.* Garden City, N.Y.: Doubleday, 1959.

———. *The Hidden Dimension.* Garden City, N.Y.: Doubleday, 1966.

———. *Beyond Culture.* Garden City, N.Y.: Doubleday, 1976.

Harré, Rom, ed. *The Social Construction of Emotions.* Oxford: Blackwell, 1986.

Hayen, André. *L'Intentionnel selon saint Thomas.* 2d ed. Bruges, Belgium: Desclée de Brouwer, 1954.

———. "La connaissance par connaturalité." In *La communication de l'être d'après saint Thomas d'Aquin,* 238–60. Louvain, Belgium: Desclée de Brouwer, 1957.

Heath, T. Review of *Creative Intuition in Art and Poetry,* by Jacques Maritain. *The Thomist* 17 (1954).

Heidegger, Martin. *What is Philosophy?* Translated by Jean T. Wilde and William Kluback. New Haven, Conn.: College and University Press, 1955.

———. *An Introduction to Metaphysics.* Translated by Ralph Mannheim. Garden City, N.Y.: Doubleday, 1959.

———. *Kant and the Problem of Metaphysics.* Translated by James S. Churchill. Bloomington: Indiana University Press, 1962a.

———. *Being and Time.* Translated by John Macquarrie and Edward Robinson. New York: Harper, 1962b.

———. *Discourse on Thinking: A Translation of Gelassenheit.* Translated by John M. Anderson and E. Hans Freund. New York: Harper, 1966.

———. *What Is Called Thinking?* Translated by Fred D. Wieck and J. Glenn Gray. New York: Harper, 1968.

———. *Identity and Difference.* Translated by Joan Stambaugh. New York: Harper, 1969.

———. "The Origin of a Work of Art." In *Poetry, Language, Thought.* Translated by Albert Hofstadter. New York: Harper, 1971.

———. "The End of Philosophy and the Task of Thinking." In *On Time and Being.* Translated by Joan Stambaugh. New York: Harper, 1972.

———. *Early Greek Thinking.* Translated by David F. Krell and Frank A. Capuzzi. New York: Harper, 1975.

———. "The Age of the World Picture." In *The Question Concerning Technology and Other Essays.* Translated by William Lovitt. New York: Harper, 1977a.

———. "What is Metaphysics?" In *Basic Writings,* edited by D. F. Krell, 91–112. New York: Harper, 1977b.

———. *The Fundamental Concepts of Metaphysics: World, Finitude, Solitude.* Translated by William McNeill and Nicolas Walker. Bloomington: Indiana University Press, 1995.

———. *Being and Time: A Translation of Sein und Zeit.* Translated by Joan Stambaugh. Albany: State University of New York Press, 1996.

Henry, Michel. "Does the Concept 'Soul' Mean Anything?" Translated by Girard Etzkorn. *Philosophy Today* 13 (1969) 94-114.

——— *The Essence of Manifestation.* Translated by Girard Etzkorn. The Hague: Nijhoff, 1973.

———. *Philosophy and Phenomenology of the Body.* Translated by Girard Etzkorn. The Hague: Nijhoff, 1975.

Heron, John. "The Phenomenology of Social Encounter: The Gaze." *Philosophy and Phenomenological Research* 31 (1970): 243–64.

Hildebrand, Dietrich von. *Ethics.* Chicago: Franciscan Herald, 1953.

———. *Metaphysik der Gemeinschaft: Untersuchungen über Wesen und Wert der Gemeinschaft.* 2d ed. Regensburg, Germany: Habbel, 1955.

———. "Die geistigen Formen der Affektivität." *Philosophischen Jahrbuch der Görresgesellschaft* 68 (1960): 180–190.

———. "Phenomenology of Value in a Christian Philosophy." In *Christian Philosophy and Religious Renewal,* edited by George F. McLean, 3–19. Washington, D.C.: Catholic University of America Press, 1966.

———. *The Heart: An Analysis of Human and Divine Affectivity.* Chicago: Franciscan Herald, 1977.

Hillman, James. *Emotion: A Comprehensive Phenomenology of Theories and Their Meanings for Therapy.* Evanston, Ill.: Northwestern University Press, 1961.

Hume, David. *A Treatise of Human Nature.* Oxford: Oxford University Press, 1888.

Hurley, Kathleen, and Theodore Dobson. *What's My Type?* San Francisco: HarperSan Francisco, 1991

———. *My Best Self.* San Francisco: HarperSan Francisco, 1993.

Janeck, Axel. *Cor humanum. Herzanatomie in der graphischen Darstellung —ein kulturgeschictlicher Überblick.* Nuremberg, Germany: Sandoz AG, 1983.

Jefferson, Thomas. Letter to Maria Cosway (12 Oct. 1786). In *The Papers of Thomas Jefferson*, 10: 443–54. Edited by Julian Boyd. Princeton, N.J.: Princeton University Press, 1954.

Kadowaki, Johannes. *Cognitio Secundum Connaturalitatem Iuxta S. Thomam.* Bern, Switzerland: Herbert Lang/Frankfurt, Germany: Peter Lang, 1974.

Kapleau, Philip. *The Three Pillars of Zen.* Garden City: Anchor, 1980.

Keane, Helen Virginia. "Knowledge by Connaturality in St. Thomas Aquinas." Ph.D. diss., Marquette University, Milwaukee, Wis., 1966.

Kerr, Fergus. *Theology after Wittgenstein.* Oxford: Basil Blackwell, 1986.

Kestenbaum, Victor. *The Phenomenological Sense of John Dewey: Habit and Meaning.* Atlantic Highlands, N.J.: Humanities Press, 1977.

Khatchadourian, Haig. "Rational/Irrational in Dostoevsky, Nietzsche and Aristotle." *Journal of the British Society for Phenomenology* 11 (1980): 107–15.

Kierkegaard, Søren. *Søren Kierkegaard's Journals and Papers*, Vol. 2, F–K. Translated by Howard V. Hong and Edna H. Hong. Bloomington: Indiana University Press, 1970.

Klubertanz, George P. *The Philosophy of Human Nature.* New York: Appleton, 1953.

———. *Habits and Virtues.* New York: Appleton-Century-Crofts, 1965.

Kwant, Rémy C. *Encounter.* Translated by Robert C. Adolfs. Pittsburgh, Pa.: Duquesne University Press, 1960.

Lamb, Matthew L. *History, Method, and Theology: A Dialectical Comparison of Wilhelm Dilthey's Critique of Historical Reason and Ber-*

nard Lonergan's Meta-Methodology. Missoula, Mont.: Scholars Press, 1978.

Langer, Susanne K. *Philosophy in a New Key: A Study in the Symbolism of Reason, Rite, and Art.* New York: Penguin, 1942.

———. *Feeling and Form.* New York: Charles Scribner's Sons, 1953.

———. *Philosophical Sketches.* Baltimore, Md.: John Hopkins University Press, 1962.

———. *Mind: An Essay on Human Feeling.* Baltimore, Md.: Johns Hopkins University Press, 1967 (vol. 1), 1972 (vol. 2), and 1982 (vol. 3).

Lavalette, Henri de. "Le théoricien de l'amour." *Recherches de science religieuse* [*Memorial Pierre Rousselot (1878–1915)*] 53 (1965): 462–94.

Lebacqz, Joseph. "La connaissance par connaturalité." In *Certitude et volonté,* 113–28. Louvain, Belgium: Desclée de Brouwer, 1962.

Le Blond, Jean-Marie. "La philosophie thomiste." *Recherches de science religieuse* [*Memorial Pierre Rousselot (1878–1915)*] 53 (1965): 391–421.

Levinas, Emmanuel. *Totality and Infinity: An Essay on Exteriority.* Translated by Alphonso Lingis. Pittsburgh: Duquesne University Press, 1969).

———. *The Theory of Intuition in Husserl's Phenomenology.* Translated by André Orianne. Evanston: Northwestern University Press, 1973.

———. *Otherwise than Being or Beyond Essence.* Translated by Alphonso Lingis. The Hague: Nijhoff. 1981.

———. "La conscience non-intentionnelle." In *Entre nous. Essais sur le penser-à-l'autre,* 141–51. Paris: Grasset, 1991.

———. *Emmanuel Levinas: Basic Philosophical Writings.* Edited by Adriaan T. Peperzak, Simon Critchley, and Robert Bernasconi. Bloomington: Indiana University Press, 1996.

Lewisohn, R. *Histoire entière du coeur.* Paris: Plon, 1959.

Lonergan, Bernard J. F. *Insight: A Study of Human Understanding.* New York: Philosophical Library, 1957.

———. "Cognitional Structure." In *Spirit as Inquiry. Studies in Honor of Bernard Lonergan. Continuum* 2 (1964): 530–42.

———. *The Subject.* Milwaukee, Wi.: Marquette University Press, 1968.

———. *Grace and Freedom: Operative Grace in the Thought of St. Thomas Aquinas.* Edited by J. Patout Burns. New York: Herder, 1971.

———. *Method in Theology.* New York: Herder, 1972.

———. *A Third Collection.* Edited by Frederick E. Crowe. New York: Paulist Press, 1985.

———. *Understanding and Being: The Halifax Lectures on Insight.* Edited by Elizabeth A. Morelli and Mark D. Morelli. 2d ed., rev. and augmented. Toronto: University of Toronto Press, 1990.

———. *Topics in Education: The Cincinnati Lectures of 1959 on the Philosophy of Education.* Edited by Frederick E. Crowe, and Robert M. Doran. Toronto: University of Toronto Press, 1993.

———. *Philosophical and Theological Papers 1958–1964.* Edited by Edited by Robert C. Croken, Frederick E. Crowe, and Robert M. Doran. Toronto: University of Toronto Press, 1996.

———. *The Lonergan Reader.* Edited by Mark D. Morelli and Elizabeth A. Morelli. Toronto: University of Toronto Press, 1997.

Louth, Andrew. *The Origins of the Christian Mystical Tradition.* Oxford: Clarendon Press, 1981.

MacLean, Paul D. "Sensory and Perceptive Factors in Emotional Functions of the Triune Brain." In *Explaining Emotions,* edited by A. O. Rorty, 9-36. Berkeley and Los Angeles: University of California Press, 1980.

———. *The Triune Brain in Evolution: Role in Paleocerebral Functions.* New York: Plenum Press, 1990.

Macquarrie, John. *Existentialism.* New York: Penguin, 1972.

Madison, Gary B. "Merleau-Ponty's Destruction of Logocentrism." In *Merleau-Ponty Vivant,* edited by Martin C. Dillon, 117–52. Albany: Albany: State University of New York Press, 1991.

Maguire, Daniel C. *The Gifts of the Holy Spirit in John of St. Thomas.* Rome: Gregorian University Press, 1969.

Marin-Sola, F. "L'évolution dogmatique par voie affective ou expérimentale" and "Autres observations sur la voie affective." In *L'évolution homogène du dogme catholique,* Tome 1: 353–92. Imprimerie et Librairie de l'Œuvre de Saint-Paul: Fribourg, Switzerland, 1924.

Marion, Jean-Luc. "L'être et l'affection. A propos de *La conscience affective* de F. Alquié." *Archives de philosophie* 43 (1980): 433–41.

Maritain, Jacques. *Man and the State.* Chicago: University of Chicago Press, 1951.

————. "On Knowledge through Connaturality." In *The Range of Reason*, 22–29. New York: Scribner's, 1952.

————. *Creative Intuition in Art and Poetry*. New York: Pantheon Books, 1953.

————. *The Degrees of Knowledge*. New York: Scribner's, 1959.

Marx, Karl. *Zur Kritik der politischen Ökonomie*. Berlin: Dietz Verlag, 1951.

McCool, Gerald A. *The Neo-Thomists*. Milwaukee, Wi.: Marquette University Press, 1995.

McDermott, John M. "Un inédit de P. Rousselot: 'Idéalisme et thomisme.'" *Archives de Philosophie* 42 (1979): 91-126.

————. *Love and Understanding: The Relation of Will and Intellect in Pierre Rousselot's Christological Vision*. Rome: Gregorian University Press, 1983.

McInerny, Ralph. "Apropos of Art and Connaturality." *The Modern Schoolman* 35 (1958): 173–89.

Meinong, Alexius. *On Emotional Presentation*. Translated and intro. by Marie-Luise Schubert Kalsi. Foreword by J.N. Findlay. Evanston, Ill.: Northwestern University Press, 1972.

Merleau-Ponty, Maurice. *Phenomenology of Perception*. Translated by Colin Smith. London: Routledge & Kegan Paul, 1962.

————. *The Structure of Behavior*. Translated by Alden L. Fisher. Boston: Beacon Press, 1963.

————. *The Primacy of Perception*. Translated by James M. Edie. Evanston, Ill.: Northwestern University Press, 1964a.

————. *Signs*. Translated by Richard C. McCleary. Evanston, Ill.: Northwestern University Press, 1964b.

————. *The Visible and the Invisible*. Translated by Alphonso Lingis. Evanston, Ill.: Northwestern University Press, 1968.

Miller, Barry. *The Range of Intellect*. London: Routledge, 1963.

Moreno, Antonio. "The Nature of St. Thomas' Knowledge 'Per Connaturalitatem.'" *Angelicum* 47(1970): 44–62.

Nédoncelle, Maurice. *God's Encounter with Man: A Contemporary Approach to Prayer*. Translated by A. Manson. New York: Sheed & Ward, 1964.

Noble, Henri-Dominique. "La connaissance affective." *Revue des Sciences Philosophiques et Théologiques* 7 (1913): 637–62.

Owens, Thomas J. *Phenomenology and Intersubjectivity: Contemporary Interpretations of the Interpersonal Situation.* The Hague: Nijhoff, 1970.

Ossa, Manuel. "Blondel et Rousselot." *Recherches de science religieuse* [*Memorial Pierre Rousselot (1878–1915)*] 53 (1965): 522–43.

Palmer, Helen. *The Enneagram.* San Francisco: HarperSan Francisco, 1988.

Péghaire, Julien. *Intellectus et Ratio selon S. Thomas d'Aquin.* Paris: Vrin/Ottawa: Institut d'Études Médiévales, 1936.

Pfänder, Alexander. *Phenomenology of Willing and Motivation and Other Phænomenologica.* Translated by Herbert Spiegelberg. Evanston, Ill.: Northwestern University Press, 1967.

Poole, Roger. *Towards Deep Subjectivity.* New York: Harper, 1972.

Poster, Marc. *Existential Marxism in Postwar France: From Sartre to Althusser.* Princeton, N.J.: Princeton University Press, 1975.

Pradines, Maurice. *Traité de psychologie générale,* 3 vols. 2d ed. Paris, 1946.

Racette, Jean. "Michel Henry's Philosophy of the Body." Translated by Robert Lechner. *Philosophy Today* 13 (1969): 83–94.

Rahner, Karl. "The Doctrine of the 'Spiritual Senses' in the Middle Ages." In *Theological Investigations,* vol. 16. Translated by David Morland. New York: Crossroad/Seabury, 1979.

———. *Hearer of the Word: Laying the Foundation for a Philosophy of Religion.* Translated by Joseph Donceel from the 1st ed. New York: Continuum, 1994.

Reagan, C., and D. Stewart, eds. "The Antinomy of Human Reality and the Problem of Philosophical Anthropology." *The Philosophy of Paul Ricoeur. An Anthology of His Work.* Boston: Beacon Press, 1978.

Restak, Richard M. *The Modular Brain.* New York: Scribner's, 1994.

Ricoeur, Paul. *Fallible Man.* Translated by Charles Kelbley. Chicago: Regnery, 1965. Rev. ed. New York: Fordham University Press, 1986.

———. *Husserl: An Analysis of His Phenomenology.* Translated by Edward G. Ballard and Lester E. Embree. Evanston, Ill.: Northwestern University Press, 1967.

———. *Freud and Philosophy: An Essay on Interpretation.* Translated by Denis Savage. New Haven, Conn.: Yale University Press, 1970.

————. "Foreword" to *The Phenomenology of Feeling* by Stephan Strasser, xi-xiv. Pittsburgh, Pa.: Duquesne University Press, 1977,

Riordan, Kathleen. "Gurdjieff." In *Transpersonal Psychologies*, edited by Charles Tart, 281–328. New York: Harper, 1975.

Riso, Don Richard. *Personality Types: Using the Enneagram for Self-Discovery.* Boston: Houghton Mifflin, 1987.

———— *Understanding the Enneagram: The Practical Guide to Personality Types.* Boston: Houghton Mifflin, 1990.

————. *Discovering Your Personality Type.* Boston: Houghton Mifflin, 1992.

Rodier, Jacques. *L'ordre du coeur.* Paris: J. Vrin, 1981.

Rohr, Richard, and Andreas Ebert. *Discovering the Enneagram.* Translated by Peter Heinegg. New York: Crossroad, 1993.

Rohr, Richard, et al. *Experiencing the Enneagram.* Edited by A. Ebert and Marion Küstenmacher. Translated by Peter Heinegg. New York: Crossroad, 1994.

Roldan, Alejandro. *Metafisica del sentimiento: Ensayo de psicologia afectiva. Aplicaciones a la ontologia y axiologia.* Madrid: Instituto "Luis Vives" de Filosofia. Consejo superior de investigaciones cientificas, 1956.

Roland-Gosselin, Marie-Dominique. "De la connaissance affective." *Revue des Sciences Philosophiques et Théologiques* 27 (1938): 5–26.

Rorty, Amélie Oksenberg, ed. *Explaining Emotions.* Berkeley and Los Angeles: University of California Press, 1980.

Rousselot, Pierre. *L'Intellectualisme de Saint Thomas.* Paris: Beauchesne, 1908; 2d ed. 1924; 3d ed. 1935.

————. *Pour l'histoire du problème de l'amour au Moyen Âge.* Munster: Aschendorffsche Buchhandlund, 1908. *Love in the Middle Ages.* Translated by Alan Vincelette and Pol Vandevelde. Milwaukee, Wis.: Marquette University Press, forthcoming, 1998. (Volume 2 of Pierre Roussleot's Collected Philosophical Works.)

Rousselot, Pierre. "Amour spirituel et synthèse aperceptive." In *Revue de Philosophie* 17 (1910a) 225–40.*(see end of Rousselot entries).

————. "Métaphysique thomiste et critique de la connaissance." In *Revue Néo-scolastique de Louvain* 17 (1910b) 476–509.*(see end of Rousselot entries).

————. "L'Être et l'Esprit." In *Revue de Philosophie* 17 (1910c) 561–74.*(see end of Rousselot entries).

———. "Les yeux de la foi." In *Recherches de Science Religieuse* 1 (1910d): 241–59 and 444–75. *The Eyes of Faith.* Translated by Joseph Donceel. Intro. by John M. McDermott. New York: Fordham University Press, 1990.

———. "L'Esprit de saint Thomas d'après un livre récent" In *Études* 128 (1911) 614–29.

———. *The Intellectualism of Saint Thomas.* Translated by James E. O'Mahony. New York: Sheed & Ward, 1935. New translation *The Intellecutlaism of Thomas Aquinas* by Andrew Tallon. Milwaukee, Wis.: Marquette University Press, 1997. (Volume 1 of Pierre Roussleot's Collected Philosophical Works.)

———. "Intellectualisme." In *Dictionnaire Apologétique de la Foi Catholique* 2, 2: 1066–1081. Edited by A. d'Alès. Paris, 1914.

———. "Théorie des concepts par l'unité fonctionnelle suivant les principes de saint Thomas. Synthèse aperceptive et connaissance d'amour vécue." In *Archives de Philosophie* 23 (1960) 573–607. Includes letter of 29 janvier 1914 important for theme of connaturality. *(see end of Rousselot entries).

———. "Idéalisme et thomisme." In *Archives de Philosophie* 42 (1979): 103–26. * These 5 articles will be translated and published as Volume 3 of Pierre Roussleot's Collected Philosophical Works. Milwaukee, Wis.: Marquette University Press.

Roy, Lucien. *Lumière et sagesse: La grâce mystique dans la théologie de saint Thomas d'Aquin.* Montreal, Canada: L'Immaculée-Conception, 1948.

Saliers, Don E. *The Soul in Paraphrase: Prayer and the Religious Affections.* New York: Seabury, 1980.

Sartre, Jean-Paul. *The Emotions: Outline of a Theory.* Translated by Bernard Frechtman. New York: Philosophical Library, 1948a.

———. *The Psychology of Imagination.* Secaucus: Citadel Press, 1948b.

———. *Being and Nothingness: An Essay on Phenomenological Ontology.* Translated by Hazel E. Barnes. New York: Washington Square Press, 1953a.

———. *The Transcendence of the Ego: An Existentialist Theory of Consciousness.* Translated by Forrest Williams & Robert Kirkpatrick. New York: Noonday Press, 1957.

———. *Imagination: A Psychological Critique.* Translated by Forrest Williams. Ann Arbor: University of Michigan Press, 1962.

————. *Search for a Method.* Translated by Hazel E. Barnes. New York: Vintage Books, 1953b.

————. *Critique of Dialectical Reason and Theory of Practical Ensembles.* Translated by Alan Sheridan Smith. London: NCB, 1976.

Scheler, Max. *Der Formalismus in der Ethik und die materiale Wertethik.* Collected Edition, vol. 2. Bern, Switzerland: Francke Verlag, 1954.

————. "Ordo Amoris." In *Selected Philosophical Essays,* translated by David R. Lachterman, 98–135. Evanston, Ill.: Northwestern University Press, 1973.

Schrag, Calvin O. *Experience and Being: Prolegomena to a Future Ontology.* Evanston, Ill.: Northwestern University Press, 1969.

Sheehan, Thomas. "Heidegger's Philosophy of 'Mind.'" In *Contemporary Philosophy: A New Survey,* edited by G. Fløisdad, 287–318. The Hague: Nijhoff, 1983.

————. *Karl Rahner: The Philosophical Foundations.* Athens: Ohio University Press, 1987.

Shelton, Charles M. *Morality of the Heart.* New York: Crossroad, 1990.

Simon, Yves R. *Critique de la connaissance morale.* Paris: Desclée de Brouwer, 1934.

————. *Philosophy of Democratic Government.* Chicago: University of Chicago Press, 1951.

————. "Introduction to the Study of Practical Wisdom." *The New Scholasticism* 35 (1961).

————. *The Definition of Moral Virtue.* Edited by Vukan Kuic. New York: Fordham University Press, 1986.

Simonin, Henri-Dominique. "La lumière de l'amour: Essai sur la connaissance affective." *La vie spirituelle,* suppl. 46 (1936): 65–72.

Smith, Quentin. *The Felt Meanings of the World: A Metaphysics of Feeling.* West Lafayette, Ind.: Purdue University Press, 1986.

Smith, Stephen G. *The Argument to the Other: Reason beyond Reason in the Thought of Karl Barth and Emmanuel Levinas.* Chico, Calif.: Scholars Press, 1983.

————. *The Concept of the Spiritual. An Essay in First Philosophy.* Philadelphia: Temple University Press, 1988.

Solomon, Robert C. *The Passions.* Garden City, N.Y: Anchor Books, 1976.

Sousa, Ronald de. *The Rationality of Emotion.* Cambridge, Mass.: MIT Press, 1987.

Spiegelberg, Herbert. *The Phenomenological Movement: An Historical Introduction.* 2 vols. 2d ed. The Hague: Nijhoff, 1964.

Stein, Edith. *On the Problem of Empathy.* Translated by Waltraut Stein. Washington, D.C.: ICS Publications, 1989.

Strasser, Stephan. *The Idea of Dialogal Phenomenology.* Translated by Henry J. Koren. Pittsburgh, Pa.: Duquesne University Press, 1969.

———. "Feeling as Basis of Knowing and Recognizing the Other as an Ego." In *Feelings and Emotions: The Loyola Symposium,* edited by Magda B. Arnold, 291–307. New York: Academic Press, 1970.

———. *The Phenomenology of Feeling: An Essay on the Phenenoma of the Heart.* Translated by Robert E. Wood. Pittsburgh: Duquesne University Press, 1977.

Sweeney, Robert D. "The Affective 'A Priori.'" In *The Phenomenological Realism of the Possible Worlds: The 'A Priori,' Activity and Passivity of Consciousness, Phenomenology and Nature,* edited by Anna-Teresa Tymieniecka, 80-97. Dordrecht, The Netherlands: Reidel, 1974.

Tallon, Andrew. "Spirit, Matter, Becoming: Karl Rahner's *Spirit in the World* (*Geist in Welt*)," in *The Modern Schoolman,* 48 (1971): 151-65.

———. "Person and Community: Buber's Category of the Between." *Philosophy Today* 17 (1973): 62–83.

———. "Spirit, Freedom, History: Karl Rahner's *Hearers of the Word* (*Hörer des Wortes*)." *The Thomist,* 38 (1974): 908-36.

———. "Emmanuel Levinas and the Problem of Ethical Metaphysics." *Philosophy Today* 20 (1976a): 53–66.

———. "Emmanuel Levinas's *Autrement qu'être ou au-delà de l'essence.*" *Man and World* 9, (1976b): 451–62.

———. "Intentionality, Intersubjectivity, and the Between: Buber and Levinas on Affectivity and the Dialogical Principle." *Thought* 53 (1978) 292–309.

———. "Personal Becoming: Karl Rahner's Metaphysical Anthropology." *The Thomist,* 53 (1979): i-v +1-177.

———. *Personal Becoming: Karl Rahner's Metaphysical Anthropology.* 2d ed. Milwaukee, Wis.: Marquette University Press, 1982a.

————. "Love in the Heart Tradition." In *Phenomenology and the Understanding of Human Destiny*, edited by Stephen Skousgaard, 335-53. Washington, D.C.: University Press of America, 1982b.

————. "Love and the Logic of the Heart." *Listening: Journal of Religion and Culture* 18 (1983) 5-22.

————. "Connaturality in Aquinas and Rahner. A Contribution to the Heart Tradition." *Philosophy Today* 28 (1984a): 138–47.

————. "The Meaning of the Heart Today: Revising a Paradigm with Levinas and Rahner." *Journal of Religious Studies* 11 (1984b) 59–74.

————. "Religious Belief and the Emotional Life: Faith, Love, and Hope in the Heart Tradition." In *The Life of Religion: Philosophy and the Nature of Religious Belief*, edited by Stanley Harrison and Richard Taylor, 17–38. Washington, D.C.: University Press of America, 1986.

————. "This is Not Levinas's Other." *Philosophy & Theology* 4 (1989): 206–18.

————. "Affectivity in Ethics: Lonergan, Rahner, and Others in the Heart Tradition." In *Religion and Economic Ethics*, edited by Joseph F. Gower, 87–122. Lanham, Md.: University Press of America, 1990.

————. "The Concept of the Heart in Strasser's Phenomenology of Feeling." *American Catholic Philosophical Quarterly* 66 (1992a): 341–60.

————. "The Heart in Rahner's Philosophy of Mysticism." *Theological Studies* 53 (1992b): 700–28.

————. "The Experience of God in Relation to Rahner's Philosophy of the Heart. *Philosophy & Theology* 7 (1992c): 193–210.

————. "Prophecy, Prayer, and Affectivity: For a Religion of the Heart." In *Tradition and Renewal: The Centennial of Louvain's Institute of Philosophy*, vol. 3, edited by David A. Boileau and John A. Dick, 117–41. Leuven: Leuven University Press, 1993.

————. "Affection, Cognition, Volition: The Triadic Meaning of Heart in Ethics." *American Catholic Philosophical Quarterly* 66 (1994a): 211–32.

————. "Editor's Introduction." In *Hearer of the Word* by Karl Rahner. New York: Continuum, 1994b, ix–xxii.

————. "The Role of the Connaturalized Heart in *Veritatis Splendor*." In *Veritatis splendor: American Responses*, edited by Michael

E. Allsopp and John J. O'Keefe, 137–56. Kansas City: Sheed & Ward, 1995a.

———. "Nonintentional Affectivity, Affective Intentionality, and the Ethical in Levinas's Philosophy." In *Ethics as First Philosophy: The Significance of Emmanuel Levinas for Philosophy, Literature and Religion*. Edited by Adriaan T. Peperzak, 107–21. New York: Routledge, 1995b.

———. "Triune Consciousness and Some Recent Books on Affectivity." *American Catholic Philosophical Quarterly* 70 (1996): 243–73.

———. "Lonergan and Rousselot on Connaturality, Affection, and Consciousness." In Festschrift for Gerard A. McCool, edited by Anthony J. Cernera. Hartford, Conn.: Sacred Heart University Press, forthcoming.

Tart, Charles, ed. *Transpersonal Psychologies*. New York: Harper, 1975.

Theunissen, Michael. *Der Andere: Studien zur Sozialontologie der Gegenwart*. Berlin: de Gruyter Verlag, 1965. *The Other: Studies in the Social Ontology of Husserl, Heidegger, Sartre, and Buber* is an English translation of part of this work. Translated by Christopher Macann. Cambridge, Mass.: M.I.T Press,1984.

Titus, Craig Steven. "The Development of Virtue and 'Connaturality' in Thomas Aquinas' Works," Ph.D. diss., University of Fribourg, Switzerland, 1990.

Tracy, David. *The Achievement of Bernard Lonergan*. New York: Herder & Herder, 1970.

Turski, W. George. *Toward a Rationality of Emotions: An Essay in the Philosophy of Mind*. Athens: Ohio University Press, 1994.

Veldman, Frans. *Haptonomie. Science de l'affectivité*. Translated by Paul Scheurer. Revised by Bernard This and Frans Veldman. Paris: Presses Universitaires de France, 1989.

Vella, Arthur G. *Love Is Acceptance. A psychological and theological investigation of the mind of St. Thomas Aquinas*. Rome: Gregorian University Press, 1964.

White, Victor. "Thomism and 'Affective Knowledge.'" in *Blackfriars* 35 (1944): 321–28.

Whitmont, E. *The Symbolic Quest: Basic Concepts of Analytical Psychology*. Princeton, N.J.: Princeton University Press, 1969.

Wyschogrod, Edith. *Saints and Postmodernism: Revisioning Moral Philosophy*. Chicago: University of Chicago Press, 1990.

Windle, M. "Temperament and personality attributes of children of alcoholics." In *Children of Alcoholics*, edited by M. Windle and J. Searles, 129–67. New York: Guilford Press, 1990.

Wood, Robert E. *Martin Buber's Ontology*. Evanston, Ill.: Northwestern University Press, 1969.

————. "Translator's Introduction" to *The Phenomenology of Feeling*, by Stephan Strasser, 3–39. Pittsburgh, Pa.: Duquesne University Press, 1977.

————. *A Path into Metaphysics: Phenomenological, Hermeneutical, and Dialogical Studies*. Albany: State University of New York Press, 1990.

Index